Contents

Introduction

This is the fourth edition of *Education and Training Statistics for the United Kingdom* and again provides an integrated overview of statistics on education and training in the UK. It largely follows the format of last year's volume, however, there have been a number of changes in the 2000 volume:

- The source for educational expenditure figures in Tables 1.1 and 1.2 is now HM Treasury, taken from Public Expenditure Statistical Analysis (PESA). Data are not therefore directly comparable with that shown in previous editions.

- A new table 1.3 showing average spending per pupil in nursery & primary, and secondary schools in the UK replaces the previous table showing unit costs for England only.

- Table 3.2 now shows UK data for participation in education and government-supported training and replaces the previous tables 3.2 and 3.3 which contained data for England only.

- Tables 3.6, 3.8 and 3.10 previously shown, have been split into separate tables for further education and for higher education as the data presented are not on a comparable basis. The FE tables [new Tables 3.5, 3.8, and 3.11] show **whole year** figures (for 1998/99) to give a more complete coverage throughout the year, whilst the HE tables [new Tables 3.6, 3.9 and 3.12] record **annual snapshot** data (for 1999/00). New Table 3.7 (overseas students by country of origin), is now restricted to HE students only.

- Table 3.15 from the 1999 edition has been dropped, as data are largely duplicated in other tables, and a new table (3.25) shows a summary of job-related training received or never offered.

- Table 4.1 has been restructured to give (in part (i)) the proportion of the population of a "typical age" (i.e. generally either pupils in their last year of compulsory schooling, or aged 16-18 at the start of the academic year, depending on the type of examination) obtaining various GCE, GCSE, SCE and GNVQ/GSVQ qualifications. Part (ii) gives overall numbers for those of all ages obtaining these qualifications.

International Chapter
The international chapter (Chapter 7), last seen in the 1998 volume, has been reintroduced into the 2000 volume, as more up-to date data are now available from the Organisation for Economic Co-operation and Development (OECD) publication Education at a Glance 2000.

Regional Analyses
Where regional analyses are given they are on the basis of Government Office Regions (GORs). These have been the primary classification for the presentation of regional statistics since April 1997.

Contributions
The efforts of the statistics teams in DfEE, National Assembly for Wales, Scottish Executive, Northern Ireland Department of Education and Northern Ireland Department of Higher and Further Education, Training and Employment, who have contributed data for the volume, are again greatly appreciated. In DfEE the people responsible for bringing all the data together and producing the 2000 volume were John Canlin, Dave Walton, Suzanne Trowsdale, James Chapman, Harj Guram, Adele Lingard and Paul Blackett.

Chapter 1
Expenditure

CHAPTER 1: EXPENDITURE

Key Facts

- Total managed education expenditure on services by public authorities in the UK in 1998-99 was £38.4 billion, of which £1.8 billion was directly on under fives, and £22.5 billion was on schools. (**Table 1.1**)

- Total managed expenditure by public authorities on education services in the UK in 1998-99 represented 4.5 per cent of Gross Domestic Product, compared with 5.0 per cent in 1994-95. (**Table 1.2**)

- In 1998-99 average spending per pupil in nursery & primary schools in the UK (£1,880) represented a real terms increase of almost 14 per cent since 1988-89; conversely the figure for secondary schools (£2,530) represented a decrease of almost 2 per cent over the same period. (**Table 1.3**)

CHAPTER 1: EXPENDITURE - LIST OF TABLES

EXPENDITURE
Total Managed Education Expenditure on services by function and economic category (1)

United Kingdom   Financial year 1 April 1998-31 March 1999(2)   £ million

	Local education authorities	Central government(3)	Total		Local education authorities	Central government(3)	Total
Under fives				**Student support (inc mandatory awards & access funds)**			
Pay (3)	1,377.6	.	1,377.6	Pay (3)	.	4.5	4.5
Other current expenditure on goods and services (4)	288.6	.	288.6	Other current expenditure on goods and services (4)	.	13.7	13.7
Subsidies (5)	.	.	.	Subsidies (5)	.	375.7	375.7
Current grants to private sector (6)	.	135.2	135.2	Current grants to private sector (6)	1,933.3	129.0	2,062.3
Current transfers abroad (7)	.	.	.	Current transfers abroad (7)	.	.	.
Total current	**1,666.2**	**135.2**	**1,801.4**	**Total current**	**1,933.3**	**522.9**	**2,456.2**
Net capital expenditure on assets (8)	.	.	.	Net capital expenditure on assets (8)	.	.	.
Capital grants (9)	.	.	.	Capital grants (9)	.	.	.
Total capital	.	.	.	**Total capital**	.	.	.
Total under fives	**1,666.2**	**135.2**	**1,801.4**	**Total student support**	**1,933.3**	**522.9**	**2,456.2**
Schools				**Miscellaneous educational services, research and administration**			
Pay (3)	15,696.1	541.0	16,237.1	Pay (3)	762.5	135.4	897.9
Other current expenditure on goods and services (4)	3,772.4	210.0	3,982.4	Other current expenditure on goods and services (4)	319.7	110.9	430.6
Subsidies (5)	.	.	.	Subsidies (5)	.	.	.
Current grants to private sector (6)	356.7	543.8	900.5	Current grants to private sector (6)	5.6	475.5	481.1
Current transfers abroad (7)	.	5.8	5.8	Current transfers abroad (7)	.	.	.
Total current	**19,825.2**	**1,300.6**	**21,125.8**	**Total current**	**1,087.8**	**721.8**	**1,809.6**
Net capital expenditure on assets (8)	1,274.8	28.4	1,303.2	Net capital expenditure on assets (8)	36.4	10.0	46.4
Capital grants (9)	4.2	49.3	53.5	Capital grants (9)	3.0	7.3	10.3
Total capital	**1,279.0**	**77.7**	**1,356.7**	**Total capital**	**39.4**	**17.3**	**56.7**
Total schools	**21,104.2**	**1,378.3**	**22,482.5**	**Total miscellaneous etc**	**1,127.2**	**739.1**	**1,866.3**
Further Education				**GRAND TOTALS**			
Pay (3)	997.9	12.7	1,010.6	Pay (3)	18,834.1	702.3	19,536.4
Other current expenditure on goods and services (4)	304.7	14.1	318.8	Other current expenditure on goods and services (4)	4,697.1	347.7	5,044.8
Subsidies (5)	.	.	.	Subsidies (5)	.	425.7	425.7
Current grants to private sector (6)	52.2	3,625.1	3,677.3	Current grants to private sector (6)	2,347.8	9,583.1	11,930.9
Current transfers abroad (7)	.	.	.	Current transfers abroad (7)	.	7.9	7.9
Total current	**1,354.8**	**3,651.9**	**5,006.7**	**Total current**	**25,879.0**	**11,066.7**	**36,945.7**
Net capital expenditure on assets (8)	29.4	.	29.4	Net capital expenditure on assets (8)	1,340.6	38.4	1,379.0
Capital grants (9)	1.0	13.9	14.9	Capital grants (9)	8.2	101.6	109.8
Total capital	**30.4**	**13.9**	**44.3**	**Total capital**	**1,348.8**	**140.0**	**1,488.8**
Total further education	**1,385.2**	**3,665.8**	**5,051.0**	**TOTAL Education Expenditure**	**27,227.8**	**11,206.7**	**38,434.5**
Higher Education (5)							
Pay (3)	.	8.7	8.7				
Other current expenditure on goods and services (4)	11.7	-1.0	10.7				
Subsidies (5)	.	50.0	50.0				
Current grants to private sector (6)	.	4,674.5	4,674.5				
Current transfers abroad (7)	.	2.1	2.1				
Total current	**11.7**	**4,734.3**	**4,746.0**				
Net capital expenditure on assets (8)	.	.	.				
Capital grants (9)	.	31.1	31.1				
Total capital	.	**31.1**	**31.1**				
Total higher education	**11.7**	**4,765.4**	**4,777.1**				

Sources: HM Treasury - Public Expenditure Statistical Analysis

(1) Total Managed Expenditure on services is a definition of aggregate public spending based on the national accounts aggregate TME. It is the consolidated sum of current and capital expenditure of central and local government, and public corporations, but excludes net public service pension payments in Annually managed Expenditure (AME), debt interest payments and other accounting adjustments.

(2) Data are taken from HM Treasury public expenditure figures which are not published to the same level of detail. They are not comparable with earlier versions of this table, which used different sources.

(3) Pay and pension costs.

(4) Including general administrative expenses and purchases of other goods and services which are not of a capital nature.

(5) Payments to producers designed to reduce their prices.

(6) Including grants to households, and from the Further and Higher Education Funding Councils to further education colleges and higher education institutions for their pay and other running costs.

(7) Including net payments to European Institutions, payments from UK's development assistance, subscriptions to international organisations and pensions paid to overseas residents.

(8) Comprising expenditure on new construction, the purchase of land, buildings and other physical assets, less the proceeds from sales of similar assets and the value of net changes in the level of stocks.

(9) Grants to the private sector, nationalised industries and other public corporations.

1.2 EXPENDITURE

Summary of Total Managed Expenditure on education services (1) – time series (2)

United Kingdom		Financial Year 1 April to 31 March			£ million
	1994-95	1995-96	1996-97	1997-98	1998-99
Local education authorities					
Current	23,834.9	23,962.4	24,365.3	24,375.9	25,879.0
Capital	1,145.1	1,202.1	1,114.4	1,186.3	1,348.8
Total	**24,980.0**	**25,164.5**	**25,479.7**	**25,562.2**	**27,227.8**
Central Government					
Current	8,993.2	9,703.0	10,468.4	11,461.9	11,066.7
Capital	718.6	705.7	173.0	165.9	140.0
Total	**9,711.8**	**10,408.7**	**10,641.4**	**11,627.8**	**11,206.7**
All public authorities					
Current	32,828.1	33,665.4	34,833.7	35,837.8	36,945.7
Capital	1,863.7	1,907.8	1,287.4	1,352.2	1,488.8
Total	**34,691.8**	**35,573.2**	**36,121.1**	**37,190.0**	**38,434.5**
Gross Domestic Product (GDP, at market prices) (3)	687,345	723,782	767,716	817,286	860,186
Education expenditure as a percentage of GDP	**5.0**	**4.9**	**4.7**	**4.6**	**4.5**
GDP deflator (3)	88.980	91.538	94.482	97.162	100.000
GDP in real terms (4)	772,472	790,687	812,550	841,161	860,186
Total education expenditure in real terms (4)	**38,988.3**	**38,861.5**	**38,230.6**	**38,276.4**	**38,434.5**

Sources: HM Treasury - Public Expenditure Statistical Analysis; Office for National Statistics

(1) Total Managed Expenditure on services is a definition of aggregate public spending based on the national accounts aggregate TME. It is the consolidated sum of current and capital expenditure of central and local government, and public corporations, but excludes net public service pension payments in Annually managed Expenditure (AME), debt interest payments and other accounting adjustments.

(2) Data are taken from HM Treasury public expenditure figures which are not published to the same level of detail. They are not comparable with earlier versions of this table, which used different sources.

(3) Source: Office for National Statistics - September 2000 National Accounts first release.

(4) At 1998-99 prices.

1.3

EXPENDITURE
Average Public spending(1) per school pupils(2): by type of school(3) — time series

United Kingdom

Expenditure per pupil(£)(4)

	Nursery & Primary (5)		Secondary (5)		Total Nursery & Primary and Secondary (5)	
	Cash Terms	Real Terms(6)	Cash Terms	Real Terms(6)	Cash Terms	Real Terms(6)
1988-89	1,110	1,650	1,740	2,580	1,380	2,050
1989-90	1,220	1,690	1,910	2,640	1,510	2,090
1990-91	1,350	1,730	2,070	2,650	1,650	2,120
1991-92	1,480	1,790	2,210	2,670	1,780	2,150
1992-93	1,600	1,870	2,320	2,710	1,890	2,210
1993-94(7)	1,640	1,870	2,310	2,630	1,900	2,170
1994-95	1,670	1,880	2,340	2,630	1,930	2,170
1995-96	1,710	1,870	2,370	2,590	1,960	2,140
1996-97	1,750	1,850	2,420	2,560	2,000	2,120
1997-98(8)	1,760	1,810	2,450	2,520	2,020	2,080
1998-99(9)	1,880	1,880	2,530	2,530	2,130	2,130

Source: Department for Education and Employment; National Assembly for Wales; Scottish Executive; Northern Ireland Department of Education

(1) This table uses a different source for expenditure data from that used in Tables 1.1 and 1.2. The calculations are based on a different methodology to that used for calculating national unit costs.
(2) Pupil FTEs.
(3) Excludes Grant maintained schools.
(4) Rounded to the nearest £10.
(5) Nursery and Primary Schools and Secondary Schools include Middle Schools as deemed in England.
(6) At 1998-99 prices.
(7) Includes 1992-93 data for Wales.
(8) Includes 1998-99 data for Northern Ireland.
(9) Includes 1997-98 data for Scotland.

Chapter 2
Schools

Key Facts

- There were 10.1 million full-time and part-time pupils in 34.6 thousand schools in 1999/00, compared with 9.3 million pupils in 34.6 thousand schools in 1990/91. (**Tables 2.1, 2.2, 2.3**)

- There were 295 thousand full and part-time pupils with statements of Special Educational Needs (SEN) in 1999/00, representing 2.9% of all pupils, with 96% of SEN pupils being in maintained schools. (**Table 2.4**)

- There were 500 thousand full-time qualified teachers in the United Kingdom in 1998/99, of which two-thirds were female. Eighty-seven per cent of full-time teachers were in maintained nursery & primary and secondary schools. (**Table 2.5**)

- The average number of pupils per mainstream maintained school in 1999/00 was 48 for nursery, 232 for primary and 876 for secondary. (**Table 2.6**)

- The average class size in primary schools in the United Kingdom in 1999/00 was 26.8 pupils. The average class size in secondary schools in England and Wales was 22.1 pupils. (**Table 2.7**)

- The average class size of one-teacher classes in primary and secondary schools in England in 1999/00 was 27.1 pupils and 22.0 pupils respectively. Excluding sixth form classes, the average class size for secondary schools was 23.8. (**Table 2.7**)

- The average pupil/teacher ratio in nursery schools in 1999/00 was 24.2. In primary schools the pupil/teacher ratio was 22.7 and in secondary schools it was 16.6. The average pupil/teacher ratio for all schools was 18.1 compared to 17.3 in 1990/91. (**Table 2.8**)

- In England in 2000 at Key Stage 1, 80% of boys and 88% of girls achieved level 2 or above in English teacher assessments, a rise of 2 and 1 percentage points, respectively since 1999. Maths and Science teacher assessment and tests results also increased on the 1999 totals, with maths tests results increasing by 4 percentage points for boys and 3 percentage points for girls. In Wales, figures for 2000 also show increases in all test results and teacher assessments for English, maths and science, with both boys and girls maths test results increasing by 4 percentage points each since 1999. (**Table 2.9**)

- At Key Stage 2, the percentages of boys and girls achieving at least level 4 results in English, maths and science (in both teacher assessment and tests) in England in 2000, showed increases of between 2 and 7 percentage points since 1999. In Wales, maths test results and teacher assessments for boys were similar to 1999, but all other results and assessments for both boys and girls increased by between 1 and 6 percentage points. (**Table 2.9**)

- The percentage of Key Stage 3 girls achieving level 5 or above in English tests in England in 2000 fell by 1 percentage point (while teacher assessments for girls remained at the 1999 level). Results in maths and in science increased in both teacher assessments and tests for boys and for girls. Figures for Wales in 2000 show a decrease in test results in English for both boys and for girls (by 3 and 2 percentage points respectively), with corresponding teacher assessments remaining at the 1999 level. (**Table 2.9**)

CHAPTER 2: SCHOOLS - LIST OF TABLES

SCHOOLS
Number of schools or departments(1) by type – time series

United Kingdom   Numbers

		Academic years			
	1990/91	1995/96	1997/98	1998/99 (2)	1999/00 (3)
UNITED KINGDOM					
Public sector mainstream					
Nursery	1,364	1,486	1,681	2,329 (4)	2,826 (4)
Primary	24,135	23,441	23,230	23,125	23,052
Secondary(5)	4,790	4,463	4,434	4,418	4,406
of which					
middle deemed secondary	491	400	377	377	377
modern	171	113	113	124	148
Grammar	222	231	229	237	234
Technical	3	1	6	7	4
Comprehensive	3,696	3,509	3,499	3,465	3,440
of which 6th form colleges	116	.	.	.	.
Other	207	209	210	208	203
Non-maintained mainstream	2,508	2,436	2,499	2,482	2,456
Special - maintained }		1,456	1,419	1,428	1,427
}	1,830				
- non maintained }		109	98	94	96
Pupil referral units	.	315	332	325	322
ALL SCHOOLS	34,627	33,706	33,693	34,201	34,585
ENGLAND					
Public sector mainstream					
Nursery	566	547	533	520	514
Primary	19,047	18,480	18,312	18,234	18,158
Secondary(5)	3,897	3,594	3,567	3,560	3,550
of which					
middle deemed secondary	491	400	377	377	377
modern	171	113	113	124	148
Grammar	152	160	157	165	162
Technical	3	1	6	7	4
Comprehensive	3,042	2,876	2,870	2,844	2,822
of which 6th form colleges	114	.	.	.	.
Other	38	44	44	43	37
Non-maintained mainstream	2,289	2,266	2,244	2,231	2,204
Special - maintained }		1,191	1,164	1,148	1,134
}	1,830				
- non maintained }		72	65	61	63
Pupil referral units	.	291	309	298	295
ALL SCHOOLS	27,179	26,441	26,194	26,052	25,918
WALES					
Public sector mainstream					
Nursery	54	52	47	46	46
Primary	1,717	1,681	1,673	1,660	1,660
Secondary(5,6)	230	228	228	229	229
of which 6th form colleges	2	.	.	.	.
Non-maintained mainstream	71	62	57	54	54
Special (maintained)	61	54	50	48	48
Pupil referral units	.	24	23	27	27
ALL SCHOOLS	2,133	2,101	2,078	2,064	2,064
SCOTLAND					
Public sector mainstream					
Nursery	659	796	1,010	1,672 (4)	2,171 (4)
Primary	2,372	2,332	2,300	2,291	2,293
Secondary(6)	424	405	401	392	389
Non-maintained mainstream	131	87	176 (1)	175 (1)	176 (1)
Special- maintained	343	164	158	185	195
- non maintained	.	37	33	33	33
ALL SCHOOLS	3,929	3,821	4,078	4,748	5,257
NORTHERN IRELAND					
Grant aided mainstream					
Nursery(7)	85	91	91	91	95
Primary	999	948 (8)	945 (8)	940 (8)	941 (8)
Secondary	239	236	238	237	238
of which					
Grammar	70	71	72	72	72
Other (Secondary intermediate)	169	165	166	165	166
Non-maintained mainstream	17	21	22	22	22
Special (maintained)	46	47	47	47	50
ALL SCHOOLS	1,386	1,343	1,343	1,337	1,346

Sources: Department for Education and Employment; National Assembly for Wales; Scottish Executive; Northern Ireland Department of Education

(1) Non-maintained mainstream schools in Scotland with more than one department have been counted once for each department e.g. a school with nursery, primary and secondary departments has been counted 3 times.
(2) Revised to include 1998/99 data for Wales and nursery schools data for Scotland.
(3) Provisional. Data for Wales are for 1998/99.
(4) Nursery schools figures for Scotland include pre-school education centres and are not therefore directly comparable with earlier years.
(5) From 1993/94 excludes sixth form colleges in England and Wales which were reclassified as further education colleges on 1 April 1993.
(6) All secondary schools are classed as Comprehensive.
(7) Excludes voluntary and private pre-school education centres (268 in total in 1999/00).
(8) Includes Preparatory Departments in Grammar Schools (24 in total in 1999/00).These figures were previously excluded from the totals.

SCHOOLS
Full-time and part-time pupils by age(1), gender(2) and school type, 1999/00(3)

United Kingdom   Thousands

| | Maintained schools(4) | | | | | | | | Non-maintained | | | |
	Nursery Schools (5,6)	Nursery Classes	Other Classes (7)	Total Primary Schools	Secondary Schools	Special schools	Pupil Referral Units (8)	All maintained schools	Special schools	Other Schools (9)	All non-maintained Schools	All schools
			Primary Schools								All	
Age at 31 August 1999(10)												
All												
2-4(11)	143.8	344.8	617.5	962.3	-	6.9	-	1,113.0	0.1	71.0	71.1	1,184.1
5	-	0.7	712.6	713.3	-	4.5	-	717.9	0.1	32.7	32.8	750.7
6	-	-	717.3	717.3	-	5.1	-	722.4	0.1	32.3	32.5	754.9
7	-	-	741.5	741.5	-	5.8	0.1	747.3	0.1	35.4	35.5	782.8
8	-	-	745.7	745.7	-	6.7	0.1	752.5	0.2	37.1	37.3	789.7
9	-	-	703.7	703.7	31.8	7.4	0.1	743.0	0.2	38.7	38.9	781.9
10	-	-	683.2	683.2	41.2	8.0	0.2	732.6	0.4	39.9	40.2	772.8
11	-	-	71.2	71.2	651.1	10.2	0.2	732.6	0.5	48.4	48.9	781.6
12	-	-	0.1	0.1	702.0	11.0	0.6	713.7	0.6	48.1	48.7	762.3
13	-	-	-	-	685.7	11.4	1.0	698.1	0.7	49.4	50.1	748.2
14	-	-	-	-	678.3	11.8	2.1	692.2	0.8	50.0	50.8	743.0
15	-	-	-	-	640.1	11.2	4.4	655.7	0.9	48.7	49.6	705.3
16	-	-	-	-	238.6	4.0	0.3	242.8	0.5	41.4	41.9	284.7
17	-	-	-	-	171.5	2.9	-	174.4	0.3	37.9	38.2	212.6
18	-	-	-	-	14.6	1.9	-	16.5	0.2	5.7	5.9	22.4
19 and over	-	-	-	-	2.5	0.1	-	2.6	0.1	1.8	1.9	4.5
Total	**143.8**	**345.5**	**4,992.8**	**5,338.3**	**3,857.3**	**108.6**	**9.1**	**9,457.2**	**5.8**	**618.4**	**624.3**	**10,081.5**
of which												
England	46.3	317.6	4,117.8	4,435.3	3,181.8	91.8	8.5	7,763.8	4.8	577.3	582.0	8,345.8
Wales(3)	2.8	23.9	267.8	291.7	204.2	3.8	0.7	503.1	-	9.7	9.7	512.8
Scotland(6)	88.8	-	429.3	429.3	316.4	8.3	-	842.8	1.0	30.2	31.3	874.0
Northern Ireland(5)	6.0	4.0	177.9	182.0	155.0	4.7	-	347.6	-	1.2	1.2	348.8
Males(2)												
2-4(11)	73.8	175.9	315.9	491.8	-	4.5	-	570.0	0.1	35.4	35.4	605.4
5	-	0.4	364.6	365.0	-	3.0	-	368.0	-	16.5	16.6	384.6
6	-	-	366.7	366.7	-	3.5	-	370.2	0.1	16.3	16.4	386.6
7	-	-	379.3	379.3	-	4.0	-	383.3	0.1	18.1	18.2	401.5
8	-	-	380.1	380.1	-	4.6	0.1	384.7	0.1	19.1	19.2	403.9
9	-	-	359.0	359.0	16.3	5.0	0.1	380.4	0.2	19.9	20.0	400.5
10	-	-	347.8	347.8	20.8	5.5	0.2	374.3	0.3	20.6	20.9	395.1
11	-	-	36.4	36.4	330.2	7.0	0.2	373.7	0.4	25.0	25.3	399.1
12	-	-	-	-	357.4	7.6	0.5	365.5	0.4	24.7	25.1	390.7
13	-	-	-	-	348.7	7.8	0.9	357.3	0.5	25.6	26.1	383.4
14	-	-	-	-	344.0	8.1	1.6	353.6	0.6	25.8	26.4	380.0
15	-	-	-	-	322.6	7.5	3.1	333.3	0.6	25.2	25.8	359.1
16	-	-	-	-	113.1	2.4	0.2	115.7	0.4	21.8	22.1	137.8
17	-	-	-	-	79.5	1.7	-	81.2	0.2	20.0	20.2	101.3
18	-	-	-	-	7.8	1.1	-	8.8	0.1	3.2	3.3	12.2
19 and over	-	-	-	-	1.0	-	-	1.0	0.1	1.1	1.1	2.1
Total	**73.8**	**176.3**	**2,549.7**	**2,726.0**	**1,941.3**	**73.2**	**6.9**	**4,821.2**	**4.0**	**318.1**	**322.1**	**5,143.3**
Females(2)												
2-4(11)	68.4	168.9	301.7	470.6	-	2.4	-	541.5	-	35.6	35.6	577.1
5	-	0.4	348.0	348.4	-	1.5	-	349.8	-	16.2	16.2	366.0
6	-	-	350.6	350.6	-	1.6	-	352.2	-	16.0	16.1	368.3
7	--	-	362.2	362.2	-	1.8	-	364.0	-	17.3	17.3	381.3
8	-	-	365.6	365.6	-	2.1	-	367.7	0.1	18.0	18.1	385.8
9	-	-	344.7	344.7	15.5	2.3	-	362.5	0.1	18.8	18.9	381.4
10	-	-	335.5	335.5	20.4	2.5	-	358.4	0.1	19.3	19.4	377.8
11	-	-	34.7	34.7	320.9	3.2	-	358.8	0.2	23.4	23.6	382.4
12	-	-	-	-	344.6	3.4	0.1	348.1	0.2	23.4	23.5	371.7
13	-	-	-	-	337.0	3.6	0.2	340.8	0.2	23.8	24.0	364.8
14	-	-	-	-	334.3	3.7	0.5	338.6	0.2	24.2	24.4	363.0
15	-	-	-	-	317.5	3.7	1.3	322.4	0.3	23.5	23.8	346.2
16	-	-	-	-	125.4	1.5	0.1	127.1	0.2	19.7	19.8	146.9
17	-	-	-	-	92.0	1.2	-	93.2	0.1	17.9	18.1	111.3
18	-	-	-	-	6.9	0.8	-	7.7	0.1	2.5	2.6	10.2
19 and over	-	-	-	-	1.5	-	-	1.6	0.1	0.8	0.8	2.4
Total	**68.5**	**169.3**	**2,443.1**	**2,612.3**	**1,916.0**	**35.4**	**2.3**	**4,634.4**	**1.8**	**300.4**	**302.2**	**4,936.5**

Sources: Department for Education and Employment; National Assembly for Wales; Scottish Executive; Northern Ireland Department of Education

(1) Figures for Scotland are estimates using proportions of the stage rolls.

(2) In Northern Ireland a gender split is not collected by age but is available by year group and so this is used as a proxy. For example pupils in Year 1 are counted as age 4, pupils in Year 2 are counted as age 5 etc. The figures for males and females therefore do not sum to the totals for the "All" age groups.

(3) Provisional. Data for Wales are for 1998/99.

(4) Grant-aided schools in Northern Ireland.

(5) Excludes 3,407 children at voluntary and private pre-school centres in Northern Ireland in places funded under the Pre-School Expansion Programme which began in 1998/99.

(6) Nursery schools figures for Scotland include pre-school education centres and are not therefore directly comparable with earlier years

(7) Includes reception pupils in primary classes and, in Northern Ireland, pupils in preparatory departments of grammar schools.

(8) England and Wales only. Figures for England exclude dually registered pupils, but these are included for Wales.

(9) Age 2-4 includes pupils less than 2 years of age in England.

(10) 1 July for Northern Ireland and 31 December for Scotland.

(11) Includes the so-called rising five's (i.e. those pupils who became 5 during the autumn term).

SCHOOLS
Full-time and part-time pupils by gender and school type — time series

United Kingdom   Thousands

| | Maintained Schools(1) | | | | | | | | Non-maintained | | | |
| | | Primary Schools | | | | | | All maintained schools | | | All non-maintained schools | All schools |
	Nursery schools (4)	Nursery classes	Other classes(2)	Total Primary Schools	Secondary schools(3)	Special schools	Pupil Referral Units(5)		Special schools	Other schools		
1990/91												
All	**104.9**		**4,954.5**	**4,954.5**	**3,473.3**	**107.7**	..	**8,640.4**	**6.4**	**613.4**	**619.7**	**9,260.2**
Males	54.0		2,529.4	2,529.4	1,753.6	70.6	..	4,407.7	4.2	323.8	328.0	4,735.6
Females	50.9		2,425.1	2,425.1	1,719.7	37.1	..	4,232.8	2.2	289.6	291.8	4,524.5
1995/96												
All	**84.3**	**366.7**	**4,968.6**	**5,335.2**	**3,676.2**	**107.7**	..	**9,203.3**	**6.7**	**602.9**	**609.7**	**9,813.0**
Males	43.5	187.8	2,535.4	2,723.2	1,853.0	71.6	..	4,691.3	4.6	314.7	319.3	5,010.5
Females	40.8	178.8	2,433.2	2,612.0	1,823.2	36.1	..	4,512.1	2.2	288.3	290.4	4,802.5
1997/98												
All	**78.5**	**378.6**	**5,036.1**	**5,414.7**	**3,742.7**	**109.9**	**8.4**	**9,354.2**	**6.1**	**614.8**	**620.9**	**9,975.1**
Males	40.7	193.8	2,569.7	2,763.5	1,884.9	73.6	6.1	4,768.7	4.2	318.4	322.5	5,091.2
Females	37.8	184.8	2,466.4	2,651.2	1,857.8	36.3	2.2	4,585.5	1.9	296.5	298.4	4,883.9
1998/99(6)												
All	**79.0 (7,8)**	**379.8**	**5,026.0**	**5,405.7**	**3,793.3**	**109.8**	**8.9**	**9,396.7**	**5.7**	**617.3 (9)**	**623.0**	**10,019.7**
Males	40.9 (7,8)	194.5	2,565.1	2,759.6	1,910.6	73.8	6.7	4,791.5	3.9	317.9 (9)	321.9	5,113.4
Females	38.1 (7,8)	185.3	2,460.9	2,646.2	1,882.6	36.0	2.2	4,605.2	1.8	299.3 (9)	301.1	4,906.3
1999/00(9)												
All	**143.8 (10,11)**	**345.5**	**4,992.8**	**5,338.3**	**3,857.3**	**108.6**	**9.1**	**9,457.2**	**5.8**	**618.4**	**624.3**	**10,081.5**
Males	73.8 (10,11)	176.3	2,549.7	2,726.0	1,941.3	73.2	6.9	4,821.2	4.0	318.1	322.1	5,143.3
Females	68.5 (10,11)	169.3	2,443.1	2,612.3	1,916.0	35.4	2.3	4,634.4	1.8	300.4	302.2	4,936.5

Source: Department for Education and Employment, National Assembly for Wales, Scottish Executive, Northern Ireland Department of Education

(1) Grant aided schools in Northern Ireland.

(2) Includes reception pupils in primary schools and, in Northern Ireland, pupils in preparatory departments of grammar schools.

(3) From 1993/94 excludes sixth form colleges in England and Wales which were reclassified as Further Education colleges from 1 April 1993.

(4) For 1990/91 and 1999/00, nursery schools includes some nursery classes in primary schools for Scotland.

(5) England and Wales only. Figures for England exclude dually registered pupils, but these are included for Wales.

(6) Revised to include 1998/99 data for Wales.

(7) Includes 1997/98 data for Scotland.

(8) Includes 1,871 children at voluntary and private pre-school centres in Northern Ireland in places funded under the Pre-School Expansion Programme which began in 1998/99.

(9) Includes 1997/98 non-maintained nursery children in Scotland.

(10) Excludes 3,407 children at voluntary and private pre-school centres in Northern Ireland in places funded under the Pre-School Expansion Programme which began in 1998/99.

(11) Nursery schools figures for Scotland include pre-school education centres and are not therefore directly comparable with earlier years.

SCHOOLS
2.4 Full-time and part-time pupils with Special Educational Needs (SEN)(1) by type of school, 1999/00(2)

United Kingdom   Thousands and *percentages*

	UK(2)	England	Wales(2)	Scotland(3)	N Ireland
ALL SCHOOLS					
Total Pupils	10,085.2	8,345.8	512.8	874.4	352.2
SEN pupils with statements	294.5	252.9	17.1	16.1	8.5
Incidence(%)(3)	*2.9*	*3.0*	*3.3*	*1.8*	*2.4*
MAINTAINED SCHOOLS(4)					
Nursery(5,6)					
Total Pupils	147.3	46.3	2.8	88.8	9.4
SEN pupils with statements	1.0	0.5	-	0.4	0.1
Incidence(%)(3)	*0.7*	*1.0*	*1.2*	*0.5*	*0.7*
Placement(%)(7)	*0.3*	*0.2*	*0.2*	*2.7*	*0.8*
Primary(8)					
Total Pupils	5,340.5	4,435.3	291.7	431.4	182.0
SEN pupils without statements(9)	896.7	886.0	-	10.7	-
SEN pupils with statements	84.9	72.5	6.2	3.9	2.2
Pupils with statements - Incidence(%)(3)	*1.6*	*1.6*	*2.1*	*0.9*	*1.2*
Pupils with statements - Placement(%)(7)	*28.8*	*28.7*	*36.3*	*24.5*	*26.3*
Secondary					
Total Pupils	3,855.2	3,181.8	204.2	314.3	155.0
SEN pupils without statements(9)	549.7	541.4	-	8.3	-
SEN pupils with statements	93.6	79.8	6.8	4.8	2.3
Pupils with statements - Incidence(%)(3)	*2.4*	*2.5*	*3.3*	*1.5*	*1.5*
Pupils with statements - Placement(%)(7)	*31.8*	*31.6*	*39.6*	*29.8*	*26.9*
Special(10,11)					
Total Pupils	108.6	91.8	3.8	8.3	4.7
SEN pupils with statements	101.0	86.9	3.7	6.5	3.9
Incidence(%)(3)	*93.0*	*94.6*	*96.1*	*78.7*	*83.3*
Placement(%)(7)	*34.3*	*34.4*	*21.4*	*40.7*	*46.0*
Pupil Referral Units(10)					
Total Pupils	9.1	8.5	0.7	.	.
SEN pupils with statements(9)	2.0	1.8	0.2	.	.
Incidence(%)(3)	*21.4*	*20.8*	*28.3*	.	.
Placement(%)(7)	*0.7*	*0.7*	*1.1*	.	.
OTHER SCHOOLS					
Independent					
Total Pupils	618.7	577.3	9.7	30.5	1.2
SEN pupils with statements(9)	7.1	6.8	0.2	-	..
Incidence(%)(3)	*1.1*	*1.2*	*2.5*	*0.1*	..
Placement(%)(7)	*2.4*	*2.7*	*1.4*	*0.2*	..
Non-maintained Special(10)					
Total Pupils	5.8	4.8	.	1.0	.
SEN pupils with statements	4.9	4.6	.	0.3	.
Incidence(%)(3)	*84.7*	*96.6*	.	*30.7*	.
Placement(%)(7)	*1.7*	*1.8*	.	*2.0*	.

Sources: Department for Education and Employment; National Assembly for Wales; Scottish Executive; Northern Ireland Department of Education

(1) For Scotland, pupils with a Record of Needs.

(2) Provisional. Data for Wales are for 1998/99.

(3) Incidence of pupils - the number of pupils with statements within each school type expressed as a proportion of the total number of pupils on roll in each school type.

(4) Grant-Aided schools in Northern Ireland.

(5) Includes pupils in Voluntary and Private Pre-School Centres in Northern Ireland funded under the Pre-School Expansion Programme which began in 1998/99.

(6) Nursery schools figures for Scotland include pre-school education centres and are not therefore directly comparable with earlier years.

(7) Placement of pupils - the number of pupils with statements within each school type expressed as a proportion of the number of pupils with statements in all schools.

(8) Includes nursery classes (except for Scotland, where they are included with Nursery schools) and reception classes in primary schools.

(9) UK totals are slight undercounts as data are not available for Wales and not applicable for Northern Ireland.

(10) England figures exclude dually registered pupils.

(11) Including general and hospital special schools.

2.5

SCHOOLS
Qualified teachers by type of school and gender — time series

	(i) Full-time teachers				Thousands
	Public sector mainstream schools		Non-maintained	All Special	Total
	Nursery and Primary	Secondary(2)	mainstream schools	schools	All Schools
All teachers					
Great Britain					
1990/91	200.3	223.2	44.9	18.2	486.6
1995/96	203.3	212.2	48.6	16.6	480.6
1996/97	202.7	211.3	48.2	16.4	478.6
1997/98(1)	201.1	209.6	49.1	16.0	476.0
United Kingdom					
1998/99	210.5	223.0	50.5	16.7	500.6
of which:					
England & Wales	181.1	190.6	47.9	14.0	433.4
Scotland	21.3	22.2	2.5	2.0	48.0
Northern Ireland	8.1	10.2	0.1	0.7	19.2
Males					
Great Britain					
1990/91	35.8	116.0	20.6	5.8	178.2
1995/96	33.8	103.4	21.1	5.3	163.5
1996/97	33.0	101.6	20.6	5.2	160.4
1997/98(1)	31.9	99.3	20.1	5.0	156.4
United Kingdom					
1998/99	32.9	103.9	20.8	5.1	162.8
of which:					
England & Wales	29.9	88.8	19.7	4.5	142.9
Scotland	1.5	10.9	1.1	0.4	13.9
Northern Ireland	1.5	4.3	-	0.1	5.9
Females					
Great Britain					
1990/91	164.5	107.1	24.3	12.4	308.4
1995/96	169.5	108.8	27.4	11.3	317.0
1996/97	169.7	109.7	27.6	11.2	318.2
1997/98(1)	169.2	110.3	28.5	11.0	319.0
United Kingdom					
1998/99	177.6	119.1	29.6	11.6	337.8
of which:					
England & Wales	151.2	101.8	28.1	9.4	290.6
Scotland	19.8	11.3	1.4	1.6	34.1
Northern Ireland	6.6	5.9	0.1	0.6	13.2

	(ii) Part-time teachers(3)				Thousands
	Public sector mainstream schools		Non-maintained	All Special	Total
	Nursery and Primary	Secondary(2)	mainstream schools	schools	All Schools
All teachers					
Great Britain					
1990/91	..	..	..	..	30.0
1995/96	18.7	17.6	8.9	1.5	46.7
1996/97	17.8	15.7	9.4	1.4	44.3
1997/98	18.0	16.2	10.7	1.4	46.4
United Kingdom					
1998/99	19.7	16.8	9.9	1.5	48.0

Sources: Department for Education and Employment; National Assembly for Wales; Scottish Executive; Northern Ireland Department of Education

(1) Includes revised data for England and Wales.

(2) From 1993/94 excludes sixth form colleges in England and Wales which were reclassified as further education colleges on 1 April 1993.

(3) Full-time equivalents of part-time teachers.

2.6

Schools, and pupils by size of school(1) or department(2), by school type, 1999/00(3)

United Kingdom					(i) Number of schools							Numbers
	25 and under	26 to 50	51 to 100	101 to 200	201 to 300	301 to 400	401 to 600	601 to 800	801 to 1,000	1,001 to 1,500	1,501 and over	Total
United Kingdom(3)												
Public sector mainstream												
Nursery(4,5)	1,086	819	901	286	2	-	-	-	-	-	-	3,094
Primary(6)	333	1,112	2,706	5,534	7,248	3,534	2,338	225	21	1	-	23,052
Secondary(7)	6	8	11	63	112	217	652	834	950	1,333	220	4,406
Pupil referral units	210	60	39	10	2	-	1	-	-	-	-	322
Non-maintained mainstream(2,8)	234	245	333	593	374	220	196	109	84	67	1	2,456
Special	175	334	626	360	26	2	-	-	-	-	-	1,523
All schools	**2,044**	**2,578**	**4,616**	**6,846**	**7,764**	**3,973**	**3,187**	**1,168**	**1,055**	**1,401**	**221**	**34,853**
England												
Public sector mainstream												
Nursery	-	46	307	160	1	-	-	-	-	-	-	514
Primary	65	554	1,898	4,226	6,216	2,980	2,017	185	17	-	-	18,158
Secondary	-	1	1	44	91	156	503	671	755	1,135	193	3,550
Pupil referral units	189	57	36	10	2	-	1	-	-	-	-	295
Non-maintained mainstream(8)	171	192	302	558	350	204	184	98	80	64	1	2,204
Special	72	242	545	319	17	2	-	-	-	-	-	1,197
All schools	**497**	**1,092**	**3,089**	**5,317**	**6,677**	**3,342**	**2,705**	**954**	**852**	**1,199**	**194**	**25,918**
Wales(3)												
Public sector mainstream												
Nursery	3	14	26	3	-	-	-	-	-	-	-	46
Primary	49	177	270	523	423	151	64	3	-	-	-	1,660
Secondary	-	-	-	-	-	11	35	52	47	72	12	229
Pupil referral units	21	3	3	-	-	-	-	-	-	-	-	27
Non-maintained mainstream	11	10	5	9	7	5	2	5	-	-	-	54
Special	3	11	23	9	2	-	-	-	-	-	-	48
All schools	**87**	**215**	**327**	**544**	**432**	**167**	**101**	**60**	**47**	**72**	**12**	**2,064**
Scotland												
Public sector mainstream												
Nursery(4)	826	741	488	115	1	-	-	-	-	-	-	2,171
Primary	200	271	312	542	474	299	182	12	1	-	-	2,293
Secondary	6	7	8	13	8	13	50	66	106	100	12	389
Non-maintained mainstream(2)	43	38	21	25	15	11	10	6	4	3	-	176
Special	93	72	44	15	4	-	-	-	-	-	-	228
All schools	**1,168**	**1,129**	**873**	**710**	**502**	**323**	**242**	**84**	**111**	**103**	**12**	**5,257**
Northern Ireland												
Grant aided mainstream												
Nursery(5)	257	18	80	8	-	-	-	-	-	-	-	363
Primary(6)	19	110	226	243	135	104	75	25	3	1	-	941
Secondary(7)	-	-	2	6	13	37	64	45	42	26	3	238
Non-maintained mainstream	9	5	5	1	2	-	-	-	-	-	-	22
Special	7	9	14	17	3	-	-	-	-	-	-	50
All schools	**292**	**142**	**327**	**275**	**153**	**141**	**139**	**70**	**45**	**27**	**3**	**1,614**

Sources: Department for Education and Employment; National Assembly for Wales; Scottish Executive; Northern Ireland Department of Education

(1) School size on a pupil headcount basis.
(2) Non-maintained mainstream schools in Scotland with more than one department have been counted once for each department e.g. a school with nursery, primary and secondary departments has been counted 3 times.
(3) Provisional. Data for Wales are for 1998/99.
(4) Nursery schools figures for Scotland include pre-school education centres and are not therefore directly comparable with earlier years.
(5) Northern Ireland figures include 268 Voluntary and Private Pre-School Centres including 3,407 pupils, funded under the Pre-School Expansion Programme which began in 1998/99.
(6) Includes 24 preparatory departments attached to Grammar Schools in Northern Ireland.
(7) Includes Voluntary Grammar Schools in Northern Ireland.
(8) Includes City Technology Colleges.
(9) Includes pupils in nursery classes in primary schools in Scotland.
(10) Includes pupils in nursery classes and reception classes, except for Scotland - see footnote (9).

SCHOOLS

Schools, and pupils by size of school(1) or department(2), by school type, 1999/00(3)

United Kingdom   (ii) Number of pupils   Thousands

	25 and under	26 to 50	51 to 100	101 to 200	201 to 300	301 to 400	401 to 600	601 to 800	801 to 1,000	1,001 to 1,500	1,501 and over	Total
United Kingdom(3)												
Public sector mainstream												
Nursery(4,5,9)	15.4	31.1	64.3	35.9	0.5	-	-	-	-	-	-	147.3
Primary(6,10)	5.7	43.6	204.8	850.6	1,767.3	1,221.6	1,077.9	149.5	18.3	1.2	-	5,340.5
Secondary(7)	0.1	0.3	0.8	9.9	28.7	76.6	332.8	586.7	852.7	1,599.6	369.4	3,857.6
Pupil referral units	2.3	2.1	2.6	1.3	0.4	-	0.4	-	-	-	-	9.1
Non-maintained mainstream(8)	3.4	9.4	24.4	88.3	91.5	76.0	93.3	76.3	75.5	78.1	2.8	619.0
Special	2.7	12.7	45.6	46.8	5.8	0.7	-	-	-	-	-	114.4
All schools	**29.6**	**99.2**	**342.6**	**1,032.8**	**1,894.3**	**1,374.8**	**1,504.5**	**812.5**	**946.5**	**1,678.8**	**372.2**	**10,087.9**
England												
Public sector mainstream												
Nursery	-	2.0	23.7	20.4	0.2	-	-	-	-	-	-	46.3
Primary(10)	1.3	22.4	145.3	653.2	1,515.8	1,030.5	929.5	122.7	14.8	-	-	4,435.3
Secondary	-	0.1	0.1	7.0	23.4	55.1	257.7	472.0	678.7	1,364.1	323.6	3,181.8
Pupil referral units	1.9	2.0	2.4	1.3	0.4	-	0.4	-	-	-	-	8.5
Non-maintained mainstream(8)	2.5	7.3	22.2	83.2	85.9	70.2	87.9	68.7	72.0	74.5	2.8	577.3
Special	1.1	9.6	39.8	41.4	3.9	0.7	-	-	-	-	-	96.6
All schools	**6.8**	**43.3**	**233.5**	**806.5**	**1,629.7**	**1,156.5**	**1,275.5**	**663.4**	**765.4**	**1,438.6**	**326.5**	**8,345.8**
Wales(3)												
Public sector mainstream												
Nursery	0.1	0.5	1.8	0.4	-	-	-	-	-	-	-	2.8
Primary(10)	0.9	6.8	20.1	79.1	101.8	51.3	29.6	2.0	-	-	-	291.7
Secondary	-	-	-	-	-	3.6	17.2	35.9	41.4	86.2	19.9	204.2
Pupil referral units	0.3	0.1	0.2	-	-	-	-	-	-	-	-	0.7
Non-maintained mainstream	0.2	0.4	0.4	1.3	1.5	1.7	0.8	3.4	-	-	-	9.7
Special	0.1	0.5	1.7	1.2	0.4	-	-	-	-	-	-	3.8
All schools	**1.6**	**8.3**	**24.2**	**82.0**	**103.8**	**56.6**	**47.6**	**41.3**	**41.4**	**86.2**	**19.9**	**512.8**
Scotland												
Public sector mainstream												
Nursery(4,9)	12.3	28.1	33.8	14.4	0.3	-	-	-	-	-	-	88.8
Primary	3.1	10.0	23.1	83.4	116.8	103.5	82.8	7.8	0.8	-	-	431.4
Secondary	0.1	0.2	0.6	1.9	2.0	4.7	26.0	47.1	95.2	118.7	20.2	316.6
Non-maintained mainstream	0.6	1.5	1.5	3.6	3.7	4.0	4.6	4.2	3.6	3.5	-	30.8
Special	1.4	2.2	3.1	1.8	0.9	-	-	-	-	-	-	9.4
All schools	**17.5**	**42.0**	**62.0**	**105.1**	**123.7**	**112.2**	**113.4**	**59.0**	**99.6**	**122.3**	**20.2**	**877.0**
Northern Ireland												
Grant aided mainstream												
Nursery(5)	3.0	0.5	5.0	0.8	-	-	-	-	-	-	-	9.4
Primary(6,10)	0.4	4.3	16.3	34.9	32.8	36.3	36.0	17.0	2.7	1.2	-	182.0
Secondary(7)	-	-	0.2	1.0	3.3	13.2	31.9	31.7	37.5	30.5	5.7	155.0
Non-maintained mainstream	0.2	0.2	0.3	0.2	0.4	-	-	-	-	-	-	1.2
Special	0.1	0.4	1.1	2.4	0.7	-	-	-	-	-	-	4.7
All schools	**3.7**	**5.4**	**22.9**	**39.3**	**37.2**	**49.5**	**68.0**	**48.7**	**40.2**	**31.7**	**5.7**	**352.2**

Sources: Department for Education and Employment; National Assembly for Wales; Scottish Executive; Northern Ireland Department of Education
See previous page for footnotes.

2.7 SCHOOLS
Average class size(1), by Government Office Region(2) – time series

United Kingdom   Numbers

	One teacher classes		All classes(3)	
	Primary	Secondary(4,5)	Primary	Secondary(4)
1990/91				
Great Britain	..	..	26.4	21.0
North East	26.0	20.6	26.5	21.6
North West	27.1	20.4	27.5	21.1
Yorkshire and the Humber	25.9	20.5	26.4	21.2
East Midlands	26.1	20.1	26.5	20.9
West Midlands	26.3	20.6	26.8	21.1
Eastern	26.0	20.9	26.4	21.7
London	25.8	20.7	26.2	21.4
South East	26.7	20.7	27.1	21.4
South West	26.4	20.9	26.7	21.4
England	26.3	20.6 [21.9]	26.8	21.3
Wales	..	19.5	24.8	21.0
Scotland	..	..	24.7	18.5
1995/96				
Great Britain	..	..	27.1	21.6
North East	27.1	22.0	27.2	22.5
North West	27.7	21.8	28.0	22.0
Yorkshire and the Humber	27.6	21.9	27.9	22.1
East Midlands	27.6	21.6	27.8	21.9
West Midlands	27.3	21.8	27.6	22.0
Eastern	26.6	21.3	26.8	21.6
London	27.0	21.7	27.3	22.0
South East	27.3	21.4	27.4	21.6
South West	27.3	21.8	27.4	22.0
England	27.3	21.7 [23.4]	27.5	21.9
Wales	..	..	25.9	20.2
Scotland	..	..	24.8	19.5
1996/97				
Great Britain(6)	..	..	27.3	21.5
North East	27.2	22.0	27.3	22.4
North West	27.9	21.8	28.1	22.0
Yorkshire and the Humber	27.9	21.9	28.1	22.1
East Midlands	27.8	21.6	28.0	21.9
West Midlands	27.4	22.0	27.6	22.1
Eastern	26.9	21.3	27.0	21.5
London	27.1	21.7	27.3	21.9
South East	27.5	21.3	27.6	21.4
South West	27.5	21.7	27.6	21.8
England	27.5	21.7 [23.4]	27.6	21.9
Wales	..	..	25.9	20.6
Scotland(6)	..	..	24.9	19.2

Source: Department for Education and Employment, National Assembly for Wales, Scottish Executive, Northern Ireland Department of Education

(1) Maintained schools only.
(2) Government Office Regions in England and each UK country.
(3) Includes classes where more than one teacher may be present.
(4) Figures throughout the table exclude sixth form colleges in England and Wales, which were reclassified as further education colleges from 1 April 1993.
(5) Figures in [brackets] are for pupils aged mainly under 16 (i.e. excluding sixth forms).
(6) Includes 1997/98 data for Scotland.
(7) Great Britain.
(8) Excludes preparatory departments attached to Grammar schools.
(9) Includes revised data for England, Wales and Scotland.
(10) England and Wales.
(11) Includes 1998/99 data for Wales.

2.7

United Kingdom   Numbers

	One teacher classes		All classes(3)	
	Primary	Secondary(4,5)	Primary	Secondary(4)
1997/98				
United Kingdom	..	..	27.3	21.6 (7)
North East	27.3	22.2	27.4	22.4
North West	28.0	21.8	28.2	22.0
Yorkshire and the Humber	28.2	22.1	28.4	22.3
East Midlands	28.0	21.7	28.2	21.9
West Midlands	27.5	22.0	27.7	22.1
Eastern	27.2	21.2	27.3	21.5
London	27.3	21.7	27.5	21.9
South East	27.8	21.4	27.9	21.5
South West	27.9	22.0	28.0	22.1
England	27.7	21.7 [23.6]	27.8	21.9
Wales	..	..	26.4	20.6
Scotland	..	..	24.9	19.2
Northern Ireland	..	..	24.1 (8)	..
1998/99				
United Kingdom(9)	..	..	27.1	21.9 (10)
North East	26.7	22.3	26.9	22.6
North West(9)	27.7	21.8	27.9	22.0
Yorkshire and the Humber	27.7	22.2	27.9	22.3
East Midlands	27.6	21.8	27.7	22.0
West Midlands(9)	27.0	22.0	27.2	22.0
Eastern(9)	27.0	21.3	27.2	21.7
London	27.3	21.8	27.5	22.1
South East	27.7	21.7	27.8	21.8
South West	27.7	22.0	27.8	22.2
England(9)	27.5	21.9 [23.7]	27.6	22.0
Wales(9)	..	..	25.6	20.7
Scotland(9)	24.9	..	24.9	..
Northern Ireland	..	..	24.3 (8)	..
1999/00				
United Kingdom	..	..	26.8	22.1 (10)
North East	26.2	22.1	26.3	22.2
North West	27.1	22.0	27.3	22.1
Yorkshire and the Humber	27.2	22.3	27.4	22.4
East Midlands	27.4	22.1	27.5	22.3
West Midlands	26.9	22.0	27.1	22.1
Eastern	26.8	21.7	26.9	21.9
London	27.3	22.0	27.5	22.2
South East	27.3	21.9	27.4	22.0
South West	27.3	22.2	27.4	22.3
England	27.1	22.0 [23.8]	27.3	22.2
Wales	..	..	25.2	20.7 (11)
Scotland	24.5	..	24.6	..
Northern Ireland	..	..	24.1 (8)	..

Source: Department for Education and Employment, National Assembly for Wales, Scottish Executive, Northern Ireland Department of Education

For footnotes see previous page.

SCHOOLS

Pupil/teacher(1) ratios(2) by type of school and Government Office Region(3) – time series

United Kingdom   Numbers

| | Public sector mainstream(4) | | | Non-maintained mainstream schools | Pupil Referral Units(8) | Special schools | | All schools |
	Nursery Schools	Primary Schools(5)	Secondary Schools(6,7)			Maintained	Non-maintained	
1990/91								
United Kingdom	21.6	22.0	15.2	10.7	.	5.9	..	17.3
North East	19.3	22.3	15.6	12.5	.	6.1	4.7	18.0
North West	19.3	22.8	15.4	12.6	.	5.7	5.0	18.1
Yorkshire and the Humber	18.1	21.9	15.5	11.6	.	5.8	4.7	17.6
East Midlands	19.1	22.4	15.2	10.5	.	5.7	5.4	17.5
West Midlands	24.0	22.4	15.5	10.6	.	6.3	3.9	17.7
Eastern	18.7	22.4	16.2	10.7	.	5.8	5.0	17.6
London	16.9	20.6	15.3	11.6	.	5.1	4.8	16.6
South East	18.1	22.8	16.2	9.9	.	7.0	4.8	17.0
South West	19.2	22.4	16.0	9.8	.	6.5	4.9	17.2
England	19.1	22.2	15.7	10.8	.	6.0	4.8	17.4
Wales	20.6	22.3	15.4	9.8	.	6.3	.	18.2
Scotland	25.7	19.5	12.2	10.5	.	4.5	..	15.2
Northern Ireland	24.7	22.9	14.7	11.0	.	6.9	.	18.1
1995/96(6)								
United Kingdom	21.3	22.7	16.1	10.3	..	6.3	..	18.0 (9)
North East	21.3	23.7	17.1	11.9	5.7	7.1	5.0	19.3
North West	20.0	23.7	16.6	11.7	4.1	5.8	4.5	18.9
Yorkshire and the Humber	18.7	23.8	17.0	11.3	4.6	6.5	3.8	19.2
East Midlands	19.2	24.1	16.8	10.1	2.9	6.2	5.2	18.9
West Midlands	23.3	23.5	16.7	10.4	3.1	7.1	3.6	18.7
Eastern	19.3	22.7	16.5	10.1	4.3	6.6	4.1	17.9
London	16.4	21.6	15.8	10.8	5.2	5.5	5.5	17.0
South East	17.0	23.0	16.7	9.4	3.9	7.1	4.7	17.2
South West	20.4	23.6	17.1	9.4	4.1	6.9	4.9	18.2
England	19.2	23.2	16.6	10.2	4.3	6.7	4.6	18.2
Wales	19.5	22.5	16.0	10.1	..	6.7	.	18.7
Scotland	24.3	19.5	12.9	11.0	.	4.8	3.7	15.5
Northern Ireland	23.9	20.4	14.7	10.9	.	6.7	.	17.1
1996/97(6)								
United Kingdom	21.3	22.8	16.2	10.4	..	6.4	..	18.1 (9)
North East	20.3	23.8	17.1	11.8	8.5	7.3	5.0	19.3
North West	19.6	23.9	16.6	11.9	4.5	6.2	4.7	19.1
Yorkshire and the Humber	18.6	24.1	17.2	11.4	5.1	6.5	3.8	19.5
East Midlands	17.9	24.4	17.0	10.5	2.9	6.2	5.7	19.2
West Midlands	22.9	23.6	16.9	10.4	3.8	7.0	3.1	18.8
Eastern	18.8	23.0	16.6	10.1	3.9	6.8	4.3	18.0
London	16.9	21.9	15.9	10.7	4.7	5.7	6.7	17.1
South East	16.3	23.2	16.7	9.5	3.7	7.1	4.6	17.3
South West	20.5	23.7	17.1	9.6	4.4	7.1	5.1	18.3
England	18.9	23.4	16.7	10.3	4.3	6.6	4.6	18.3
Wales	19.3	22.6	16.2	10.0	..	6.7	.	18.8
Scotland	24.7	19.6	13.2	11.5	.	4.8	3.5	15.8
Northern Ireland	23.4	19.8	14.5	9.7	.	6.4	.	16.7

Sources: Department for Education and Employment; National Assembly for Wales; Scottish Executive; Northern Ireland Department of Education

(1) Qualified teachers only for all countries.
(2) Includes full-time equivalents of part-time pupils and teachers.
(3) Government Office Regions in England and each UK country.
(4) Includes grant-maintained schools from 1990/91.
(5) Includes preparatory departments attached to grammar schools in Northern Ireland.
(6) From 1993/94 excludes sixth form colleges in England and Wales which were reclassified as further education colleges from 1 April 1993.
(7) Includes voluntary grammar schools in Northern Ireland from 1990/91, formerly allocated to the non-maintained sector.
(8) Pupil Referral Units refer to England only.
(9) Excludes Pupil Referral Units as information on teachers is not collected for Wales.
(10) Revised to include 1998/99 data for Wales.
(11) Includes 1997/98 nursery data for Scotland.
(12) Provisional. Includes 1998/99 data for Wales.
(13) Nursery schools figures for Scotland include pre-school education centres and are not therefore directly comparable with earlier years.

2.8

SCHOOLS
Pupil/teacher(1) ratios(2) by type of school and Government Office Region(3) – time series

United Kingdom

Numbers

	Public sector mainstream(4)			Non-maintained mainstream schools	Pupil Referral Units(8)	Special schools		All schools
	Nursery Schools	Primary Schools(5)	Secondary Schools(6,7)			Maintained	Non-maintained	
1997/98(6)								
United Kingdom	20.7	23.1	16.4	10.2	..	6.5	..	18.2 (9)
North East	20.0	23.9	17.4	11.8	6.1	7.6	4.9	19.5
North West	19.3	24.0	16.7	11.7	5.0	6.4	5.1	19.2
Yorkshire and the Humber	17.7	24.5	17.4	11.5	4.8	6.7	3.7	19.7
East Midlands	17.0	24.6	17.2	10.5	3.2	6.2	5.2	19.3
West Midlands	22.5	23.9	17.0	10.2	3.8	7.0	3.3	19.0
Eastern	19.0	23.3	16.7	9.9	3.1	6.8	3.9	18.1
London	16.7	22.2	16.0	10.9	4.6	5.8	5.8	17.3
South East	16.5	23.6	16.9	9.2	4.1	7.2	4.8	17.4
South West	19.5	24.2	17.3	9.5	4.5	7.2	5.1	18.5
England	18.6	23.7	16.9	10.2	4.3	6.7	4.7	18.5
Wales	18.2	23.0	16.5	9.9	..	6.9	.	19.1
Scotland	23.1	19.9	13.2	10.7	.	4.7	3.3	15.8
Northern Ireland	24.4	19.9	14.5	9.3	.	6.7	.	16.7
1998/99(6,10,11)								
United Kingdom	20.6	22.9	16.5	10.0	..	6.4	..	18.1 (9)
North East	19.6	23.5	17.4	11.7	4.8	7.3	4.9	19.2
North West	19.0	23.9	16.8	11.3	4.7	6.5	5.0	19.0
Yorkshire and the Humber	18.5	24.1	17.5	11.1	4.9	6.7	3.7	19.6
East Midlands	17.8	24.2	17.3	10.0	4.1	6.2	5.1	19.2
West Midlands	22.3	23.6	17.0	10.1	4.2	7.0	3.6	18.8
Eastern	19.0	23.3	16.9	9.6	5.1	6.9	4.5	18.2
London	16.3	22.3	16.1	10.5	5.4	5.9	5.7	17.3
South East	16.4	23.6	17.1	9.2	4.6	6.1	4.7	17.5
South West	19.6	24.0	17.5	9.5	4.2	6.9	5.2	18.5
England	18.4	23.5	17.0	10.0	4.5	6.7	4.7	18.4
Wales(10)	18.4	22.3	16.5	9.8	..	6.8	.	18.8
Scotland(11)	23.1	19.4	13.0	10.4	.	4.4	3.3	15.4
Northern Ireland	23.7	19.9	14.6	10.0	.	6.4	.	16.7
1999/00(6,12,13)								
United Kingdom	24.2	22.7	16.6	9.9	..	6.3	..	18.1 (9)
North East	20.0	23.1	17.3	11.7	5.7	7.2	5.1	19.1
North West	18.7	23.4	16.8	11.0	4.6	6.4	4.8	18.8
Yorkshire and the Humber	18.0	23.7	17.5	10.9	4.8	6.7	3.7	19.4
East Midlands	17.1	24.0	17.5	9.8	4.3	6.2	5.0	19.1
West Midlands	21.9	23.5	17.1	9.9	4.3	7.0	3.3	18.7
Eastern	17.8	23.1	17.2	9.6	2.7	6.9	5.0	18.2
London	16.3	22.3	16.5	10.6	4.2	5.8	5.8	17.4
South East	16.3	23.2	17.3	8.9	4.4	7.0	4.5	17.3
South West	18.1	23.7	17.7	9.2	4.3	6.7	5.2	18.4
England	18.1	23.3	17.2	9.9	4.3	6.6	4.6	18.3
Wales(12)	18.4	22.3	16.5	9.8	..	6.8	.	18.8
Scotland(13)	31.3	19.1	12.9	10.3	.	4.2	3.1	15.4
Northern Ireland	25.7	20.2	14.7	8.8	.	6.2	.	16.8

Sources: Department for Education and Employment; National Assembly for Wales; Scottish Executive; Northern Ireland Department of Education

See previous page for footnotes

SCHOOLS

Proportion of pupils reaching or exceeding expected standards, by key stage, subject and gender – time series

England, Wales and Northern Ireland   Percentages

	England				Wales				Northern Ireland			
	Tests		Teacher assessment		Tests		Teacher assessment		Tests		Teacher assessment	
	Boys	Girls	Boys	Girls	Boys	Girls	Boys	Girls	Boys	Girls	Boys	Girls
1995												
Key Stage 1(1)												
English	.	.	76	86	.	.	74	84	..	..	..	..
Reading	73	83	74	84	73	83	72	83	..	..	..	..
Writing	76	85	72	83	73	84	70	81	..	..	..	..
Maths	77	81	76	80	77	81	74	80	..	..	..	..
Science	.	.	83	86	.	.	82	84	..	..	..	..
Key Stage 2(2)												
English	42	56	50	63	41	56	50	65	..	..	..	..
Maths	44	45	53	56	46	50	55	61	..	..	..	..
Science	71	68	63	64	70	70	66	69	..	..	..	..
Key Stage 3(3)												
English	45	64	53	72	44	62	47	65	..	..	..	..
Maths	57	58	60	63	52	53	56	61	..	..	..	..
Science	57	54	59	61	54	52	56	58	..	..	..	..
1996												
Key Stage 1(1)												
English	.	.	74	84	.	.	73	84	..	..	..	..
Reading	73	83	73	83	72	83	72	84	..	..	..	..
Writing	74	85	71	82	72	84	70	82	..	..	..	..
Maths	81	84	80	83	80	84	78	84	..	..	..	..
Science	.	.	83	85	.	.	81	85	..	..	..	..
Key Stage 2(2)												
English	50	65	53	68	48	65	53	68	..	..	..	..
Maths	54	54	58	62	56	56	60	64	..	..	..	..
Science	61	63	64	67	64	66	66	70	..	..	..	..
Key Stage 3(3)												
English	48	66	51	70	47	65	48	68	..	..	..	..
Maths	56	58	60	64	53	56	58	62	..	..	..	..
Science	57	56	59	61	55	55	57	60	..	..	..	..
1997												
Key Stage 1(1)												
English	.	.	75	85	.	.	75	86	..	..	..	..
Reading	75	85	75	85	74	85	75	85	..	..	..	..
Writing	75	85	72	83	74	85	72	83	..	..	..	..
Maths	82	85	82	86	82	86	82	86	..	..	..	..
Science	.	.	84	86	.	.	82	86	..	..	..	..
Key Stage 2(2)												
English	57	70	57	70	57	70	58	71	..	..	..	..
Maths	63	61	63	65	63	64	64	68	..	..	..	..
Science	68	69	68	70	70	73	70	74	..	..	..	..
Key Stage 3(3)												
English	48	67	52	70	48	68	51	69	..	..	..	..
Maths	60	60	62	65	58	58	60	64	..	..	..	..
Science	61	60	60	63	61	60	60	64	..	..	..	..

Sources: Department for Education and Employment; National Assembly for Wales; Northern Ireland Department of Education

(1) Percentage of pupils achieving level 2 or above.
(2) Percentage of pupils achieving level 4 or above.
(3) Percentage of pupils achieving level 5 or above.
(4) Revised.
(5) Figures for England and Wales are provisional.

CONTINUED
SCHOOLS
Proportion of pupils reaching or exceeding expected standards, by key stage, subject and gender – time series

England, Wales and Northern Ireland

Percentages

| | England | | | | Wales | | | | Northern Ireland | | | |
| | Tests | | Teacher assessment | | Tests | | Teacher assessment | | Tests | | Teacher assessment | |
	Boys	Girls	Boys	Girls	Boys	Girls	Boys	Girls	Boys	Girls	Boys	Girls
1998(4)												
Key Stage 1(1)												
English	.	.	76	86	.	.	75	85	.	.	91	95
Reading	75	85	76	85	74	84	74	84	..	..	..	..
Writing	76	86	73	84	74	85	72	83	..	..	..	..
Maths	83	86	83	87	82	87	82	86	.	.	92	94
Science	.	.	85	87	.	.	84	87	.	.	.	.
Key Stage 2(2)												
English	57	73	59	72	56	74	57	73	.	.	61	73
Maths	59	58	64	66	60	62	63	68	.	.	69	75
Science	70	69	70	72	69	69	69	73	.	.	.	.
Key Stage 3(3)												
English	56	73	53	71	53	72	52	72	62	79	..	..
Maths	60	59	62	65	60	60	62	65	63	69	..	..
Science	57	55	60	63	56	54	59	62	65	70	..	..
1999(4)												
Key Stage 1(1)												
English	.	.	78	87	.	.	76	87	.	.	92	96
Reading	78	86	78	86	75	86	76	86	..	..	..	..
Writing	78	88	75	85	76	87	73	85	..	..	..	..
Maths	85	88	84	88	84	88	83	88	.	.	93	95
Science	.	.	85	88	.	.	84	88	.	.	.	.
Key Stage 2(2)												
English	65	76	62	74	63	74	61	73	.	.	64	75
Maths	69	69	69	70	67	67	68	70	.	.	71	77
Science	79	78	75	76	77	77	75	76	.	.	.	.
Key Stage 3(3)												
English	55	73	55	73	54	70	54	71	58	77	65	80
Maths	62	62	63	66	60	60	62	64	68	72	68	75
Science	55	55	59	62	55	55	59	60	63	68	67	73
2000(5)												
Key Stage 1(1)												
English	.	.	80	88	.	.	77	88	..	..	..	..
Reading	79	88	80	88	77	87	77	87	..	..	..	..
Writing	80	89	77	87	78	88	75	87	..	..	..	..
Maths	89	91	87	89	88	92	85	90	..	..	..	..
Science	.	.	87	89	.	.	86	90	..	..	..	..
Key Stage 2(2)												
English	70	79	65	76	67	80	62	76	..	..	..	..
Maths	72	71	72	73	67	71	68	72	..	..	..	..
Science	84	85	78	80	79	82	76	80	..	..	..	..
Key Stage 3(3)												
English	55	72	56	73	51	68	54	71	..	..	..	..
Maths	64	65	65	68	60	61	63	66	..	..	..	..
Science	61	58	60	63	60	58	59	62	..	..	..	..

Sources: Department for Education and Employment; National Assembly for Wales; Northern Ireland Department of Education

See previous page for footnotes

Chapter 3
Post Compulsory Education and Training
(a) Institutions and Staff
(b) Participation Rates
(c) Students and Starters
(d) Job Related Training

CHAPTER 3: POST- COMPULSORY EDUCATION AND TRAINING

Key Facts

(A) INSTITUTIONS AND STAFF

- There were 88 universities, 58 other higher education institutions and 516 further education colleges (of which 105 were 6th form colleges) in the UK in 1990/00. **(Table 3.1)**

- There were 74 thousand full-time higher education lecturers and 58 thousand full-time further education lecturers in the United Kingdom in 1998/99. **(Table 3.1)**

(B) PARTICIPATION RATES

- 70% of 16 year olds and 57% of 17 year olds were in post-compulsory education either at school or in full-time further education in 1997/98. **(Table 3.2)**

- In Spring 2000 14% of people of working age had received job-related training in the last four weeks. Employees are more likely to receive job-related training than the self-employed, the unemployed or the economically inactive. **(Table 3.3)**

(C) STUDENTS AND STARTERS

- There were just over 4 million further education students in the United Kingdom during the academic year 1998/99, of which three quarters were part time. **(Table 3.5)**

- There were just over 2 million higher education students in the United Kingdom in the academic year 1999/00, of which nearly 880 thousand were part time. Of these 2 million students, roughly 400,000 were postgraduate students, 1 million were first degree students and 600,000 were other undergraduate students. **(Table 3.6)**

- In 1999/00 25,100 students from Greece were in full-time higher education in the UK, the highest of any overseas country. **(Table 3.7)**

- There were nearly 3.5 million new entrants to further education in 1998/99, of whom just over 2.6 million were part time. **(Table 3.11)**

- There were 900,000 new entrants to higher education in 1999/00 of which over 40% were part time. **(Table 3.12)**

TEC Delivered Government-Supported Training Programmes

(i) Work-Based Training for Young People (WBTYP)

Modern Apprenticeships (MAs)
- There were 88,700 new starts on Advanced Modern Apprenticeship schemes (AMAs) in England and Wales in 1999-00, a slight increase on the 1998-99 figure of 87,400. **(Table 3.13)**

- The overall number of participants in AMAs increased by 3% between 1998-99 and 1999-00 to 139,400 and represented almost half of work-based training for young people participants. **(Table 3.10)**

Foundation Modern Apprenticeships (FMAs)
- There were 97,100 new starts on Foundation Modern Apprenticeships (FMAs) in 1999-00, more than double the figure in 1998-99 (41,900). **(Table 3.13)**

- FMA participants accounted for around a quarter of work-based training for young people participants as at March 2000. **(Table 3.10)**

- Female starts on FMAs in 1999-00 (53% of total) outnumbered Male starts (47%). **(Table 3.14)**

Other Training (OT)
- As a result of increases in other schemes for young people, the number of new starts on Other Training (OT) programmes in England and Wales in 1999-00, fell to 80,000, almost two-fifths less than the number of new starts in 1998-99. **(Table 3.13)**

- The proportion of starts on OT with a disability remained at 7% in 1999-00, but the proportion identified as having literacy or numeracy needs rose from 13% to 18% between 1998-99 and 1999-00. The proportion of ethnic minority starts also rose to 11% in 1999-00, an increase of three percentage points since 1998-99. **(Table 3.14)**

(ii) Work-Based Learning for Adults
- As at March 2000, there were 34,500 people on the Work-Based Learning for Adults programme in England and Wales, compared to 34,700 the previous year and 124,900 in March 1991. **(Table 3.10)**

- There were 108,300 new starts on Work-Based Learning for Adults in England and Wales in 1999-00 compared to 102,900 in 1998-99, but still significantly lower than recruitment in 1990-91. This long-term fall in starts reflects the fall in unemployment during this period. **(Table 3.13)**

- The proportion of starts from ethnic minority groups rose from 18% in 1998-99 to 19% in 1999-00. 20% of those who joined WBLA programmes in 1999-00 had disabilities, a decrease of 1% since 1998-99. **(Table 3.15)**

- 21% of starts on WBTA in 1999-00 had been unemployed for more than 3 years before joining, a similar proportion to 1998-99. **(Table 3.15)**

(D) JOB RELATED TRAINING

- In Spring 2000 people in the South West region (16.3%) were more likely to have received job-related training in the last four weeks than people in any other region. People in Northern Ireland (9.6%) were least likely to have received training. The pattern was similar for employees receiving job-related training. **(Table 3.16)**

- 18.6% of Black employees, 15.2% of those of Indian, Pakistani or Bangladeshi origin, and 21.1% of other non-white employees had received job-related training compared with 16.0% of white employees. **(Table 3.17)**

- People with high levels of qualifications were much more likely than those with low or no qualifications to have received job-related training. **(Table 3.17)**

- In Spring 2000, 8.3% of employees had received off-the-job training in the last four weeks, 4.6% received only on-the-job training and 3.2% received both types of training. **(Table 3.17)**

- Employees in public administration, education and health were more likely than employees in other industries to have received job-related training. Those employed in agriculture, forestry and fishing were least likely to receive training. **(Table 3.18)**

- Much of the job-related training received by employees is of short duration; in Spring 2000, 33.2% of the training received by employees lasted for less than a week. **(Table 3.21)**

- The economically inactive tend to receive job-related training that is of a longer duration than the training received by employees. **(Table 3.21)**

- A Further Education college or university is the most common location for off-the-job training. The employer's premises are also a common location for employees' off-the-job training. **(Table 3.22)**

- In Spring 2000, young employees had spent, on average, more hours on job-related training *in the last week* than older employees. Male recipients spent more hours in training than females. **(Table 3.23)**

- In 2000, 26.2% of employees in seasonal/casual temporary employment had undertaken job-related training in the last thirteen weeks compared to 16.9% in 1995. **(Table 3.24)**

- 29.3% of employees had received job-related training *in the last thirteen weeks*, 16.1% had received job-related training *in the last four weeks*, and 8.9% had received *job-related training in the last week*. 32.4% of employees had never been offered training by their current employer. **(Table 3.25)**

CHAPTER 3: POST-COMPULSORY EDUCATION AND TRAINING - LIST OF TABLES

POST-COMPULSORY EDUCATION AND TRAINING – INSTITUTIONS AND STAFF
Number of establishments of further and higher education by type, and lecturers by gender time series

United Kingdom	(i) Number of establishments of further and higher education				Numbers
		Academic years			
	1990/91	1995/96	1997/98	1998/99 (1,2)	1999/00 (3)
UNITED KINGDOM					
Universities (including Open University)(4)	48	89	88	88	88
Other higher education institutions }		66	63	58	58
}	588				
Further education colleges }		543	533	553	516
of which 6th form colleges	.	110	108	107	105
ENGLAND					
Universities (including Open University)(4)	37	72	71	70	70
Other higher education institutions }		50	48	47	47
}	460				
Further education colleges }		453	443	435	428
of which 6th form colleges	.	110	108	107	105
WALES					
Universities(4)	1	2	2	2	2
Other higher education institutions }		5	4	4	4
}	38				
Further education colleges }		26	26	24	24
SCOTLAND					
Universities(4)	8	13	13	14	14
Other higher education institutions }		9	9	5	5
}	64				
Further education colleges }		47	47	47	47
NORTHERN IRELAND					
Universities	2	2	2	2	
Colleges of Education	2	2	2	2	2
Further education colleges	24	17	17	17	17

United Kingdom	(ii) Number of full-time lecturers, by gender				Thousands
		Academic years			
	1990/91	1995/96	1997/98	1998/99 (5)	1999/00
All					
Further and Higher Education Institutions	122	127	133 (6)	132	..
of which					
Further Education Institutions(FEIs)(7,8)	..	60 (9)	60 (6)	58	..
Higher Education Institutions(HEIs)(4,10,11)	..	67	73	74	..
Males					
Further and Higher Education Institutions	89	84	86 (6)	85	..
of which					
Further Education Institutions(FEIs)(7,8)	..	34 (9)	34 (6)	33	..
Higher Education Institutions(HEIs)(4,10,11)	..	49	52	52	..
Females					
Further and Higher Education Institutions	33	44	47 (6)	47	..
of which					
Further Education Institutions(FEIs)(7,8)	..	26 (9)	26 (6)	26	..
Higher Education Institutions(HEIs)(4,10,11)	..	18	21	22	..

Sources: Department for Education and Employment; National Assembly for Wales; Scottish Executive; Northern Ireland Department of Higher and Further Education, Training and Employment

(1) Revised to include 1998/99 further education colleges data for Wales.
(2) Figures for universities in Scotland have been revised to include one former college which became a university; higher education institution figures now reflect a number of college mergers.
(3) Provisional. Includes 1998/99 further education college figures for Wales.
(4) From 1993/94 includes former polytechnics and colleges which became universities as a result of the Further and Higher Education Act 1992.
(5) Includes 1997/98 further education institution data for England.
(6) Includes 1996/97 further education institution data for Northern Ireland.
(7) Figures for England relate to staff whose primary role is teaching, and do not include other staff whose primary role is supporting teaching and learning or other.
(8) Scotland figures include full-time equivalent (rather than headcount) staff in academic departments only. Cross-college staff are excluded.
(9) Excludes Wales.
(10) Excludes the Open University.
(11) Non-clinical academic staff paid wholly by the institution.

POST-COMPULSORY EDUCATION AND TRAINING – PARTICIPATION RATES

16 and 17 year olds participating in post-compulsory education(1) and government supported training - time series

United Kingdom
Percentages(2)

1995/96

	16 year olds					17 year olds				
		In further education(3)		Government-supported training	All in full-time education and			In further education(3)		Government-supported training	All in full-time education and
	At school	Full-time	Part-time	(GST)	GST(4)	At school	Full-time	Part-time	(GST)	GST(4)
Region of study										
United Kingdom	37.3	33.6	8.4	..	..	28.1	29.1	9.9	..	..
North East	24.3	37.8	8.5	19.0	80.0	18.0	30.6	11.2	18.8	66.4
North West	24.0	42.3	9.0	14.5	78.9	19.5	34.7	10.6	15.5	68.0
Yorkshire and the Humber	29.9	35.6	9.1	13.7	77.4	22.4	29.0	10.6	15.3	65.2
East Midlands	35.6	30.8	8.3	12.4	77.5	27.4	27.4	9.7	14.6	67.9
West Midlands	30.1	38.2	8.7	12.9	79.7	24.1	33.1	10.2	12.7	68.6
Eastern	39.6	34.9	5.9	9.1	82.8	31.4	30.7	7.9	11.3	72.4
London	39.1	36.7	4.5	5.4	80.8	28.6	33.7	6.0	6.7	68.4
South East	38.8	37.5	5.0	6.3	81.9	31.1	32.4	6.6	8.5	71.2
South West	38.8	36.8	6.7	9.8	84.0	31.1	31.5	7.9	11.7	73.2
England	33.8	37.1	7.1	10.8	80.4	26.4	31.8	8.7	12.2	69.2
Wales	37.3	33.2	10.1	11.8	82.2	27.9	27.9	8.5	14.6	70.3
Scotland(5,6)	66.5	8.8	19.0	10.4	85.8	40.1	9.6	19.9	13.8	63.4
Northern Ireland	46.1	29.9	11.2	..	..	35.4	28.8	14.3	..	..

1996/97

	16 year olds					17 year olds				
		In further education(3)		Government-supported training	All in full-time education and			In further education(3)		Government-supported training	All in full-time education and
	At school	Full-time	Part-time	(GST)	GST(4)	At school	Full-time	Part-time	(GST)	GST(4)
Region of study										
United Kingdom	37.5	33.1	8.1	..	..	28.4	29.4	10.0	..	..
North East	25.3	36.3	8.7	17.8	78.8	18.7	31.2	10.6	19.1	68.5
North West	23.8	41.2	9.5	13.5	77.0	19.1	34.5	10.7	15.4	67.7
Yorkshire and the Humber	30.0	34.4	10.1	13.6	76.7	23.3	29.4	11.3	14.8	66.2
East Midlands	36.0	30.9	8.1	11.5	77.6	28.6	26.7	9.5	12.7	67.0
West Midlands	30.9	35.9	9.2	11.0	76.6	23.4	31.6	10.6	13.2	67.1
East	40.4	34.5	6.5	7.4	81.8	31.1	29.7	7.9	10.2	70.2
London	38.7	35.3	4.7	5.2	78.7	28.6	32.7	6.1	6.8	67.6
South East	38.8	36.1	5.1	5.9	80.3	30.6	31.2	6.4	8.2	69.4
South West	38.6	36.0	6.5	8.5	82.0	31.0	30.5	8.1	10.7	71.1
England	34.0	35.9	7.4	9.8	78.8	26.4	31.1	8.8	11.8	68.3
Wales	37.3	33.9	11.1	10.6	81.9	28.0	28.9	9.3	14.8	71.7
Scotland(5)	66.7	9.9	11.0	4.6	81.2	40.5	10.4	14.9	16.2	67.1
Northern Ireland	45.7	29.2	11.5	..	..	36.9	28.5	13.3	..	..

Source: Department for Education and Employment; National Assembly for Wales; Scottish Executive; Northern Ireland Department of Education

(1) Excluding higher education.

(2) As a percentage of the estimated 16 year old and 17 year old population respectively.

(3) Including sixth form colleges and a small element of further education in higher education institutions in England.

(4) Figures for England exclude overlap between full-time education and government-supported training.

(5) The estimates of 16 year olds at school exclude those pupils who leave school in the Winter term at the minimum statutory school-leaving age.

(6) Figures shown for government supported training are not directly comparable with later years.

(7) Including a small element of further education in higher education institutions in England.

(8) Figures for England and Wales exclude overlap between full-time education and government-supported training.

(9) Participation in part-time FE should not be aggregated with full-time FE or schools activity due to the unquantifiable overlap with these activities.

CONTINUED
POST-COMPULSORY EDUCATION AND TRAINING – PARTICIPATION RATES
16 and 17 year olds participating in post-compulsory education(1) and government supported training - time series

United Kingdom   Percentages(2)

	1997/98									
	16 year olds					17 year olds				
		In further education(3)		Government-supported training	All in full-time education and		In further education(3)		Government-supported training	All in full-time education and
	At school	Full-time	Part-time	(GST)	GST(4)	At school	Full-time	Part-time	(GST)	GST(4)
Region of study										
United Kingdom	37.9	32.5	8.0	..	..	28.2	28.2	9.2	..	..
North East	25.4	34.9	7.4	17.9	77.6	19.5	29.7	9.4	17.8	66.6
North West	24.3	40.8	8.5	13.3	77.4	19.4	33.9	10.2	14.7	67.5
Yorkshire and the Humber	30.9	33.6	9.1	12.8	76.3	23.4	27.6	11.0	14.7	64.9
East Midlands	36.7	29.7	7.9	11.2	76.7	29.1	25.9	9.3	13.2	67.1
West Midlands	30.7	35.4	8.3	11.0	76.0	24.5	30.7	10.3	12.4	66.7
East	40.2	33.1	5.7	7.0	79.9	32.0	28.4	7.4	9.2	68.9
London	39.7	35.0	4.4	5.4	79.7	28.9	32.2	6.0	6.2	67.0
South East	39.7	35.2	4.7	5.8	80.4	30.6	29.7	6.1	7.7	67.5
South West	38.4	34.4	6.1	9.0	80.9	30.9	29.7	7.5	10.5	70.4
England	34.4	35.1	6.7	9.7	78.5	26.8	30.1	8.4	11.2	67.4
Wales	36.8	31.8	12.6	16.6	85.3	28.2	27.2	9.7	15.1	70.5
Scotland(5)	68.1	10.9	12.6	9.1	88.1	38.8	10.9	15.2	15.8	65.5
Northern Ireland(9)	45.0	27.5	17.8	..	..	36.6	28.2	13.2	..	..

Source: Department for Education and Employment; National Assembly for Wales; Scottish Executive; Northern Ireland Department of Education

See previous page for footnotes.

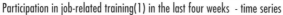

POST-COMPULSORY EDUCATION AND TRAINING – PARTICIPATION RATES

3.3

Participation in job-related training(1) in the last four weeks - time series

United Kingdom: People of working age(2)

Thousands and percentages(3)

	1991	1996(4,5)	1997(4,5)	1998(4,5)	1999(4,5)	2000(4)
Numbers (thousands)						
All People						
All	4,471	4,656	4,876	4,951	5,087	5,196
Males	2,385	2,353	2,423	2,489	2,510	2,516
Females	2,086	2,303	2,453	2,463	2,577	2,680
Employees(6,7)						
All	3,268	3,271	3,473	3,599	3,723	3,833
Males	1,745	1,643	1,709	1,806	1,830	1,872
Females	1,522	1,628	1,764	1,793	1,893	1,961
Self-employed(7,8)						
All	185	199	191	217	229	238
Males	128	126	123	146	144	140
Females	57	73	67	71	85	98
ILO unemployed(9)						
All	142	196	201	169	166	166
Males	78	117	113	87	92	87
Females	64	80	88	82	75	79
Economically inactive(10)						
All	561	811	850	818	839	841
Males	251	361	379	358	357	349
Females	310	449	471	460	482	491
Percentages(3)						
All People						
All	12.7	13.1	13.6	13.7	14.1	14.3
Males	13.0	12.6	12.9	13.2	13.2	13.2
Females	12.5	13.5	14.3	14.3	15.0	15.5
Employees(6,7)						
All	14.9	14.8	15.4	15.6	15.9	16.1
Males	14.7	14.1	14.3	14.7	14.7	14.7
Females	15.1	15.6	16.7	16.8	17.3	17.8
Self-employed(7,8)						
All	5.7	6.4	6.0	7.0	7.6	8.1
Males	5.1	5.4	5.2	6.4	6.4	6.4
Females	7.5	9.7	8.6	9.0	11.4	13.0
ILO unemployed(9)						
All	5.7	8.5	10.0	9.6	9.6	10.4
Males	4.9	7.6	8.7	8.0	8.4	8.8
Females	7.0	10.2	12.2	12.3	11.6	12.8
Economically inactive(10)						
All	8.0	10.4	10.9	10.3	10.7	10.9
Males	11.6	12.6	12.9	11.8	11.9	11.7
Females	6.4	9.1	9.6	9.4	10.0	10.3

Source: Labour Force Survey, Spring of each year(11)

(1) Job-related training includes both on and off-the-job training.

(2) Working age is defined as males aged 16-64 and females aged 16-59.

(3) Expressed as a percentage of the total number of people in each group.

(4) Due to a change in the LFS questionnaire, data from Summer 1994 onwards are not comparable with earlier figures.

(5) Figures have been revised as a result of revisions to quarterly LFS data from Autumn 1993 to Autumn 1999 to better reflect population changes over this period.

(6) Employees are those in employment excluding the self-employed, unpaid family workers and those on government employment and training programmes.

(7) The split into employees and self-employed is based on respondents' own assessment of their employment status.

(8) Self-employed are those in employment excluding employees, unpaid family workers and those on government employment and training programmes.

(9) Unemployed according to the International Labour Office (ILO) definition.

(10) Economically inactive are those who are neither in employment nor ILO unemployed and includes students.

(11) Users of these data should read the LFS entry in Annex A, as it contains important information about the LFS and the concepts and definitions used.

POST COMPULSORY EDUCATION AND TRAINING: PARTICIPATION RATES

3.4

Participation in job-related training(1) in the last four weeks by economic activity and age, 2000

United Kingdom: People of working age(2)

Thousands and *percentages(3)*

	Thousands			Percentages(3)		
	All	Males	Females	All	Males	Females
All people						
All	5,196	2,516	2,680	14.3	13.2	15.5
16-19	715	371	344	24.6	25.0	24.3
20-24	866	442	425	24.9	25.0	24.9
25-29	658	320	338	16.2	15.4	17.0
30-39	1,347	666	681	14.3	13.9	14.7
40-49	1,014	437	577	12.9	11.1	14.7
50-64	596	280	316	6.9	5.6	8.7
Employees(4,5)						
All	3,833	1,872	1,961	16.1	14.7	17.8
16-19	374	190	184	26.1	26.5	25.8
20-24	531	271	260	23.3	22.2	24.7
25-29	522	267	256	17.3	16.1	18.7
30-39	1,087	565	523	16.1	15.3	17.0
40-49	833	359	474	15.0	12.7	17.4
50-64	485	221	264	10.2	8.3	12.5
Self-employed(5,6)						
All	238	140	98	8.1	6.4	13.0
16-19	*	*	*	*	*	*
20-24	10	*	*	12.2	*	*
25-29	20	10	10	9.0	6.1	16.4
30-39	73	41	31	8.8	7.0	13.5
40-49	80	46	34	9.3	7.4	14.1
50-64	54	36	18	5.8	4.9	9.2
ILO unemployed(7)						
All	166	87	79	10.4	8.8	12.8
16-19	42	23	20	14.9	13.7	16.5
20-24	34	22	13	14.3	14.2	14.5
25-29	17	*	*	8.6	*	*
30-39	33	14	19	9.1	6.6	12.6
40-49	23	12	11	9.1	8.0	10.7
50-64	17	*	*	6.3	*	*
Economically inactive(8)						
All	841	349	491	10.9	11.7	10.3
16-19	231	117	114	21.4	21.8	21.0
20-24	277	136	141	32.5	42.3	26.6
25-29	94	33	61	15.1	23.2	12.7
30-39	139	38	101	9.7	13.3	8.8
40-49	66	15	51	5.8	4.5	6.3
50-64	33	11	22	1.3	0.8	1.8

Source: Labour Force Survey, Spring 2000(9)

(1) Job-related training includes both on and off-the-job training.
(2) Working age is defined as males aged 16-64 and females aged 16-59.
(3) Expressed as a percentage of the total number of people in each group.
(4) Employees are those in employment excluding the self-employed, unpaid family workers and those on government employment and training programmes.
(5) The split into employees and self-employed is based on respondents' own assessment of their employment status.
(6) Self-employed are those in employment excluding employees, unpaid family workers and those on government employment and training programmes.
(7) Unemployed according to the International Labour Office (ILO) definition.
(8) Economically inactive are those who are neither in employment nor ILO unemployed.
(9) Users of these data should read the LFS entry in Annex A, as it contains important information about the LFS and the concepts and definitions used.

POST COMPULSORY EDUCATION AND TRAINING: STUDENTS AND STARTERS

Students in further education(1) by country of study, type of course, mode of study(2), gender and subject group, during 1998/99

United Kingdom   (i) Home and Overseas Students   Thousands

	United Kingdom		England(3)		Wales		Scotland(4)		Northern Ireland	
	Full-time	Part-time	Full-time	Part-time	Full-time	Part-time	Full-time	Part-time	Full-time	Part-time
All										
Medicine & Dentistry	-	-	-	-			-	-	-	-
Subjects Allied to Medicine	105.9	161.3	101.2	145.7	-	-	3.3	13.9	1.5	1.7
Biological Sciences	1.0	1.4	0.9	0.5	-	-	0.1	0.9	-	-
Vet. Science, Agriculture & related	36.1	150.6	35.0	144.7	-	-	1.0	5.3	0.1	0.6
Physical Sciences	14.7	10.5	14.0	5.4	-	-	0.7	5.0	-	0.1
Mathematical and Computing Sciences(5)	129.0	288.4	127.7	277.3	-	-	0.1	3.0	1.3	8.1
Engineering & Technology	50.3	113.0	43.6	91.4	-	-	4.8	17.9	2.0	3.6
Architecture, Building & Planning	26.7	49.5	21.2	40.2	-	-	3.0	8.0	2.5	1.3
Social Sciences	15.7	62.0	11.2	46.8	-	-	3.8	12.3	0.7	2.9
Business & Financial Studies	105.5	295.2	90.4	221.8	-	-	9.8	60.6	5.3	12.7
Librarianship & Info Science(5)	11.6	64.4	7.5	12.3	-	-	3.6	51.8	0.4	0.4
Languages	21.9	83.8	21.5	68.8	-	0.1	0.4	13.3	-	1.6
Humanities	6.8	9.4	6.4	7.2	-	-	0.4	2.2	-	-
Creative Arts & Design	67.9	65.9	63.3	54.8	0.1	-	2.4	7.8	2.2	3.3
Education(6)	17.1	48.2	15.5	26.8	-	0.4	1.0	18.4	0.6	2.4
Combined, general	151.9	210.1	144.9	154.3	0.2	5.5	2.6	33.3	4.2	17.0
Unknown	302.8	1,364.3	259.3	1,208.0	43.5	156.3	-	-	-	-
All subjects	**1,065.0**	**2,977.9**	**963.5**	**2,506.1**	**43.9**	**162.4**	**37.0**	**253.6**	**20.6**	**55.8**
Males										
Medicine & Dentistry	-	-	-	-			-	-	-	-
Subjects Allied to Medicine	33.8	61.4	33.6	57.2	-	-	0.2	4.0	0.1	0.2
Biological Sciences	0.3	0.4	0.3	0.2	-	-	-	0.2	-	-
Vet. Science, Agriculture & related	16.1	55.6	15.4	51.9	-	-	0.7	3.4	-	0.3
Physical Sciences	10.2	6.0	9.9	3.4	-	-	0.3	2.5	-	0.1
Mathematical and Computing Sciences(5)	60.3	106.6	59.2	102.5	-	-	0.1	1.4	1.0	2.7
Engineering & Technology	47.0	103.4	40.5	85.1	-	-	4.6	14.9	1.9	3.4
Architecture, Building & Planning	25.4	45.0	20.1	37.7	-	-	2.8	6.0	2.5	1.3
Social Sciences	1.9	9.0	1.4	6.2	-	-	0.5	2.5	-	0.3
Business & Financial Studies	46.9	110.4	40.6	83.7	-	-	4.4	23.8	1.8	2.8
Librarianship & Info Science(5)	6.4	24.8	3.8	4.8	-	-	2.4	19.9	0.2	0.1
Languages	8.9	29.8	8.7	24.5	-	-	0.2	4.7	-	0.6
Humanities	3.2	3.9	3.0	3.2	-	-	0.1	0.7	-	-
Creative Arts & Design	25.3	12.5	23.4	9.9	-	-	1.1	2.1	0.8	0.5
Education(6)	10.0	18.0	9.4	9.8	-	0.1	0.3	7.3	0.4	0.8
Combined, general	73.1	84.7	69.7	60.5	0.1	2.0	1.3	15.9	2.0	6.4
Unknown	162.8	585.3	142.3	520.9	20.4	64.4	-	-	-	-
All subjects	**531.6**	**1,257.0**	**481.3**	**1,061.5**	**20.6**	**66.6**	**19.0**	**109.5**	**10.7**	**19.4**
Females										
Medicine & Dentistry	-	-	-	-			-	-	-	-
Subjects Allied to Medicine	72.1	99.9	67.6	88.5	-	-	3.1	9.9	1.4	1.5
Biological Sciences	0.6	0.9	0.6	0.3	-	-	0.1	0.6	-	-
Vet. Science, Agriculture & related	20.1	95.0	19.6	92.8	-	-	0.4	1.9	0.1	0.3
Physical Sciences	4.5	4.5	4.2	2.0	-	-	0.3	2.5	-	-
Mathematical and Computing Sciences(5)	68.8	181.8	68.5	174.8	-	-	-	1.6	0.2	5.4
Engineering & Technology	3.3	9.5	3.1	6.3	-	-	0.2	3.0	-	0.3
Architecture, Building & Planning	1.3	4.5	1.1	2.5	-	-	0.2	1.9	-	0.1
Social Sciences	13.8	53.0	9.8	40.6	-	-	3.3	9.8	0.7	2.6
Business & Financial Studies	58.6	184.8	49.8	138.1	-	-	5.4	36.8	3.4	9.9
Librarianship & Info Science(5)	5.1	39.6	3.8	7.5	-	-	1.2	31.8	0.2	0.3
Languages	13.0	54.0	12.7	44.4	-	-	0.2	8.6	-	1.0
Humanities	3.6	5.5	3.4	4.0	-	-	0.2	1.5	-	-
Creative Arts & Design	42.6	53.4	39.8	44.9	-	-	1.3	5.7	1.4	2.8
Education(6)	7.1	30.1	6.2	17.1	-	0.3	0.7	11.1	0.2	1.6
Combined, general	78.7	125.4	75.2	93.8	0.1	3.6	1.3	17.4	2.2	10.6
Unknown	140.0	779.0	116.9	687.1	23.1	91.9	-	-	-	-
All subjects	**533.4**	**1,720.9**	**482.3**	**1,444.6**	**23.3**	**95.8**	**18.0**	**144.1**	**9.9**	**36.4**

Sources: Department for Education and Employment; National Assembly for Wales; Scottish Executive; Northern Ireland Department of Higher and Further Education, Training and Employment

(1) Further education figures are whole year counts and differ from the higher education tables which use annual snapshots. Data for Northern Ireland however, are collected on a snapshot basis.
(2) Full-time includes sandwich, and for Scotland, short full-time. Part-time comprises both day and evening, including block release (except for Scotland) and open/distance learning.
(3) Excludes approximately 241,600 students in further education institutions in England since the information cannot be broken down in this way. External institutions and specialist designated colleges are also excluded.
(4) Figures for Scotland further education institutions are enrolments rather than headcounts.
(5) Computing Sciences figures for further education institutions in Scotland are included with Librarianship and Information Science.
(6) Including ITT and INSET.
(7) Includes estimated breakdowns for further education students in higher education institutions.

3.5 POST COMPULSORY EDUCATION AND TRAINING: STUDENTS AND STARTERS

Students in further education(1) by country of study, type of course, mode of study(2), gender and subject group, during 1998/99

United Kingdom   (ii) of which Overseas Students   Thousands

	United Kingdom		England(3)		Wales		Scotland(4)		Northern Ireland	
	Full-time	Part-time	Full-time	Part-time	Full-time	Part-time	Full-time	Part-time	Full-time	Part-time
All										
Medicine & Dentistry	-	-	-	-	-	-	-	-	-	-
Subjects Allied to Medicine	0.6	1.9	0.6	1.9	-	-	-	-	0.1	-
Biological Sciences	-	-	-	-	-	-	-	-	-	-
Vet. Science, Agriculture & related	0.5	2.1	0.5	2.0	-	-	-	0.1	-	-
Physical Sciences	0.1	0.1	0.1	-	-	-	-	-	-	-
Mathematical and Computing Sciences(5)	2.1	2.2	2.1	2.1	-	-	-	-	-	0.1
Engineering & Technology	1.0	2.0	0.9	1.6	-	-	-	0.3	-	0.1
Architecture, Building & Planning	0.2	0.7	0.2	0.7	-	-	-	-	-	-
Social Sciences	0.1	0.4	-	0.3	-	-	-	-	-	0.1
Business & Financial Studies	1.4	3.2	1.3	2.7	-	-	-	0.3	0.1	0.2
Librarianship & Info Science(5)	0.6	0.6	0.6	0.5	-	-	-	0.1	-	-
Languages	6.9	17.8	6.8	15.0	-	-	0.1	2.8	-	-
Humanities	0.1	-	0.1	-	-	-	-	-	-	-
Creative Arts & Design	1.0	0.6	0.9	0.5	-	-	-	-	0.1	0.1
Education(6)	0.1	0.3	0.1	0.1	-	-	-	0.1	-	-
Combined, general	2.9	3.3	2.8	2.8	-	-	-	0.4	-	0.1
Unknown	10.1	56.1	10.0	54.4	0.1	1.7	-	-	-	-
All subjects	**27.6**	**91.4**	**26.8**	**84.7**	**0.1**	**1.7**	**0.2**	**4.2**	**0.5**	**0.8**
of which European Union(7)	9.2	18.2	8.5	13.9	-	0.4	0.1	3.1	0.5	0.8
Other Europe(7)	1.2	4.9	1.2	4.6	-	-	-	0.3	-	-
Commonwealth(7)	3.2	3.9	3.1	3.7	-	-	-	0.2	-	-
Other Countries(7)	14.0	64.3	13.9	62.4	0.1	1.3	0.1	0.6	-	-
Males										
Medicine & Dentistry	-	-	-	-	-	-	-	-	-	-
Subjects Allied to Medicine	0.2	0.6	0.2	0.6	-	-	-	-	-	-
Biological Sciences	-	-	-	-	-	-	-	-	-	-
Vet. Science, Agriculture & related	0.2	0.7	0.2	0.7	-	-	-	-	-	-
Physical Sciences	0.1	0.1	0.1	-	-	-	-	-	-	-
Mathematical and Computing Sciences(5)	0.9	0.8	0.9	0.8	-	-	-	-	-	-
Engineering & Technology	0.9	1.8	0.8	1.4	-	-	-	0.3	-	0.1
Architecture, Building & Planning	0.2	0.7	0.1	0.6	-	-	-	-	-	-
Social Sciences	-	0.1	-	0.1	-	-	-	-	-	-
Business & Financial Studies	0.6	1.8	0.6	1.5	-	-	-	0.2	-	-
Librarianship & Info Science(5)	0.2	0.2	0.2	0.2	-	-	-	0.1	-	-
Languages	2.7	4.9	2.6	3.8	-	-	0.1	1.1	-	-
Humanities	-	-	-	-	-	-	-	-	-	-
Creative Arts & Design	0.3	0.1	0.3	0.1	-	-	-	-	-	-
Education(6)	0.1	0.1	-	0.1	-	-	-	0.1	-	-
Combined, general	1.1	1.3	1.1	1.1	-	-	-	0.2	-	-
Unknown	5.7	21.6	5.6	20.6	-	0.9	-	-	-	-
All subjects	**13.1**	**34.7**	**12.8**	**31.5**	**-**	**0.9**	**0.1**	**2.0**	**0.1**	**0.2**
of which European Union(7)	3.7	6.5	3.5	4.5	-	0.2	0.1	1.5	0.1	0.2
Other Europe(7)	0.4	1.0	0.4	0.9	-	-	-	0.1	-	-
Commonwealth(7)	1.8	2.0	1.8	1.8	-	-	-	0.2	-	-
Other Countries(7)	7.2	25.2	7.1	24.2	-	0.7	-	0.3	-	-
Females										
Medicine & Dentistry	-	-	-	-	-	-	-	-	-	-
Subjects Allied to Medicine	0.5	1.3	0.4	1.2	-	-	-	-	0.1	-
Biological Sciences	-	-	-	-	-	-	-	-	-	-
Vet. Science, Agriculture & related	0.3	1.3	0.3	1.3	-	-	-	-	-	-
Physical Sciences	-	-	-	-	-	-	-	-	-	-
Mathematical and Computing Sciences(5)	1.2	1.4	1.2	1.3	-	-	-	-	-	0.1
Engineering & Technology	0.1	0.2	0.1	0.2	-	-	-	-	-	-
Architecture, Building & Planning	-	-	-	-	-	-	-	-	-	-
Social Sciences	0.1	0.3	-	0.2	-	-	-	-	-	0.1
Business & Financial Studies	0.8	1.5	0.7	1.2	-	-	-	0.1	0.1	0.2
Librarianship & Info Science(5)	0.4	0.4	0.4	0.3	-	-	-	0.1	-	-
Languages	4.3	13.0	4.2	11.3	-	-	0.1	1.7	-	-
Humanities	-	-	-	-	-	-	-	-	-	-
Creative Arts & Design	0.7	0.5	0.6	0.4	-	-	-	-	0.1	0.1
Education(6)	-	0.2	-	0.1	-	-	-	0.1	-	-
Combined, general	1.7	2.0	1.7	1.8	-	-	-	0.2	-	0.1
Unknown	4.4	34.5	4.4	33.7	-	0.8	-	-	-	-
All subjects	**14.5**	**56.6**	**14.0**	**53.1**	**0.1**	**0.8**	**0.1**	**2.2**	**0.3**	**0.6**
of which European Union(7)	5.5	11.7	5.1	9.4	-	0.2	0.1	1.6	0.3	0.6
Other Europe(7)	0.8	3.9	0.8	3.7	-	-	-	0.2	-	-
Commonwealth(7)	1.4	1.9	1.3	1.8	-	-	-	0.1	-	-
Other Countries(7)	6.8	39.1	6.8	38.2	-	0.6	-	0.3	-	-

Sources: Department for Education and Employment; National Assembly for Wales; Scottish Executive; Northern Ireland Department of Education

See previous page for footnotes.

POST COMPULSORY EDUCATION AND TRAINING: STUDENTS AND STARTERS

3.6 Students in higher education(1) by type of course, mode of study(2), gender and subject group, 1999/00(3,4)

United Kingdom (i) Home and Overseas Students Thousands

	Postgraduate level						First degree		Other Undergraduate		Total higher education students	
	PHD's & equivalent		Masters and Others		Total Postgraduate							
	Full-time	Part-time	Full-time	Part-time	Full-time	Part-time	Full-time	Part-time	Full-time	Part-time	Full-time	Part-time
All												
Medicine & Dentistry	2.3	3.3	2.9	5.2	5.2	8.4	29.5	0.1	0.1	-	**34.8**	**8.6**
Subjects Allied to Medicine	1.6	1.7	2.8	14.5	4.4	16.2	50.2	22.5	53.3	43.0	**108.0**	**81.7**
Biological Sciences	5.8	4.0	4.0	4.9	9.8	8.9	64.2	3.0	2.5	1.7	**76.5**	**13.6**
Vet. Science, Agriculture & related	0.9	0.6	1.2	0.9	2.2	1.5	10.4	0.3	4.7	2.1	**17.3**	**3.9**
Physical Sciences	6.0	3.4	4.5	3.0	10.5	6.4	47.5	2.1	1.8	2.8	**59.8**	**11.3**
Mathematical and Computing Sciences(5)	2.3	1.8	9.3	7.5	11.5	9.3	66.6	4.9	13.6	16.2	**91.7**	**30.4**
Engineering & Technology	5.5	4.4	9.0	8.5	14.5	12.9	74.4	7.1	12.6	26.9	**101.5**	**46.8**
Architecture, Building & Planning	0.5	0.5	3.8	4.9	4.3	5.5	20.6	5.4	4.1	9.4	**29.0**	**20.3**
Social Sciences	3.9	4.6	20.3	21.7	24.2	26.3	109.6	11.3	11.2	22.4	**145.0**	**60.0**
Business & Financial Studies	1.4	2.1	17.2	45.2	18.6	47.3	106.1	11.6	37.6	78.7	**162.3**	**137.6**
Librarianship & Info Science(5)	0.2	0.3	2.5	2.8	2.6	3.1	15.5	0.7	7.2	7.9	**25.3**	**11.7**
Languages	2.3	2.5	4.2	4.2	6.5	6.7	57.3	3.5	3.8	13.7	**67.6**	**23.9**
Humanities	2.3	2.9	3.6	5.5	5.9	8.4	31.6	2.4	0.7	8.4	**38.2**	**19.3**
Creative Arts & Design	0.5	0.9	5.3	3.6	5.8	4.5	76.4	3.1	12.4	5.8	**94.6**	**13.4**
Education(6)	0.8	3.6	23.5	42.7	24.3	46.2	48.2	4.2	3.9	15.6	**76.4**	**66.1**
Combined, general	0.6	0.8	2.1	30.4	2.7	31.2	104.2	10.0	11.9	153.1	**118.8**	**194.2**
Unknown	-	-	0.1	0.8	0.1	0.8	7.8	2.9	5.1	18.0	**13.0**	**21.7**
All subjects	36.9	37.4	116.3	206.3	153.1	243.6	920.1	95.1	186.4	425.7	**1,259.7**	**764.4**
Males												
Medicine & Dentistry	1.0	1.8	1.3	2.6	2.3	4.4	13.6	0.1	0.1	-	**16.0**	**4.5**
Subjects Allied to Medicine	0.7	0.7	0.9	4.0	1.6	4.7	12.1	2.5	7.9	4.1	**21.6**	**11.3**
Biological Sciences	2.5	1.9	1.6	1.7	4.1	3.5	24.4	1.2	1.3	0.6	**29.7**	**5.3**
Vet. Science, Agriculture & related	0.5	0.4	0.6	0.4	1.1	0.8	4.1	0.1	2.4	1.2	**7.7**	**2.1**
Physical Sciences	4.1	2.4	2.7	1.8	6.8	4.2	29.5	1.2	1.0	1.6	**37.3**	**7.1**
Mathematical and Computing Sciences(5)	1.8	1.4	6.5	5.2	8.3	6.6	50.8	3.7	10.0	10.0	**69.1**	**20.3**
Engineering & Technology	4.5	3.7	7.2	7.4	11.7	11.1	62.9	6.6	11.1	24.9	**85.7**	**42.6**
Architecture, Building & Planning	0.3	0.4	2.4	3.2	2.7	3.6	15.0	4.4	3.3	8.0	**21.0**	**16.0**
Social Sciences	2.1	2.6	9.0	9.5	11.1	12.0	43.9	4.7	2.7	5.1	**57.7**	**21.9**
Business & Financial Studies	0.9	1.4	9.8	25.4	10.7	26.7	50.6	5.0	16.2	32.2	**77.5**	**63.8**
Librarianship & Info Science(5)	0.1	0.1	0.9	1.0	0.9	1.1	5.9	0.2	4.6	4.3	**11.4**	**5.7**
Languages	1.0	1.1	1.4	1.4	2.4	2.5	15.9	1.1	1.2	5.1	**19.5**	**8.7**
Humanities	1.4	1.7	1.7	2.7	3.1	4.4	14.6	1.0	0.3	2.9	**18.0**	**8.3**
Creative Arts & Design	0.3	0.5	2.2	1.6	2.5	2.0	31.1	1.0	6.3	2.1	**39.9**	**5.2**
Education(6)	0.3	1.7	7.2	12.7	7.5	14.4	12.7	1.0	2.0	4.5	**22.2**	**19.8**
Combined, general	0.3	0.5	1.1	18.4	1.4	18.9	44.5	3.6	4.8	66.3	**50.7**	**88.8**
Unknown	-	-	-	0.3	-	0.3	3.5	1.2	2.5	8.2	**6.1**	**9.8**
All subjects	21.8	22.1	56.5	99.3	78.3	121.4	435.1	38.6	77.7	181.2	**591.1**	**341.2**
Females												
Medicine & Dentistry	1.3	1.5	1.6	2.6	2.9	4.0	15.8	-	0.1	-	**18.8**	**4.1**
Subjects Allied to Medicine	0.9	1.0	1.9	10.5	2.8	11.5	38.2	19.9	45.4	38.9	**86.4**	**70.4**
Biological Sciences	3.3	2.1	2.4	3.2	5.7	5.3	39.8	1.9	1.2	1.0	**46.7**	**8.2**
Vet. Science, Agriculture & related	0.4	0.2	0.6	0.5	1.0	0.7	6.3	0.2	2.3	0.9	**9.6**	**1.7**
Physical Sciences	1.9	1.0	1.8	1.2	3.7	2.2	18.1	0.9	0.7	1.2	**22.5**	**4.3**
Mathematical and Computing Sciences(5)	0.5	0.4	2.7	2.3	3.2	2.7	15.8	1.2	3.6	6.2	**22.6**	**10.1**
Engineering & Technology	1.1	0.7	1.8	1.1	2.8	1.8	11.5	0.5	1.5	2.0	**15.8**	**4.2**
Architecture, Building & Planning	0.2	0.2	1.5	1.7	1.6	1.9	5.6	1.0	0.8	1.4	**8.0**	**4.3**
Social Sciences	1.8	2.0	11.3	12.2	13.1	14.3	65.7	6.6	8.5	17.2	**87.3**	**38.1**
Business & Financial Studies	0.5	0.7	7.4	19.9	7.8	20.6	55.5	6.7	21.4	46.6	**84.7**	**73.8**
Librarianship & Info Science(5)	0.1	0.1	1.6	1.9	1.7	2.0	9.6	0.5	2.6	3.5	**13.9**	**6.0**
Languages	1.3	1.4	2.8	2.8	4.1	4.2	41.4	2.4	2.6	8.6	**48.1**	**15.2**
Humanities	0.9	1.2	1.9	2.8	2.8	4.0	17.0	1.5	0.4	5.5	**20.2**	**11.0**
Creative Arts & Design	0.3	0.4	3.1	2.1	3.4	2.5	45.3	2.1	6.1	3.7	**54.7**	**8.3**
Education(6)	0.5	1.9	16.3	29.9	16.8	31.9	35.5	3.2	1.9	11.2	**54.2**	**46.2**
Combined, general	0.3	0.3	1.0	11.9	1.3	12.3	59.6	6.4	7.1	86.8	**68.0**	**105.5**
Unknown	-	-	0.1	0.5	0.1	0.5	4.3	1.7	2.6	9.8	**6.9**	**11.9**
All subjects	15.0	15.3	59.8	106.9	74.9	122.2	485.0	56.5	108.7	244.5	**668.6**	**423.2**

Sources: Department for Education and Employment; National Assembly for Wales; Scottish Executive; Northern Ireland Department of Higher and Further Education, Training and Employment

(1) Higher education institutions include Open University students. Part-time figures include dormant modes, those writing up at home and on sabbaticals which are not included in HESA SFR38.
(2) Full-time includes sandwich, and for Scotland, short full-time. Part-time comprises both day and evening, including block release (except for Scotland) and open/distance learning.
(3) Provisional. Figures for higher education students in further education institutions (except for Northern Ireland) relate to 1998/99.
(4) Figures for students (other than in Scotland further education institutions) are snapshots counted at a particular point in the year [December for UK HE institutions and FE institutions in Wales, November for FE institutions in England and Northern Ireland]. Students starting courses after these dates will not therefore be counted. Figures for Scotland, however, are whole year (not snapshot) enrolments (rather than headcounts) for 1998/99.
(5) Computing Sciences figures for further education institutions in Scotland are included with Librarianship and Information Science.
(6) Including ITT and INSET.
(7) Numbers in grouped countries do not sum to overall student numbers due to overlaps.

3.6 POST COMPULSORY EDUCATION AND TRAINING: STUDENTS AND STARTERS

Students in higher education(1) by type of course, mode of study(2), gender and subject group, 1999/00(3,4)

United Kingdom   (ii) of which Overseas Students   Thousands

| | Postgraduate level | | | | | | First degree | | Other Undergraduate | | Total higher education students | |
| | PHD's & equivalent | | Masters and Others | | Total Postgraduate | | | | | | | |
	Full-time	Part-time	Full-time	Part-time	Full-time	Part-time	Full-time	Part-time	Full-time	Part-time	Full-time	Part-time
All												
Medicine & Dentistry	0.6	0.4	1.3	0.6	2.0	1.0	2.6	-	0.1	-	4.6	1.0
Subjects Allied to Medicine	0.5	0.3	0.9	1.0	1.3	1.3	3.6	0.4	3.6	0.3	8.5	2.1
Biological Sciences	1.4	0.7	1.2	0.5	2.6	1.3	4.5	0.1	0.4	0.1	7.5	1.5
Vet. Science, Agriculture & related	0.4	0.3	0.6	0.1	1.0	0.4	1.0	0.1	0.3	0.1	2.3	0.5
Physical Sciences	1.7	0.8	1.5	0.5	3.2	1.4	2.6	0.1	0.4	0.1	6.2	1.5
Mathematical and Computing Sciences(5)	1.1	0.5	2.7	1.0	3.8	1.6	5.5	0.4	0.9	0.4	10.2	2.3
Engineering & Technology	2.9	1.6	5.1	1.8	8.0	3.4	16.9	0.5	1.9	0.3	26.8	4.2
Architecture, Building & Planning	0.3	0.2	1.4	0.7	1.6	0.9	3.2	0.1	0.6	0.1	5.4	1.1
Social Sciences	2.2	1.7	8.6	3.7	10.8	5.4	11.7	0.9	1.6	0.4	24.1	6.6
Business & Financial Studies	0.9	0.7	11.3	6.3	12.2	7.0	16.0	0.8	3.1	0.9	31.2	8.7
Librarianship & Info Science(5)	0.1	0.1	0.8	0.4	0.8	0.5	1.5	0.1	0.2	0.1	2.5	0.6
Languages	1.1	0.9	2.1	1.0	3.1	1.9	4.1	0.4	2.9	1.3	10.1	3.6
Humanities	1.0	0.8	1.5	0.4	2.5	1.3	1.2	-	0.6	0.1	4.3	1.4
Creative Arts & Design	0.2	0.2	2.1	0.3	2.3	0.5	7.4	0.1	0.8	0.2	10.5	0.8
Education(6)	0.5	1.0	2.3	2.8	2.7	3.8	1.4	0.3	0.3	0.6	4.5	4.7
Combined, general	0.2	0.2	1.1	0.7	1.3	0.9	9.0	0.3	9.4	1.6	19.7	2.8
Unknown	-	-	-	-	-	-	0.4	-	0.2	0.3	0.5	0.3
All subjects	**15.0**	**10.3**	**44.6**	**22.0**	**59.5**	**32.3**	**92.4**	**4.7**	**27.1**	**6.8**	**179.1**	**43.8**
of which European Union(7)	4.7	3.1	17.2	7.3	21.9	10.4	48.6	1.9	15.2	3.3	85.7	15.6
Other Europe(7)	1.1	0.8	3.2	1.6	4.3	2.4	7.9	0.2	0.9	0.4	13.1	3.0
Commonwealth(7)	3.0	2.1	9.4	5.7	12.4	7.8	23.0	1.2	3.7	1.0	39.1	9.9
Other Countries(7)	6.3	4.5	15.6	7.8	21.9	12.3	15.7	1.5	7.5	2.3	45.1	16.1
Males												
Medicine & Dentistry	0.4	0.2	0.6	0.4	1.0	0.6	1.2	-	-	-	2.2	0.6
Subjects Allied to Medicine	0.2	0.1	0.3	0.4	0.6	0.6	0.9	0.1	0.8	-	2.3	0.7
Biological Sciences	0.7	0.4	0.5	0.2	1.2	0.6	1.4	0.1	0.1	-	2.7	0.7
Vet. Science, Agriculture & related	0.3	0.2	0.4	0.1	0.6	0.3	0.4	-	0.2	-	1.3	0.3
Physical Sciences	1.1	0.5	0.9	0.4	2.0	0.9	1.4	-	0.2	0.1	3.7	1.0
Mathematical and Computing Sciences(5)	0.8	0.4	1.9	0.7	2.7	1.1	3.9	0.3	0.6	0.2	7.3	1.7
Engineering & Technology	2.4	1.3	4.2	1.6	6.6	2.9	14.3	0.4	1.5	0.3	22.4	3.6
Architecture, Building & Planning	0.2	0.1	0.8	0.5	1.0	0.6	1.9	0.1	0.3	0.1	3.2	0.8
Social Sciences	1.3	1.0	4.3	2.1	5.6	3.2	5.4	0.5	0.6	0.1	11.7	3.8
Business & Financial Studies	0.6	0.5	6.6	4.0	7.2	4.5	8.1	0.4	1.6	0.5	16.9	5.4
Librarianship & Info Science(5)	-	-	0.2	0.1	0.3	0.2	0.5	-	0.1	-	0.8	0.2
Languages	0.4	0.4	0.6	0.4	1.0	0.7	1.0	0.2	0.8	0.5	2.8	1.4
Humanities	0.6	0.5	0.7	0.3	1.4	0.7	0.5	-	0.2	0.1	2.1	0.8
Creative Arts & Design	0.1	0.1	0.8	0.1	0.9	0.2	2.5	-	0.3	0.1	3.6	0.3
Education(6)	0.2	0.5	0.6	1.1	0.9	1.6	0.4	0.1	0.1	0.2	1.3	1.9
Combined, general	0.1	0.1	0.6	0.5	0.7	0.6	4.0	0.1	3.6	0.5	8.2	1.3
Unknown	-	-	-	-	-	-	0.2	-	0.1	0.2	0.3	0.2
All subjects	**9.6**	**6.4**	**24.0**	**12.8**	**33.6**	**19.3**	**48.0**	**2.5**	**11.3**	**2.9**	**92.9**	**24.7**
of which European Union(7)	2.7	1.8	9.2	4.0	11.9	5.8	24.8	1.0	5.9	1.4	42.6	8.2
Other Europe(7)	0.7	0.5	1.6	0.9	2.3	1.4	3.6	0.1	0.4	0.1	6.3	1.6
Commonwealth(7)	2.0	1.3	5.7	3.7	7.7	5.0	12.9	0.7	1.9	0.5	22.5	6.3
Other Countries(7)	4.2	2.9	7.9	4.5	12.2	7.5	8.1	0.8	3.1	1.0	23.4	9.2
Females												
Medicine & Dentistry	0.3	0.2	0.7	0.2	1.0	0.4	1.4	-	-	-	2.4	0.4
Subjects Allied to Medicine	0.2	0.2	0.5	0.6	0.7	0.7	2.7	0.3	2.8	0.3	6.2	1.3
Biological Sciences	0.7	0.4	0.7	0.3	1.4	0.7	3.1	0.1	0.3	0.1	4.8	0.8
Vet. Science, Agriculture & related	0.1	0.1	0.3	-	0.4	0.1	0.5	-	0.1	-	1.1	0.2
Physical Sciences	0.6	0.3	0.6	0.2	1.2	0.5	1.1	-	0.2	-	2.5	0.5
Mathematical and Computing Sciences(5)	0.2	0.1	0.9	0.3	1.1	0.4	1.5	0.1	0.3	0.2	2.9	0.7
Engineering & Technology	0.5	0.3	0.9	0.2	1.5	0.5	2.6	-	0.4	-	4.4	0.5
Architecture, Building & Planning	0.1	0.1	0.6	0.2	0.7	0.3	1.3	-	0.2	-	2.3	0.3
Social Sciences	0.9	0.7	4.3	1.5	5.2	2.2	6.2	0.3	0.9	0.3	12.4	2.8
Business & Financial Studies	0.3	0.2	4.7	2.3	5.0	2.5	7.9	0.4	1.5	0.4	14.3	3.3
Librarianship & Info Science(5)	-	0.1	0.5	0.3	0.6	0.3	1.0	-	0.1	-	1.6	0.4
Languages	0.6	0.5	1.5	0.6	2.1	1.1	3.1	0.3	2.1	0.8	7.3	2.2
Humanities	0.4	0.3	0.8	0.2	1.2	0.5	0.7	-	0.3	0.1	2.2	0.6
Creative Arts & Design	0.1	0.1	1.4	0.2	1.5	0.3	4.9	0.1	0.5	0.1	6.9	0.5
Education(6)	0.2	0.5	1.6	1.7	1.9	2.2	1.1	0.2	0.2	0.4	3.1	2.8
Combined, general	0.1	0.1	0.5	0.3	0.6	0.3	5.0	0.2	5.9	1.0	11.5	1.6
Unknown	-	-	-	-	-	-	0.2	-	0.1	0.1	0.3	0.1
All subjects	**5.4**	**3.9**	**20.6**	**9.1**	**25.9**	**13.0**	**44.4**	**2.2**	**15.9**	**3.9**	**86.2**	**19.1**
of which European Union(7)	2.0	1.4	8.0	3.3	10.0	4.6	23.8	0.9	9.3	1.9	43.0	7.4
Other Europe(7)	0.4	0.3	1.6	0.8	2.0	1.1	4.2	0.1	0.5	0.2	6.7	1.4
Commonwealth(7)	1.0	0.7	3.7	2.0	4.7	2.8	10.1	0.5	1.8	0.5	16.6	3.7
Other Countries(7)	2.0	1.5	7.7	3.3	9.7	4.8	7.6	0.7	4.4	1.3	21.7	6.9

Sources: Department for Education and Employment; National Assembly for Wales; Scottish Executive; Northern Ireland Department of Higher and Further Education, Training and Employment

See previous page for footnotes.

POST COMPULSORY EDUCATION AND TRAINING: STUDENTS AND STARTERS

3.7 Full-time students from overseas in higher education, by type of course, gender and country, 1999/00(1,2) and time series

United Kingdom   Thousands

1999/00 RANK	1998/99 RANK	TOP FIFTY NAMED COUNTRIES	1980/81 All	1998/99 All	1998/99 Males	1998/99 Females	1999/00 All	1999/00 Males	1999/00 Females	PhD	Masters	Total post-graduate	First degree	Other under-graduate	Total Higher Education
1	(1)	Greece	2.5	24.6	9.8	14.8	25.1	15.2	9.9	1.0	6.9	8.0	16.5	0.7	25.1
2	(4)	Germany	1.3	11.1	5.7	5.4	11.4	5.5	5.9	0.9	2.0	2.9	5.4	3.1	11.4
3	(3)	France	0.7	11.4	5.8	5.7	11.3	5.6	5.7	0.6	2.2	2.8	5.3	3.2	11.3
4	(2)	Irish Republic	0.5	12.8	7.6	5.2	11.2	4.4	6.8	0.4	1.4	1.8	7.0	2.5	11.2
5	(5)	Malaysia	13.3	10.6	4.5	6.1	8.9	5.2	3.7	0.6	1.2	1.9	6.7	0.3	8.9
6	(6)	USA	2.9	8.5	4.8	3.7	8.7	3.7	5.0	0.9	2.1	3.0	1.5	4.2	8.7
7	(7)	Spain	0.2	6.1	3.2	2.9	6.4	3.0	3.4	0.3	1.1	1.4	2.8	2.2	6.4
8	(8)	Hong Kong	7.2	5.1	2.4	2.7	5.2	2.8	2.5	0.1	0.9	1.0	4.0	0.3	5.2
9	(14)	China	0.2	3.0	1.4	1.6	5.0	2.5	2.5	0.7	2.3	3.1	1.3	0.6	5.0
10	(11)	Italy	0.1	4.5	2.4	2.1	4.9	2.3	2.6	0.7	1.1	1.7	2.0	1.2	4.9
11	(10)	Japan	0.3	4.6	2.9	1.7	4.8	1.7	3.2	0.3	1.6	1.9	1.9	1.0	4.8
12	(9)	Singapore	1.6	4.7	1.7	2.9	4.0	2.5	1.6	0.2	0.5	0.7	3.3	0.1	4.0
13	(12)	Norway	0.5	3.8	2.2	1.6	3.8	1.6	2.1	0.1	0.6	0.7	2.9	0.2	3.8
14	(13)	Sweden	0.1	3.2	2.0	1.2	3.5	1.3	2.2	0.1	0.5	0.6	2.3	0.6	3.5
15	(17)	India	0.9	2.9	1.0	1.8	3.1	2.1	0.9	0.3	1.5	1.8	1.0	0.3	3.1
16	(16)	Cyprus	1.5	2.9	1.4	1.5	3.1	1.6	1.4	0.1	0.6	0.7	2.3	0.1	3.1
17	(15)	Taiwan	..	3.0	1.7	1.2	3.0	1.3	1.8	0.4	1.6	2.0	0.9	0.2	3.0
18	(18)	Finland	-	2.4	1.6	0.9	2.4	0.8	1.6	0.1	0.2	0.2	1.8	0.3	2.4
19	(19)	Canada	0.7	2.1	1.1	1.0	2.2	1.0	1.2	0.4	0.9	1.3	0.5	0.4	2.2
20	(22)	Belgium	0.1	1.9	0.9	1.0	2.0	1.0	1.0	0.1	0.4	0.5	1.2	0.3	2.0
21	(21)	Thailand	0.2	2.0	1.0	0.9	2.0	0.9	1.1	0.5	0.9	1.4	0.5	0.1	2.0
22	(23)	Kenya	1.1	1.9	1.0	1.0	2.0	1.0	1.0	0.1	0.3	0.4	1.5	0.1	2.0
23	(20)	Netherlands	0.1	2.0	1.0	0.9	1.9	0.9	1.0	0.1	0.4	0.6	1.0	0.4	1.9
24	(25)	Nigeria	5.2	1.7	0.8	0.9	1.8	1.0	0.8	0.1	0.6	0.6	1.1	0.1	1.8
25	(24)	Portugal	0.2	1.8	0.8	0.9	1.8	1.0	0.9	0.3	0.4	0.7	0.9	0.2	1.8
26	(26)	South Korea	0.1	1.7	0.6	1.0	1.7	1.0	0.7	0.4	0.6	1.0	0.6	0.1	1.7
27	(27)	Denmark	-	1.5	0.9	0.6	1.6	0.7	0.9	0.1	0.4	0.5	0.9	0.3	1.6
28	(32)	Zimbabwe	0.9	1.1	0.6	0.5	1.6	0.7	0.9	0.1	0.1	0.2	0.4	1.0	1.6
29	(28)	Pakistan	0.8	1.5	0.3	1.2	1.5	1.2	0.3	0.2	0.7	0.8	0.6	0.1	1.5
30	(29)	Turkey	0.7	1.4	0.5	0.9	1.3	0.7	0.6	0.2	0.5	0.7	0.5	0.1	1.3
31	(34)	Austria	-	1.0	0.5	0.5	1.1	0.5	0.6	0.1	0.2	0.3	0.6	0.3	1.1
32	(33)	Switzerland	0.2	1.0	0.5	0.5	1.1	0.5	0.5	0.1	0.2	0.3	0.6	0.2	1.1
33	(36)	Sri Lanka	1.2	0.9	0.3	0.6	1.0	0.6	0.4	0.1	0.2	0.3	0.6	0.1	1.0
34	(35)	Saudi Arabia	0.4	1.0	0.2	0.7	1.0	0.8	0.2	0.3	0.3	0.6	0.3	0.1	1.0
35	(37)	Oman	-	0.9	0.3	0.6	1.0	0.7	0.2	0.1	0.2	0.3	0.5	0.2	1.0
36	(30)	Brunei	1.0	1.2	0.6	0.6	1.0	0.5	0.5	-	0.1	0.1	0.8	0.1	1.0
37	(39)	Mauritius	0.4 (3)	0.8	0.4	0.5	0.9	0.5	0.4	-	0.2	0.2	0.6	0.2	0.9
38	(44)	Russia	..	0.7	0.4	0.4	0.9	0.4	0.5	0.1	0.3	0.4	0.5	-	0.9
39	(31)	Israel	0.2	1.2	0.4	0.7	0.9	0.6	0.3	0.1	0.2	0.3	0.5	-	0.9
40	(42)	Mexico	0.4	0.8	0.3	0.5	0.9	0.6	0.3	0.3	0.5	0.8	-	-	0.9
41	(38)	Australia	0.5	0.8	0.4	0.5	0.9	0.4	0.4	0.2	0.3	0.5	0.2	0.1	0.9
42	(41)	Indonesia	0.3	0.8	0.3	0.5	0.9	0.5	0.4	0.2	0.5	0.6	0.2	-	0.9
43	(45)	Ghana	0.7	0.7	0.3	0.5	0.8	0.5	0.3	0.1	0.3	0.3	0.3	0.1	0.8
44	(40)	Botswana	0.1	0.8	0.3	0.5	0.7	0.5	0.3	-	0.2	0.2	0.5	0.1	0.7
45	(43)	Brazil	0.5	0.8	0.4	0.4	0.7	0.4	0.3	0.2	0.3	0.5	0.2	-	0.7
46	(46)	South Africa	0.4	0.7	0.3	0.4	0.7	0.4	0.3	0.1	0.3	0.4	0.2	0.1	0.7
47	(48)	Jordan	1.2	0.6	0.2	0.4	0.6	0.4	0.2	0.1	0.2	0.4	0.2	-	0.6
48	(47)	United Arab Emirates	0.1	0.6	0.2	0.4	0.6	0.4	0.2	0.1	0.1	0.2	0.4	-	0.6
49	(-)	Luxembourg	-	0.5	0.2	0.2	0.6	0.3	0.3	-	0.1	0.1	0.5	-	0.6
50	(-)	Iran	6.6	0.5	0.1	0.4	0.5	0.4	0.1	0.3	0.1	0.4	0.1	-	0.5
		Other/unknown	17.5	14.5	6.2	8.3	15.1	8.7	6.4	2.3	5.3	7.6	6.1	1.8	15.1
		TOTAL	75.6	176.6	84.5	92.1	179.1	92.9	86.2	15.0	44.6	59.5	92.4	27.1	179.1

Full-time students from overseas
of which

			1980/81	1998/99	M	F	All	M	F	PhD	Masters	Total PG	First degree	Other UG	Total HE
		European Union(4)	6.3 (5)	85.4	42.8	42.6	85.7	42.6	43.0	4.7	17.2	21.9	48.6	15.2	85.7
		Other Europe(4)	2.6 (5)	12.6	6.4	6.2	13.1	6.3	6.7	1.1	3.2	4.3	7.9	0.9	13.1
		Commonwealth(4)	39.6 (5)	40.1	17.1	23.0	39.1	22.5	16.6	3.0	9.4	12.4	23.0	3.7	39.1
		Other Countries	27.0 (5)	42.1	19.9	22.2	45.1	23.4	21.7	6.3	15.6	21.9	15.7	7.5	45.1

Sources: Department for Education and Employment; National Assembly for Wales; Scottish Executive; Northern Ireland Department of Higher and Further Education, Training and Employment

(1) Provisional. Figures for higher education students in further education institutions (except for Northern Ireland) relate to 1998/99.
(2) Figures for students (other than in Scotland further education institutions) are snapshots counted at a particular point in the year [December for UK HE institutions and FE institutions in Wales, November for FE institutions in England and Northern Ireland]. Students starting courses after these dates will not therefore be counted. Figures for Scotland, however, are whole year (not snapshot) enrolments (rather than headcounts) for 1998/99.
(3) Data are for 1981/82.
(4) Except for 19980/81 Gibraltar is included in both EC and Commonwealth figures, and Cyprus and Malta are included in Other Europe and Commonwealth figures. Numbers in grouped countries do not sum to overall student numbers due to overlaps.
(5) Estimated.

3.8

POST COMPULSORY EDUCATION AND TRAINING: STUDENTS AND STARTERS
Students in further education(1) by country of study, mode of study(2), gender and age(3), during 1998/99

United Kingdom   Home and Overseas Students   Thousands

	United Kingdom		England(4)		Wales		Scotland(5)		Northern Ireland	
	Full-time	Part-time	Full-time	Part-time	Full-time	Part-time	Full-time	Part-time	Full-time	Part-time
All										
Age <16	9.1	56.3	7.2	29.0	0.6	3.2	1.2	21.4	0.1	2.5
16	246.5	83.7	218.7	58.8	13.1	3.9	7.6	15.3	7.2	5.6
17	214.9	94.1	189.8	70.3	10.9	4.6	7.4	14.6	6.9	4.6
18	112.3	100.9	97.1	80.3	5.7	5.0	5.3	12.4	4.2	3.2
19	47.8	84.6	42.2	68.8	2.3	4.4	2.3	9.0	1.1	2.4
20	28.5	68.2	25.6	57.1	1.1	3.4	1.4	6.1	0.4	1.7
21	22.1	64.9	20.2	55.0	0.8	3.2	1.0	5.1	0.2	1.5
22	20.2	67.2	18.6	57.2	0.6	3.4	0.8	5.2	0.1	1.4
23	18.9	68.6	17.6	58.8	0.5	3.3	0.8	5.1	0.1	1.3
24	17.8	70.1	16.6	60.3	0.5	3.4	0.7	5.1	0.1	1.4
25	16.8	72.4	15.8	62.5	0.4	3.5	0.6	5.1	-	1.3
26	16.2	75.2	15.2	65.2	0.4	3.6	0.5	5.2	-	1.3
27	16.0	77.7	15.0	67.3	0.5	3.9	0.5	5.3	-	1.2
28	15.4	76.4	14.5	65.9	0.4	3.9	0.5	5.5	-	1.2
29	14.8	76.4	13.9	65.6	0.4	4.0	0.4	5.5	-	1.3
30+	243.1	1,793.8	231.1	1,539.7	5.7	102.5	6.1	127.8	0.2	23.7
Unknown	4.6	47.6	4.5	44.1	0.1	3.1	-	-	-	0.4
All ages	**1,065.0**	**2,977.9**	**963.5**	**2,506.1**	**43.9**	**162.4**	**37.0**	**253.6**	**20.6**	**55.8**
Males										
Age <16	5.3	28.9	4.2	15.7	0.4	1.7	0.8	9.9	0.1	1.6
16	122.3	43.2	107.5	31.7	6.6	2.1	4.5	7.2	3.7	2.3
17	104.7	51.5	92.0	39.2	5.2	2.7	4.0	7.7	3.5	1.9
18	58.5	54.1	50.8	42.6	2.8	2.9	2.7	7.1	2.3	1.4
19	26.4	42.0	23.3	33.5	1.2	2.5	1.3	4.9	0.6	1.1
20	15.5	31.6	13.9	26.3	0.6	1.7	0.8	3.0	0.2	0.6
21	11.6	28.0	10.6	23.8	0.4	1.4	0.5	2.3	0.1	0.5
22	10.3	27.9	9.5	23.9	0.3	1.4	0.5	2.2	0.1	0.4
23	9.8	28.5	9.2	24.5	0.2	1.3	0.4	2.2	-	0.4
24	9.1	29.2	8.5	25.4	0.2	1.4	0.3	2.0	-	0.4
25	8.2	30.0	7.7	26.3	0.2	1.3	0.3	2.0	-	0.4
26	8.0	31.4	7.6	27.6	0.2	1.4	0.2	2.0	-	0.4
27	7.8	32.5	7.4	28.5	0.2	1.4	0.2	2.1	-	0.4
28	7.4	32.0	7.1	28.1	0.1	1.5	0.2	2.1	-	0.4
29	7.1	32.1	6.8	28.0	0.1	1.5	0.2	2.2	-	0.4
30+	116.7	712.8	112.6	616.7	1.8	38.8	2.2	50.6	0.1	6.8
Unknown	2.7	21.4	2.7	19.7	-	1.6	-	-	-	0.1
All ages	**531.6**	**1,257.0**	**481.3**	**1,061.5**	**20.6**	**66.6**	**19.0**	**109.5**	**10.7**	**19.4**
Females										
Age <16	3.8	27.4	3.0	13.3	0.3	1.5	0.4	11.5	-	1.0
16	124.2	40.4	111.2	27.2	6.5	1.8	3.0	8.1	3.5	3.3
17	110.2	42.6	97.7	31.2	5.7	1.9	3.4	6.9	3.4	2.6
18	53.7	46.8	46.4	37.7	2.8	2.1	2.6	5.3	2.0	1.8
19	21.4	42.6	18.8	35.3	1.1	1.9	1.0	4.1	0.5	1.3
20	13.0	36.7	11.7	30.8	0.5	1.8	0.6	3.1	0.2	1.1
21	10.5	36.9	9.6	31.2	0.4	1.8	0.5	2.9	0.1	1.0
22	9.8	39.3	9.0	33.4	0.3	2.0	0.4	2.9	0.1	1.0
23	9.1	40.1	8.4	34.3	0.3	2.0	0.4	2.9	-	0.9
24	8.7	40.9	8.1	34.9	0.3	2.1	0.4	3.0	-	1.0
25	8.6	42.3	8.1	36.2	0.2	2.2	0.3	3.1	-	0.9
26	8.2	43.8	7.7	37.6	0.3	2.2	0.3	3.2	-	0.9
27	8.1	45.2	7.6	38.7	0.3	2.4	0.3	3.2	-	0.8
28	8.0	44.4	7.4	37.8	0.3	2.4	0.3	3.4	-	0.9
29	7.7	44.3	7.1	37.6	0.3	2.5	0.3	3.3	-	0.9
30+	126.5	1,080.9	118.5	923.0	3.9	63.7	4.0	77.3	0.1	16.9
Unknown	1.9	26.2	1.9	24.4	-	1.6	-	-	-	0.3
All ages	**533.4**	**1,720.9**	**482.3**	**1,444.6**	**23.3**	**95.8**	**18.0**	**144.1**	**9.9**	**36.4**

Sources: Department for Education and Employment; National Assembly for Wales; Scottish Executive; Northern Ireland Department of Higher and Further Education, Training and Employment

(1) Further education figures are whole year counts and differ from the higher education tables which use annual snapshots. Data for Northern Ireland however, are collected on a snapshot basis.
(2) Full-time includes sandwich, and for Scotland, short full-time. Part-time comprises both day and evening, including block release (except for Scotland) and open/distance learning.
(3) Ages as at 31 August 1998 (1 July for Northern Ireland and 31 December for Scotland).
(4) Excludes approximately 241,600 students in further education institutions in England since the information cannot be broken down in this way. External institutions and specialist designated colleges are also excluded.
(5) Figures for Scotland further education institutions are enrolments rather than headcounts.

3.9

Students in higher education(1) by level, mode of study(2), gender and age(3), 1999/00(4,5)

United Kingdom — Home and Overseas Students — Thousands

| | Postgraduate level | | | | | | First degree | | Other Undergraduate | | Total higher education students | |
| | PHD's & equivalent | | Masters and Others | | Total Postgraduate | | | | | | | |
Age	Full-time	Part-time	Full-time	Part-time	Full-time	Part-time	Full-time	Part-time	Full-time	Part-time	**Full-time**	**Part-time**
All												
<16	-	-	-	-	-	-	-	-	-	0.2	**0.1**	**0.2**
16	-	-	-	-	-	-	0.4	-	0.7	0.5	**1.1**	**0.6**
17	-	-	-	-	-	-	10.2	-	4.2	1.1	**14.4**	**1.1**
18	-	-	-	-	-	-	145.9	0.7	22.6	6.4	**168.6**	**7.1**
19	-	-	0.1	0.1	0.1	0.1	202.7	2.2	30.5	10.1	**233.3**	**12.4**
20	-	-	1.0	0.2	1.1	0.2	205.9	3.7	25.3	10.5	**232.3**	**14.5**
21	0.8	-	12.5	1.1	13.3	1.1	130.7	4.3	17.0	9.8	**161.0**	**15.2**
22	2.7	0.1	16.5	3.4	19.2	3.5	60.6	4.3	12.3	10.0	**92.0**	**17.8**
23	4.0	0.3	14.8	5.2	18.8	5.4	31.4	3.9	9.1	10.8	**59.4**	**20.2**
24	4.5	1.3	11.4	6.4	15.9	7.7	19.0	3.6	6.9	11.6	**41.7**	**22.9**
25	3.6	2.2	8.9	7.0	12.4	9.2	13.6	3.6	5.4	12.1	**31.4**	**24.9**
26	3.1	2.4	7.1	7.7	10.2	10.1	10.9	3.5	4.6	12.6	**25.6**	**26.2**
27	2.6	2.2	5.9	8.3	8.5	10.5	9.3	3.4	4.1	13.4	**21.9**	**27.3**
28	2.1	2.0	5.0	8.5	7.1	10.5	8.2	3.6	3.6	13.4	**18.9**	**27.4**
29	1.7	1.9	4.0	8.4	5.8	10.3	6.9	3.3	3.3	13.2	**16.0**	**26.7**
30+	11.7	24.9	28.6	147.7	40.3	172.6	63.8	54.5	36.5	282.7	**140.6**	**509.8**
Unknown	-	0.1	0.3	2.2	0.3	2.3	0.7	0.4	0.4	7.5	**1.4**	**10.2**
All ages	**36.9**	**37.4**	**116.3**	**206.3**	**153.1**	**243.6**	**920.1**	**95.1**	**186.4**	**425.7**	**1,259.7**	**764.4**
Males												
<16	-	-	-	-	-	-	-	-	-	0.1	**-**	**0.1**
16	-	-	-	-	-	-	0.2	-	0.3	0.3	**0.5**	**0.3**
17	-	-	-	-	-	-	4.5	-	1.8	0.6	**6.3**	**0.6**
18	-	-	-	-	-	-	66.6	0.4	10.6	3.9	**77.2**	**4.3**
19	-	-	-	-	-	-	94.4	1.3	14.2	6.3	**108.7**	**7.7**
20	-	-	0.4	0.1	0.5	0.1	96.6	2.2	11.4	6.1	**108.5**	**8.4**
21	0.4	-	5.1	0.4	5.6	0.4	64.3	2.4	7.2	5.1	**77.1**	**7.9**
22	1.6	-	7.4	1.4	9.0	1.4	32.1	2.4	5.2	4.7	**46.3**	**8.6**
23	2.4	0.1	6.9	2.1	9.3	2.2	17.1	2.0	3.9	4.7	**30.2**	**8.9**
24	2.6	0.8	5.4	2.7	8.0	3.4	10.2	1.7	2.9	4.8	**21.1**	**9.9**
25	2.1	1.3	4.3	2.9	6.3	4.3	7.1	1.6	2.3	5.1	**15.7**	**11.0**
26	1.7	1.4	3.6	3.4	5.3	4.8	5.6	1.5	1.9	5.3	**12.8**	**11.6**
27	1.5	1.3	3.1	3.6	4.5	4.9	4.7	1.5	1.7	5.7	**10.9**	**12.1**
28	1.3	1.2	2.7	4.0	3.9	5.1	4.0	1.5	1.4	5.8	**9.3**	**12.4**
29	1.0	1.1	2.2	4.0	3.2	5.1	3.3	1.4	1.3	5.9	**7.8**	**12.4**
30+	7.2	14.8	15.1	73.9	22.3	88.7	24.2	18.3	11.4	114.1	**57.9**	**221.1**
Unknown	-	-	0.2	0.8	0.2	0.8	0.4	0.2	0.2	2.8	**0.7**	**3.7**
All ages	**21.8**	**22.1**	**56.5**	**99.3**	**78.3**	**121.4**	**435.1**	**38.6**	**77.7**	**181.2**	**591.1**	**341.2**
Females												
<16	-	-	-	-	-	-	-	-	-	0.1	**-**	**0.1**
16	-	-	-	-	-	-	0.2	-	0.4	0.3	**0.6**	**0.3**
17	-	-	-	-	-	-	5.7	-	2.4	0.5	**8.1**	**0.5**
18	-	-	-	-	-	-	79.4	0.3	12.0	2.5	**91.4**	**2.7**
19	-	-	-	-	-	-	108.3	0.9	16.3	3.7	**124.6**	**4.7**
20	-	-	0.6	0.1	0.6	0.1	109.3	1.5	13.8	4.4	**123.7**	**6.0**
21	0.4	-	7.4	0.7	7.7	0.7	66.4	1.8	9.7	4.7	**83.9**	**7.3**
22	1.1	-	9.1	2.0	10.2	2.1	28.4	1.9	7.0	5.3	**45.7**	**9.3**
23	1.7	0.1	7.8	3.1	9.5	3.2	14.4	1.9	5.3	6.1	**29.1**	**11.2**
24	1.9	0.5	6.0	3.8	7.9	4.3	8.8	1.9	3.9	6.8	**20.6**	**13.0**
25	1.5	0.9	4.6	4.1	6.1	4.9	6.5	2.0	3.2	7.0	**15.8**	**13.9**
26	1.3	1.0	3.5	4.3	4.9	5.3	5.3	2.0	2.7	7.3	**12.9**	**14.6**
27	1.1	0.9	2.9	4.7	4.0	5.6	4.6	2.0	2.4	7.7	**11.0**	**15.2**
28	0.9	0.9	2.3	4.5	3.2	5.3	4.2	2.1	2.2	7.6	**9.6**	**15.0**
29	0.7	0.8	1.8	4.4	2.6	5.1	3.6	1.9	2.1	7.3	**8.2**	**14.3**
30+	4.5	10.1	13.6	73.8	18.1	84.0	39.6	36.2	25.0	168.6	**82.7**	**288.7**
Unknown	-	-	0.1	1.5	0.1	1.5	0.3	0.3	0.3	4.7	**0.7**	**6.5**
All ages	**15.0**	**15.3**	**59.8**	**106.9**	**74.9**	**122.2**	**485.0**	**56.5**	**108.7**	**244.5**	**668.6**	**423.2**

Sources: Department for Education and Employment; National Assembly for Wales; Scottish Executive; Northern Ireland Department of Higher and Further Education, Training and Employment

(1) Higher education institutions include Open University students. Part-time figures include dormant modes, those writing up at home and on sabbaticals which are not included in HESA SFR38.
(2) Full-time includes sandwich, and for Scotland, short full-time. Part-time comprises both day and evening, including block release (except for Scotland) and open/distance learning.
(3) Ages as at 31 August 1999 (1 July for Northern Ireland and 31 December for Scotland).
(4) Figures for students (other than in Scotland further education institutions) are snapshots counted at a particular point in the year [December for UK HE institutions and FE institutions in Wales, November for FE institutions in England and Northern Ireland]. Students starting courses after these dates will not therefore be counted. Figures for Scotland, however, are whole year (not snapshot) enrolments (rather than headcounts) for 1998/99.
(5) Provisional. Figures for higher education students in further education institutions (except for Northern Ireland) relate to 1998/99.

3.10

POST COMPULSORY EDUCATION AND TRAINING: STUDENTS AND STARTERS
Participants in TEC Delivered Government-Supported Training programmes by region - time series

England & Wales

Thousands

	March 91	March 96	March 98(1)	March 99(1)	March 00
Work-Based Training for Young People(2)					
Government Office Region(3)					
England & Wales	209.5	252.0	285.7	288.7	295.7
North East	19.7	17.3	19.8	20.8	22.2
North West	30.6	46.4	50.4	50.0	51.6
Yorkshire and the Humber	28.8	26.3	31.1	32.0	33.3
East Midlands(4)	22.8	23.6	27.5	25.7	25.6
West Midlands	32.3	26.3	31.9	30.4	31.5
Eastern(4)	..	24.1	25.0	25.0	24.7
London	12.7	18.4	20.1	22.2	23.8
South East	25.8	31.8	33.9	33.9	33.9
South West	20.5	21.6	25.4	26.5	27.3
England(5)	193.2	235.8	265.2	266.3	273.8
Wales	16.4	16.2	20.5	22.4	21.9
Advanced Modern Apprenticeships(6)					
England & Wales	.	27.8	118.8	135.7	139.4
North East	.	2.4	8.4	9.7	9.9
North West	.	6.5	22.1	18.9	25.4
Yorkshire and the Humber	.	3.9	13.7	14.1	14.1
East Midlands(4)	.	2.5	10.0	11.1	11.7
West Midlands	.	2.3	12.1	14.6	15.3
Eastern(4)	.	1.6	10.0	12.2	12.3
London	.	2.0	8.6	10.5	10.9
South East	.	1.7	15.4	16.6	16.9
South West	.	1.9	10.5	12.6	14.0
England(5)	.	24.8	110.8	126.5	130.4
Wales	.	3.0	8.1	9.2	9.0
Foundation Modern Apprenticeships(7)					
England & Wales	.	.	0.9	31.7	78.0
England	.	.	0.9	27.8	69.8
Wales	.	.	..	3.9	8.1
Other Training(8)					
England & Wales	209.5	224.2	166.0	121.4	72.4
England(5)	193.2	211.0	153.6	112.0	69.9
Wales	16.4	13.2	12.4	9.3	2.5
Life Skills/Skill Build					
England & Wales	.	.	.	.	5.9
England(5)	.	.	.	.	3.6
Wales	.	.	.	.	2.3
Work-Based Learning for Adults(9)					
Government Office Region(3)					
England & Wales	124.9	72.8	44.1	34.7	34.5
North East	16.0	7.3	3.2	2.6	2.4
North West	16.3	13.1	8.1	5.6	5.8
Yorkshire and the Humber	20.0	8.5	6.0	4.9	3.5
East Midlands(4)	7.0	5.6	3.0	2.2	2.1
West Midlands	15.6	6.9	4.5	3.4	3.3
Eastern(4)	..	4.8	2.8	2.2	2.0
London	18.2	10.1	7.2	7.2	8.1
South East	11.4	5.7	3.7	2.7	3.0
South West	10.2	6.3	4.0	2.4	2.4
England(5)	114.7	68.2	42.4	33.1	32.7
Wales	10.3	4.7	1.7	1.8	1.9
All participants in TEC Delivered Government-					
Supported Training programmes					
England & Wales	334.4	324.9	329.8	323.4	330.2
England	307.9	304.0	307.7	299.4	306.5
Wales	26.7	20.9	22.1	24.2	23.8

Sources: TEC Management Information; National Assembly for Wales
(1) Includes revised figures.
(2) Includes Advanced Modern Apprenticeships, Foundation Modern Apprenticeships, Other Training, and, from October 1999, Life Skills (LS) and Skill Build.
(3) Government Office Regions in England plus country totals for England and for Wales.
(4) For 1991, Eastern figures were included with East Midlands.
(5) The England figure may not be the sum of the regional figures shown due to rounding.
(6) Formerly known as Modern Apprenticeships; launched as an initiative in September 1994 and was fully operational from September 1995.
(7) Formerly known as National Traineeships which were introduced in England & Wales in September 1997, but recruitment was minimal. 1997-98 figures for Wales are not available.
(8) Other Training includes Youth Credits & Youth Training.
(9) The Employment Training programme ran from 1990 until 1993 when it was replaced by Training for Work (TfW). In 1997-98 this was replaced by Work-Based Training for Adults (WBTA) which became Work-Based Learning for Adults (WBLA) in March 1999. 1996-97 in-training figures for TfW included Pre-Vocational Pilots but from April 1997 onwards Pre-Vocational Training became part of mainstream Work-Based Learning for Adults.

3.11

New entrants to further education(1) by country of study, mode of study(2), gender and age(3), 1998/99

United Kingdom 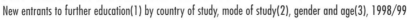 Home and Overseas Students　　　　Thousands

		United Kingdom		England(4)		Wales		Scotland(5)		Northern Ireland	
		Full-time	Part-time	Full-time	Part-time	Full-time	Part-time	Full-time	Part-time	Full-time	Part-time
All											
Age	<16	8.8	53.0	7.0	26.7	0.6	2.6	1.2	21.4	0.1	2.3
	16	241.9	80.3	215.2	56.0	12.1	3.6	7.5	15.1	7.2	5.5
	17	105.5	73.1	90.4	52.9	4.4	3.0	7.1	13.0	3.6	4.1
	18	70.7	82.0	60.6	65.8	2.8	3.1	5.1	10.3	2.3	2.9
	19	33.1	69.8	29.2	57.0	1.2	2.9	2.1	7.8	0.5	2.1
	20	22.2	57.6	20.0	48.1	0.7	2.4	1.3	5.5	0.2	1.5
	21	18.3	55.8	16.7	47.1	0.5	2.4	0.9	4.9	0.1	1.4
	22	17.4	58.7	16.0	49.8	0.4	2.6	0.8	5.0	0.1	1.3
	23	16.6	60.0	15.4	51.3	0.4	2.5	0.7	5.0	0.1	1.3
	24	15.8	61.4	14.7	52.5	0.3	2.7	0.7	4.9	0.1	1.3
	25	14.8	63.4	13.9	54.5	0.3	2.7	0.6	5.0	-	1.2
	26	14.4	65.8	13.6	56.8	0.3	2.8	0.5	5.1	-	1.2
	27	14.2	68.1	13.4	58.7	0.3	3.0	0.5	5.2	-	1.2
	28	13.8	67.2	13.0	57.6	0.3	3.0	0.5	5.4	-	1.2
	29	13.3	66.9	12.6	57.3	0.3	3.0	0.4	5.4	-	1.2
	30+	218.6	1,597.2	208.3	1,369.4	4.1	78.9	6.0	126.2	0.2	22.6
	Unknown	4.4	43.3	4.3	40.3	-	2.6	-	-	-	0.4
	All ages	**843.8**	**2,623.5**	**764.4**	**2,201.7**	**29.1**	**124.0**	**35.9**	**245.2**	**14.5**	**52.7**
Males											
Age	<16	5.2	27.2	4.0	14.4	0.3	1.4	0.8	9.9	0.1	1.4
	16	119.9	41.4	105.6	30.2	6.1	1.9	4.5	7.1	3.7	2.2
	17	56.6	37.5	48.8	27.8	2.3	1.6	3.8	6.4	1.7	1.7
	18	36.8	41.2	31.7	33.1	1.4	1.6	2.5	5.3	1.2	1.2
	19	18.3	32.6	16.2	26.4	0.6	1.5	1.2	3.8	0.3	0.9
	20	11.9	25.6	10.7	21.4	0.3	1.1	0.7	2.6	0.1	0.6
	21	9.5	23.5	8.7	19.9	0.2	1.0	0.5	2.1	0.1	0.4
	22	8.9	23.9	8.2	20.4	0.2	1.0	0.4	2.1	-	0.4
	23	8.7	24.7	8.1	21.1	0.2	1.0	0.4	2.1	-	0.4
	24	8.1	25.3	7.6	21.9	0.2	1.1	0.3	2.0	-	0.4
	25	7.3	26.0	6.8	22.6	0.1	1.0	0.3	2.0	-	0.4
	26	7.2	27.2	6.8	23.9	0.1	1.1	0.2	2.0	-	0.3
	27	7.1	28.2	6.7	24.7	0.1	1.1	0.2	2.1	-	0.4
	28	6.8	27.8	6.5	24.3	0.1	1.1	0.2	2.1	-	0.3
	29	6.5	27.8	6.2	24.1	0.1	1.1	0.2	2.2	-	0.3
	30+	107.1	633.1	103.6	546.5	1.4	30.0	2.1	50.1	0.1	6.5
	Unknown	2.6	19.0	2.6	17.6	-	1.3	-	-	-	0.1
	All ages	**428.4**	**1,091.9**	**388.7**	**920.3**	**13.8**	**50.0**	**18.5**	**103.6**	**7.4**	**18.0**
Females											
Age	<16	3.6	25.9	2.9	12.2	0.2	1.2	0.4	11.5	-	0.9
	16	122.0	38.8	109.6	25.8	6.0	1.7	3.0	8.1	3.4	3.3
	17	48.9	35.6	41.6	25.1	2.2	1.5	3.2	6.6	1.9	2.4
	18	33.9	40.9	28.9	32.7	1.4	1.5	2.5	5.0	1.1	1.7
	19	14.7	37.2	13.0	30.6	0.6	1.4	0.9	3.9	0.2	1.2
	20	10.2	32.0	9.3	26.7	0.3	1.3	0.6	3.0	0.1	1.0
	21	8.7	32.3	8.0	27.2	0.3	1.4	0.4	2.8	-	0.9
	22	8.4	34.8	7.8	29.5	0.2	1.6	0.4	2.8	-	0.9
	23	7.9	35.3	7.4	30.1	0.2	1.5	0.3	2.8	-	0.9
	24	7.7	36.1	7.2	30.6	0.2	1.6	0.3	3.0	-	0.9
	25	7.6	37.4	7.1	31.8	0.2	1.7	0.3	3.0	-	0.8
	26	7.3	38.6	6.8	32.9	0.2	1.7	0.3	3.1	-	0.8
	27	7.2	39.9	6.7	34.0	0.2	1.9	0.3	3.2	-	0.8
	28	7.0	39.3	6.6	33.3	0.2	1.9	0.3	3.3	-	0.8
	29	6.8	39.1	6.3	33.2	0.2	1.9	0.2	3.2	-	0.9
	30+	111.4	964.1	104.7	822.9	2.8	48.9	3.8	76.2	0.1	16.2
	Unknown	1.8	24.2	1.8	22.7	-	1.3	-	-	-	0.3
	All ages	**415.4**	**1,531.6**	**375.6**	**1,281.4**	**15.3**	**74.0**	**17.4**	**141.6**	**7.0**	**34.7**

Sources: Department for Education and Employment; National Assembly for Welsh; Scottish Executive; Northern Ireland Department of Higher and Further Education, Training & Employment

(1) Further education figures are whole year counts and differ from the higher education tables which use annual snapshots. Data for Northern Ireland however, are collected on a snapshot basis.
(2) Full-time includes sandwich, and for Scotland, short full-time. Part-time comprises both day and evening, including block release (except for Scotland) and open/distance learning.
(3) Ages as at 31 August 1998 (1 July for Northern Ireland and 31 December for Scotland).
(4) Excludes approximately 241,600 students in further education institutions in England since the information cannot be broken down in this way. External institutions and specialist designated colleges are also excluded. FE figures for England relate to students on year 1 of a qualification aim, which may overestimate new entrants.
(5) Figures for Scotland further education institutions are enrolments rather than headcounts.

3.12

POST COMPULSORY EDUCATION AND TRAINING: STUDENTS AND STARTERS
New entrants to higher education(1) by level, mode of study(2), gender and age(3), 1999/00(4,5)

United Kingdom · Home and Overseas Students · Thousands

| | Postgraduate level | | | | | | First degree | | Other Undergraduate | | Total higher education students | |
| | PHD's & equivalent | | Masters and Others | | Total Postgraduate | | | | | | | |
	Full-time	Part-time	Full-time	Part-time	Full-time	Part-time	Full-time	Part-time	Full-time	Part-time	Full-time	Part-time
All												
Age <16	-	-	-	-	-	-	-	-	-	0.1	0.1	0.2
16	-	-	-	-	-	-	0.4	-	0.4	0.5	0.7	0.5
17	-	-	-	-	-	-	9.8	-	3.5	0.9	13.4	1.0
18	-	-	-	-	-	-	136.6	0.5	18.9	5.4	155.5	6.0
19	-	-	0.1	0.1	0.1	0.1	72.4	0.8	16.2	6.9	88.7	7.7
20	-	-	1.0	0.1	1.0	0.1	28.7	1.2	12.2	7.1	42.0	8.4
21	0.8	-	12.3	0.9	13.1	0.9	18.4	1.4	8.9	6.6	40.4	8.9
22	1.7	0.1	15.1	1.9	16.9	1.9	11.6	1.5	7.0	7.0	35.5	10.4
23	1.2	0.1	12.3	2.5	13.5	2.6	7.6	1.4	5.2	7.8	26.2	11.8
24	1.0	0.1	9.0	2.9	10.0	3.0	5.5	1.3	3.7	8.3	19.3	12.6
25	0.7	0.1	6.9	3.2	7.6	3.3	4.1	1.4	2.8	8.4	14.6	13.1
26	0.7	0.1	5.5	3.5	6.2	3.6	3.5	1.4	2.3	8.5	12.0	13.5
27	0.6	0.1	4.6	3.6	5.1	3.8	2.9	1.3	2.1	8.8	10.2	13.9
28	0.5	0.1	3.9	3.7	4.3	3.8	2.7	1.3	1.8	8.5	8.9	13.7
29	0.4	0.1	3.0	3.5	3.5	3.7	2.3	1.3	1.7	8.1	7.4	13.1
30+	2.8	2.9	21.9	58.0	24.7	60.9	21.9	19.9	17.8	147.5	64.4	228.3
Unknown	-	-	0.3	0.9	0.3	0.9	0.4	0.3	0.3	5.7	1.1	6.8
All ages	**10.4**	**3.8**	**95.9**	**84.8**	**106.3**	**88.6**	**329.0**	**35.0**	**104.9**	**246.2**	**540.2**	**369.8**
Males												
Age <16	-	-	-	-	-	-	-	-	-	0.1	-	0.1
16	-	-	-	-	-	-	0.2	-	0.2	0.2	0.3	0.3
17	-	-	-	-	-	-	4.4	-	1.5	0.5	5.9	0.5
18	-	-	-	-	-	-	62.5	0.3	9.0	3.2	71.4	3.6
19	-	-	-	-	-	-	35.3	0.4	7.9	4.1	43.2	4.5
20	-	-	0.4	0.1	0.5	0.1	15.2	0.6	5.7	3.9	21.3	4.6
21	0.4	-	5.1	0.3	5.5	0.3	10.2	0.7	3.9	3.1	19.6	4.2
22	1.0	-	6.7	0.7	7.7	0.7	6.5	0.7	3.2	3.1	17.4	4.5
23	0.7	-	5.7	0.9	6.3	1.0	4.3	0.6	2.4	3.2	13.0	4.7
24	0.5	-	4.2	1.0	4.7	1.1	3.0	0.5	1.8	3.3	9.6	4.9
25	0.4	0.1	3.3	1.3	3.7	1.3	2.2	0.5	1.3	3.4	7.2	5.3
26	0.4	0.1	2.8	1.4	3.2	1.5	1.7	0.5	1.1	3.5	6.0	5.5
27	0.3	0.1	2.3	1.5	2.7	1.6	1.5	0.5	1.0	3.6	5.1	5.8
28	0.3	0.1	2.1	1.7	2.4	1.7	1.3	0.5	0.7	3.7	4.4	6.0
29	0.3	0.1	1.6	1.6	1.9	1.7	1.0	0.5	0.7	3.5	3.6	5.8
30+	1.7	1.6	11.4	27.2	13.1	28.8	8.0	6.4	5.9	55.2	26.9	90.4
Unknown	-	-	0.1	0.3	0.2	0.3	0.2	0.1	0.2	2.2	0.6	2.6
All ages	**6.1**	**2.0**	**45.8**	**38.1**	**51.9**	**40.1**	**157.3**	**13.0**	**46.3**	**100.1**	**255.5**	**153.2**
Females												
Age <16	-	-	-	-	-	-	-	-	-	-	-	0.1
16	-	-	-	-	-	-	0.2	-	0.2	0.3	0.4	0.3
17	-	-	-	-	-	-	5.5	-	2.1	0.5	7.5	0.5
18	-	-	-	-	-	-	74.1	0.2	9.9	2.2	84.1	2.4
19	-	-	-	-	-	-	37.1	0.4	8.4	2.7	45.5	3.2
20	-	-	0.6	0.1	0.6	0.1	13.6	0.5	6.5	3.2	20.6	3.8
21	0.3	-	7.3	0.6	7.6	0.6	8.3	0.7	4.9	3.4	20.8	4.7
22	0.7	-	8.4	1.2	9.1	1.2	5.1	0.8	3.8	3.9	18.0	5.9
23	0.5	-	6.6	1.6	7.1	1.6	3.3	0.9	2.8	4.6	13.2	7.1
24	0.4	-	4.8	1.9	5.3	1.9	2.5	0.8	1.9	4.9	9.7	7.7
25	0.3	-	3.6	1.9	3.9	2.0	2.0	0.9	1.5	4.9	7.4	7.8
26	0.3	0.1	2.7	2.1	3.0	2.1	1.7	0.8	1.3	5.0	6.0	8.0
27	0.2	0.1	2.2	2.1	2.5	2.2	1.5	0.8	1.2	5.2	5.1	8.2
28	0.2	0.1	1.8	2.0	1.9	2.0	1.5	0.8	1.0	4.8	4.5	7.7
29	0.2	0.1	1.4	1.9	1.6	2.0	1.2	0.7	1.0	4.6	3.8	7.3
30+	1.1	1.3	10.5	30.8	11.6	32.1	13.9	13.5	12.0	92.3	37.5	137.9
Unknown	-	-	0.1	0.5	0.1	0.6	0.2	0.2	0.2	3.5	0.5	4.2
All ages	**4.3**	**1.8**	**50.1**	**46.7**	**54.4**	**48.5**	**171.7**	**22.0**	**58.6**	**146.1**	**284.8**	**216.6**

Sources: Department for Education and Employment; National Assembly for Wales; Scottish Executive; Northern Ireland Department of Higher and Further Education, Training and Employment

(1) Higher Education Institution figures include Open University students.
(2) Full-time includes sandwich, and for Scotland, short full-time. Part-time comprises both day and evening, including block release (except for Scotland) and open/distance learning.
(3) Ages as at 31 August 1999 (1 July for Northern Ireland and 31 December for Scotland).
(4) Figures for students (other than in Scotland further education institutions) are snapshots counted at a particular point in the year [December for UK HE institutions and FE institutions in Wales, November for FE institutions in England and Northern Ireland]. Students starting courses after these dates will not therefore be counted. Figures for Scotland, however, are whole year (not snapshot) enrolments (rather than headcounts) for 1998/99.
(5) Provisional. Figures for higher education students in further education institutions (except for Nothern Ireland) relate to 1998/99.

POST COMPULSORY EDUCATION AND TRAINING: STUDENTS AND STARTERS
Starts in TEC Delivered Government-Supported Training programmes by region — time series

England & Wales

Thousands

	1990-91	1995-96	1997-98	1998-99(1)	1999-00
Work-Based Training for Young People(2,3)					
Government Office Region(4)					
England & Wales	244.1	279.9	274.1	243.5	258.4
North East	23.9	20.5	20.2	18.5	19.7
North West	46.5	52.2	49.3	43.4	45.9
Yorkshire and the Humber	30.7	31.3	30.0	27.9	30.1
East Midlands(5)	30.9	25.2	25.6	20.5	21.8
West Midlands	33.9	28.0	30.7	25.8	28.3
Eastern(5)	..	23.3	22.4	19.1	19.9
London	13.6	23.9	19.7	20.7	24.5
South East	24.8	32.8	32.0	26.0	26.8
South West	21.5	22.7	22.5	20.5	20.7
England(6)	225.9	259.8	252.5	222.6	237.7
Wales	18.2	20.0	21.6	20.9	20.7
Advanced Modern Apprenticeships(7)					
England & Wales	.	28.4	87.7	87.4	88.7
North East	.	2.5	6.3	6.1	6.2
North West	.	6.8	15.2	15.6	15.7
Yorkshire and the Humber	.	4.3	10.4	8.8	8.5
East Midlands(5)	.	2.7	7.7	7.1	7.4
West Midlands	.	2.4	9.0	10.2	10.5
Eastern(5)	.	1.5	7.4	8.1	7.7
London	.	1.9	7.0	8.2	9.0
South East	.	1.9	13.3	10.4	10.7
South West	.	1.8	7.0	7.8	8.4
England(6)	.	25.8	83.3	82.3	84.1
Wales	.	2.6	4.4	5.2	4.6
Foundation Modern Apprenticeships(8)					
England & Wales	.	.	0.9	41.9	97.1
England	.	.	0.9	36.8	86.6
Wales	.	.	..	5.1	10.6
Other Training(9)					
Government Office Region(4)					
England & Wales	244.1	268.1	199.6	131.5	80.0
England	225.9	250.7	181.9	119.1	78.8
Wales	18.2	17.4	17.7	12.4	1.2
Life Skills/Skill Build					
Government Office Region(4)					
England & Wales	.	.	.	.	12.9
England	.	.	.	.	6.1
Wales	.	.	.	.	6.8
Work-Based Learning for Adults(10)					
Government Office Region(4)					
England & Wales	304.6	224.4	192.6	102.9	108.3
North East	35.8	19.7	16.8	8.3	8.1
North West	52.7	39.8	35.9	16.6	16.9
Yorkshire and the Humber	44.9	26.6	22.4	11.2	10.7
East Midlands(5)	26.7	16.6	13.5	6.8	6.7
West Midlands	36.4	25.0	21.4	10.9	12.1
Eastern(5)	..	15.8	12.4	6.4	6.5
London	38.7	31.7	31.9	22.3	25.2
South East	25.4	18.5	15.2	8.3	8.9
South West	19.5	18.8	14.2	7.2	7.7
England(6)	280.2	212.4	183.6	98.1	102.7
Wales	24.4	12.1	9.0	4.8	5.6
All starts in TEC delivered Government-Supported Training programmes					
England & Wales	548.7	520.9	466.7	345.7	366.7
England	506.1	488.8	436.1	320.0	340.4
Wales	42.6	32.1	30.6	25.7	26.3

Sources: TEC Management Information; National Assembly for Wales
(1) Includes revised figures.
(2) From 1995-96, figures for Work-Based Training do not equate the sum of the starts on Modern Apprenticeships, National Traineeships and Other Training because they exclude conversions between programmes whereas the figures for individual programmes include conversions from other programmes.
(3) Includes Advanced Modern Apprenticeships, Foundation Modern Apprenticeships, Other Training, and, from October 1999, Life Skills (LS) and Skill Build.
(4) Government Office Regions in England plus country totals for England and for Wales.
(5) For 1991, Eastern figures were included with East Midlands.
(6) The England figure may not be the sum of the regional figures shown due to rounding.
(7) Formerly known as Modern Apprenticeships; launched as an initiative in September 1994 and was fully operational from September 1995.
(8) Formerly known as National Traineeships which were introduced in England & Wales in September 1997, but recruitment was minimal. 1997-98 figures for Wales are not available.
(9) Other Training includes Youth Credits & Youth Training.
(10) The Employment Training programme ran from 1990 until 1993 when it was replaced by Training for Work (TfW). In 1997-98 this was replaced by Work-based Training for Adults (WBTA) which became Work-Based Learning for Adults (WBLA) in March 1999. 1996-97 in-training figures for TfW included Pre-Vocational Pilots but from April 1997 onwards. Pre-Vocational Training became part of mainstream Work-Based Learning for Adults.

3.14 POST COMPULSORY EDUCATION AND TRAINING: STUDENTS AND STARTERS
Work-Based Training for Young People(1): characteristics of starts — time series

England & Wales

Percentages

	1990-91	1995-96	1997-98(2)	1998-99(2)	1999-00	Apr 99-Jun 99	Jul 99-Sep 99	Oct 99-Dec 99	Jan 00-Mar 00
ADVANCED MODERN APPRENTICESHIPS(3)									
As a percentage of all starters									
gender									
Males	.	67	53	53	52	45	58	53	44
Females	.	33	47	47	48	55	42	47	56
age									
16	.	23	19	19	17	8	27	15	7
17	.	24	19	19	17	18	18	17	15
18	.	20	19	19	18	19	18	19	17
19+	.	33	43	43	47	55	36	50	60
ethnic origin									
White	.	97	95	95	95	95	96	95	94
Black/African/Caribbean	.	1	1	2	2	2	1	2	2
Indian/Pakistani/ Bangladeshi/Sri Lankan	.	1	2	2	2	2	2	2	3
Other	.	1	1	1	1	1	1	1	1
special needs									
People with disabilities(4)	.	2	3	2	2	3	2	2	2
Literacy/numeracy needs	.	..	..	..	..	..	..	..	..
English/Welsh/Gaelic for speakers of other languages	.	..	..	..	..	..	..	..	..
FOUNDATION MODERN APPRENTICESHIPS(5)									
As a percentage of all starters									
gender									
Males	.	.	51	44	47	44	49	49	44
Females	.	.	49	56	53	56	51	51	56
age									
16	.	.	27	37	32	20	47	27	19
17	.	.	34	27	24	29	21	25	26
18	.	.	16	15	14	15	12	16	16
19+	.	.	23	21	29	36	19	32	40
ethnic origin									
White	.	.	93	94	94	94	94	93	93
Black/African/Caribbean	.	.	2	2	2	2	2	2	3
Indian/Pakistani/Bangladeshi/Sri Lankan	.	.	2	2	3	3	2	3	3
Other	.	.	3	1	1	1	1	1	2
special needs									
People with disabilities(4)	.	.	7	4	3	3	3	3	3
Literacy/numeracy needs	.	.	..	..	..	..	..	..	..
English/Welsh/Gaelic for speakers of other languages	.	.	..	..	..	..	..	..	..
OTHER TRAINING(6)									
As a percentage of all starters									
gender									
Males	59	53	52	54	58	57	58	59	61
Females	41	47	48	46	42	43	42	41	39
age									
16	..	37	39	42	40	29	52	37	27
17	..	24	29	32	33	41	25	33	39
18	..	9	9	10	9	9	8	10	10
over 18	..	27	23	17	18	20	15	19	24
ethnic origin									
White	92	93	93	91	89	89	90	88	90
Black/African/Caribbean	2	2	3	3	4	5	4	5	4
Indian/Pakistani/Bangladeshi/Sri Lankan	3	3	3	4	5	4	5	6	4
Other	1	2	1	1	2	2	1	2	2
special needs									
People with disabilities(4)	4	5	6	7	7	7	7	7	6
Literacy/numeracy needs	-	6	8	13	18	19	19	18	15
English/Welsh/Gaelic for speakers of other languages	1	1	1	-	-	-	-	-	

Source: Department for Education and Employment

(1) Includes Advanced Modern Apprenticeships, Foundation Modern Apprenticeships, Other Training, and, from October 1999, Life Skills (LS) and Skill Build.
(2) Includes revised figures.
(3) Formerly known as Modern Apprenticeships; launched as an initiative in September 1994 and was fully operational from September 1995.
(4) Based on trainee's self-assessment.
(5) Formerly known as National Traineeships which were introduced in England & Wales in September 1997.
(6) Other Training includes Youth Credits & Youth Training.

POST COMPULSORY EDUCATION AND TRAINING: STUDENTS AND STARTERS
Work-Based Learning for Adults(1) : characteristics of starts — time series

England & Wales

Percentages

	1990-91	1995-96	1997-98(3)	1998-99	1999-00	Apr 99-Jun 99	Jul 99-Sep 99	Oct 99-Dec 99	Jan 00-Mar 00
As a percentage of all starters									
gender									
Males	66	70	69	68	69	69	68	69	69
Females	34	30	32	32	31	31	32	31	31
age									
18-24(4)	35	27	24	.	.	.	.	.	.
25-49	58	63	64	84	82	83	82	81	82
50-59	7	10	11	16	17	17	17	18	18
unemployment duration before entry									
0-5 months	35	18	19	22	22	22	21	21	23
6-12 months	34	38	29	28	28	29	30	27	26
13-23 months	10	20	21	18	18	18	18	19	18
24-35 months	21	11	11	11	12	11	12	12	12
36+ months	.	13	19	21	21	21	20	21	20
ethnic origin									
White	88	86	85	82	81	80	81	81	81
Black/African/Caribbean	5	6	7	9	9	9	9	9	9
Indian/Pakistani/Bangladeshi/Sri Lankan	4	4	5	5	5	6	5	5	5
Other	2	3	3	4	5	5	5	5	5
special needs group									
People with disabilities(5)	11	16	19	21	20	20	20	21	21
Literacy/numeracy needs(5)	17	8	9	12	13	13	12	13	13
English/Welsh/Gaelic for speakers of other languages	3	2	3	3	6	5	6	5	6

Source: Department for Education and Employment

(1) Starts up to and including March 1993 were on Employment Training. Starts after that were on Training for Work (TfW), which superseded Employment Training and Employment Action. Differences in the coverage of the programme and its eligibility rules account for much of the change since March 1993.

(2) Prior to April 1993 Training for Work was Employment Training/Employment Action. 1996-97 starts figures for TfW include Pre-Vocational Pilots. From April 1997 onwards Pre-Vocational Training became part of mainstream work-based learning for adults (WBLA).

(3) Includes revised figures.

(4) There is no provision for 18-24 year olds on WBLA from April 1998.

(5) Based on trainee's self-assessment.

THIS PAGE HAS BEEN LEFT BLANK

POST COMPULSORY EDUCATION AND TRAINING: JOB-RELATED TRAINING
3.16 Participation in job-related training(1) in the last four weeks by economic activity and region(2), 2000

United Kingdom: People of working age(3)

Thousands and *percentages*(4)

	Thousands			Percentages(4)		
	All	Males	Females	All	Males	Females
All people						
United Kingdom	5,196	2,516	2,680	*14.3*	*13.2*	*15.5*
North East	207	97	110	*13.1*	*11.8*	*14.6*
North West	587	282	305	*14.1*	*12.8*	*15.4*
Yorkshire and the Humber	438	203	236	*14.2*	*12.4*	*16.3*
East Midlands	367	182	185	*14.3*	*13.4*	*15.2*
West Midlands	456	218	238	*14.1*	*12.7*	*15.6*
Eastern	463	228	235	*14.0*	*13.2*	*15.0*
London	710	361	348	*15.4*	*15.1*	*15.7*
South East	712	326	386	*14.5*	*12.7*	*16.5*
South West	475	242	233	*16.3*	*15.8*	*16.7*
England	4,414	2,139	2,275	*14.5*	*13.4*	*15.8*
Wales	244	123	121	*14.0*	*13.4*	*14.6*
Scotland	440	212	229	*13.9*	*12.9*	*15.0*
Northern Ireland	97	42	55	*9.6*	*8.1*	*11.2*
Employees(5,6)						
United Kingdom	3,833	1,872	1,961	*16.1*	*14.7*	*17.8*
North East	148	72	76	*15.5*	*14.0*	*17.3*
North West	458	225	232	*16.8*	*15.3*	*18.6*
Yorkshire and the Humber	329	149	180	*16.3*	*13.8*	*19.2*
East Midlands	275	138	138	*15.7*	*14.5*	*17.0*
West Midlands	339	167	173	*16.0*	*14.4*	*17.9*
Eastern	355	180	175	*15.7*	*14.8*	*16.7*
London	479	245	233	*16.9*	*16.3*	*17.6*
South East	551	252	299	*15.9*	*13.5*	*18.8*
South West	352	184	169	*17.7*	*17.4*	*18.1*
England	3,287	1,612	1,676	*16.3*	*14.9*	*18.0*
Wales	168	82	86	*15.9*	*14.5*	*17.5*
Scotland	317	153	164	*15.4*	*14.3*	*16.7*
Northern Ireland	60	25	34	*10.6*	*8.5*	*12.9*
Self-employed(6,7)						
United Kingdom	238	140	98	*8.1*	*6.4*	*13.0*
North East	*	*	*	*	*	*
North West	17	12	*	*5.7*	*5.3*	*
Yorkshire and the Humber	20	11	*	*8.9*	*6.3*	*
East Midlands	19	*	11	*9.3*	*	*18.6*
West Midlands	17	10	*	*7.6*	*6.1*	*
Eastern	20	10	10	*6.6*	*4.4*	*13.4*
London	39	24	16	*9.2*	*7.6*	*13.8*
South East	40	23	17	*8.6*	*7.0*	*12.6*
South West	29	17	12	*10.1*	*3.1*	*15.4*
England	205	117	88	*8.2*	*6.3*	*13.4*
Wales	10	*	*	*6.8*	*	*
Scotland	18	13	*	*9.5*	*8.7*	*
Northern Ireland	*	*	*	*	*	*

Source: Labour Force Survey, Spring 2000(10)

(1) Job-related training includes both on and off-the-job training.
(2) Government Office Regions in England and each UK country.
(3) Working age is defined as males aged 16-64 and females 16-59.
(4) Expressed as a percentage of the total number of people in each group.
(5) Employees are those in employment excluding the self-employed, unpaid family workers and those on government employment and training programmes.
(6) The split into employees and self-employed is based on respondents' own assessment of their employment status.
(7) Self-employed are those in employment excluding employees, unpaid family workers and those on government employment and training programmes.
(8) Unemployed according to the International Labour Office (ILO) definition.
(9) Economically inactive are those who are neither in employment nor ILO unemployed.
(10) Users of these data should read the LFS entry in Annex A, as it contains important information about the LFS and the concepts and definitions used.

3.16 POST COMPULSORY EDUCATION AND TRAINING: JOB-RELATED TRAINING
Participation in job-related training(1) in the last four weeks by economic activity and region(2), 2000

United Kingdom: People of working age(3)

Thousands and *percentages*(4)

	Thousands				*Percentages*(4)		
	All	Males	Females		All	Males	Females
ILO unemployed(8)							
United Kingdom	166	87	79		10.4	8.8	12.8
North East	*	*	*		*	*	*
North West	15	*	*		8.7	*	*
Yorkshire and the Humber	13	*	*		9.0	*	*
East Midlands	*	*	*		*	*	*
West Midlands	17	*	11		10.7	*	17.2
Eastern	*	*	*		*	*	*
London	30	17	13		11.7	10.8	13.0
South East	22	10	12		15.8	12.5	19.7
South West	16	*	*		15.6	*	*
England	138	72	66		10.7	9.2	13.0
Wales	*	*	*		*	*	*
Scotland	19	10	10		10.1	7.7	14.6
Northern Ireland	*	*	*		*	*	*
Economically inactive(9)							
United Kingdom	841	349	491		10.9	11.7	10.3
North East	38	14	24		9.5	8.6	10.1
North West	85	29	56		8.8	7.7	9.4
Yorkshire and the Humber	64	28	35		9.5	10.5	8.9
East Midlands	55	26	29		11.3	14.2	9.5
West Midlands	71	28	43		9.9	9.8	10.0
Eastern	72	29	44		11.7	13.1	10.9
London	151	68	83		13.9	16.6	12.3
South East	90	37	53		11.0	12.8	10.0
South West	68	30	39		13.0	14.7	12.0
England	694	289	405		11.0	12.0	10.4
Wales	50	24	27		11.1	12.4	10.1
Scotland	73	29	44		10.5	10.3	10.6
Northern Ireland	23	*	15		7.5	*	8.0

Source: Labour Force Survey, Spring 2000(10)

See previous page for footnotes.

3.17 POST COMPULSORY EDUCATION AND TRAINING: JOB-RELATED TRAINING

Participation by employees(1) in job-related training(2) in the last four weeks by type of training and a range of personal characteristics, 2000

United Kingdom: Employees(1) of working age(3)   Thousands and percentages(4)

	Total number of employees (thousands)	of which: receiving off-the-job training only (%)	receiving on-the-job training only (%)	receiving both on and off-the-job training (%)	receiving any training (%)
All employees	23,802	8.3	4.6	3.2	16.1
By gender					
Males	12,758	7.4	4.4	2.9	14.7
Females	11,044	9.3	4.9	3.5	17.8
By age					
16-19	1,432	13.5	6.4	6.1	26.1
20-24	2,275	10.7	6.8	5.8	23.3
25-29	3,016	8.2	5.1	3.9	17.3
30-39	6,762	8.5	4.6	3.0	16.1
40-49	5,546	8.3	4.2	2.5	15.0
50-64	4,772	5.3	3.3	1.5	10.2
By ethnic origin					
White	22,607	8.2	4.6	3.2	16.0
Non-white	1,193	9.9	4.6	3.1	17.7
of which:					
Black	366	9.1	5.8	3.7	18.6
Indian, Pakistani & Bangladeshi	537	9.2	3.5	2.5	15.2
Other non-white	291	12.3	5.3	3.5	21.1
By highest qualification held(5)					
Degree or equivalent	4,116	13.0	6.3	4.9	24.2
Higher Education qualification (below degree level)	2,325	12.9	5.9	5.1	23.8
GCE A level or equivalent	5,767	8.7	4.6	3.1	16.5
GCSE grades A* to C or equivalent	5,540	7.9	4.7	3.3	15.9
Other	3,202	4.3	3.6	1.6	9.5
None	2,611	2.0	2.2	0.6	4.8
By region					
United Kingdom	23,802	8.3	4.6	3.2	16.1
North East	958	8.0	4.1	3.4	15.5
North West	2,726	8.0	5.0	3.8	16.8
Yorkshire and the Humber	2,018	8.5	4.9	3.0	16.3
East Midlands	1,758	7.7	5.2	2.8	15.7
West Midlands	2,123	8.1	4.5	3.3	16.0
Eastern	2,266	8.4	4.2	3.1	15.7
London	2,831	9.5	4.2	3.2	16.9
South East	3,459	8.2	4.7	3.1	15.9
South West	1,986	9.7	4.7	3.4	17.7
England	20,125	8.5	4.6	3.2	16.3
Wales	1,059	8.2	4.7	3.0	15.9
Scotland	2,056	7.3	4.9	3.2	15.4
Northern Ireland	562	5.5	3.6	*	10.6
Time series (Spring of each year)(6)					
1991	21,920	8.3	4.3	2.3	14.9
1996(7)	22,092	8.5	3.9	2.4	14.8
1998(7)	23,006	8.7	4.3	2.7	15.6
1999(7)	23,392	8.7	4.4	2.9	15.9
2000	23,802	8.3	4.6	3.2	16.1

Source: Labour Force Survey, Spring 2000(8)

(1) Employees are those in employment excluding the self-employed, unpaid family workers and those on government employment and training programmes.

(2) Job-related training includes both on and off-the-job training.

(3) Working age is defined as males aged 16-64 and females aged 16-59.

(4) Expressed as a percentage of the total number of people in each group.

(5) Apart from rounding, figures may not sum to grand totals because of questions in the LFS which were unanswered or did not apply.

(6) Due to a change in the LFS questionnaire, data from Summer 1994 onwards are not comparable with earlier figures.

(7) Figures have been revised as a result of revisions to quarterly LFS data from Autumn 1993 to Autumn 1999 to better reflect population changes over this period.

(8) Users of these data should read the LFS entry in Annex A, as it contains important information about the LFS and the concepts.

3.18 POST COMPULSORY EDUCATION AND TRAINING: JOB-RELATED TRAINING
Participation by employees(1) in job-related training(2) in the last four weeks by a range of economic characteristics, 2000

United Kingdom: Employees(1) of working age(3)

Thousands and percentages(4)

	Thousands			Percentages(4)		
	All	Males	Females	All	Males	Females
All employees	3,833	1,872	1,961	16.1	14.7	17.8
By industry						
Agriculture, forestry & fishing	17	14	*	8.2	8.3	*
Energy and water supply	52	39	13	17.7	17.1	19.9
Manufacturing	509	384	125	11.5	11.6	11.1
Construction	158	135	22	11.9	11.6	13.8
Distribution, hotels & restaurants	601	280	322	12.8	12.9	12.8
Transport	188	128	59	11.3	10.6	13.5
Banking, finance & insurance	599	327	272	16.8	17.1	16.4
Public administration, education & health	1,510	476	1,034	23.6	23.9	23.5
Other services	194	86	108	15.9	14.7	17.0
By occupation						
Managers & administrators	569	352	217	15.5	14.2	18.3
Professional	730	362	367	28.5	24.5	33.9
Associate professional & technical	604	234	370	25.4	20.8	29.4
Clerical & secretarial	547	155	392	14.3	15.3	14.0
Craft & related	282	268	15	11.8	12.1	7.8
Personal & protective services	514	193	321	18.1	19.9	17.2
Sales	304	112	192	14.5	15.5	14.0
Plant & machine operatives	153	123	30	7.0	7.0	7.1
Other	127	71	56	6.9	7.2	6.5
By full-time/part-time work(5)						
Full-time	2,969	1,690	1,279	16.4	14.3	20.2
Part-time	862	181	681	15.2	18.8	14.5
of which:						
students	339	135	203	31.6	28.9	33.7
could not find full-time job	58	18	40	10.4	9.0	11.2
did not want full-time job	453	24	429	11.5	9.3	11.6
By employment status(6)						
Permanent job	3,483	1,725	1,758	15.8	14.5	17.3
Temporary job	336	138	198	21.4	18.8	23.5
of which:						
seasonal/casual work	69	26	43	19.1	16.9	20.9
contract for fixed term or task	190	73	116	24.6	20.7	27.9
agency temping	32	14	18	12.6	10.8	14.5
other	46	25	22	24.6	26.4	22.8
By socio-economic group						
Professional	376	256	120	26.0	23.2	34.8
Intermediate	1,549	696	853	21.0	17.2	25.4
Skilled (non-manual)	897	302	594	15.5	18.4	14.4
Skilled (manual)	488	370	118	11.1	10.5	13.9
Partly skilled	415	176	240	11.6	9.8	13.3
Unskilled	70	39	31	6.5	7.3	5.8
Armed Forces/Other	35	32	*	30.4	30.0	35.4

Source: Labour Force Survey, Spring 2000(7)

(1) Employees are those in employment excluding the self-employed, unpaid family workers and those on government employment and training programmes.
(2) Job-related training includes both on and off-the-job training.
(3) Working age is defined as males aged 16-64 and females aged 16-59.
(4) Expressed as a percentage of the total number of people in each group.
(5) The split between employees working full-time and part-time is based on respondents' own assessment.
(6) Apart from rounding, figures may not sum to grand totals because of questions in the LFS which were unanswered or did not apply.
(7) Users of these data should read the LFS entry in Annex A, as it contains important information about the LFS and the concepts and definitions used.

3.19 POST COMPULSORY EDUCATION AND TRAINING: JOB-RELATED TRAINING

Participation by employees(1) in job-related training(2) in the last four weeks by type of training and a range of economic characteristics, 2000

United Kingdom: Employees(1) of working age(3)   Thousands and percentages(4)

	Total number of employees (thousands)	of which: receiving off-the-job training only (4)(%)	receiving on-the-job training only (4)(%)	receiving both on and off-the-job training (4)(%)	receiving any training (4)(%)
All employees	23,802	8.3	4.6	3.2	16.1
By industry(5)					
Agriculture, forestry & fishing	210	*	*	*	8.1
Energy & water supply	292	8.1	6.0	3.6	17.7
Manufacturing	4,430	5.7	3.6	2.1	11.5
Construction	1,329	5.3	3.2	3.3	11.9
Distribution, hotels & restaurants	4,684	7.6	3.6	1.7	12.8
Transport	1,657	5.5	3.9	1.9	11.3
Banking, finance & insurance	3,570	8.6	4.7	3.4	16.8
Public administration, education & health	6,388	11.9	6.6	5.1	23.6
Other services	1,218	8.5	4.1	3.3	15.9
By occupation(5)					
Managers & administrators	3,664	8.9	3.9	2.7	15.5
Professional	2,559	14.8	7.4	6.2	28.5
Associate professional & technical	2,383	12.0	7.0	6.3	25.4
Clerical & secretarial	3,826	7.5	4.5	2.3	14.3
Craft & related	2,400	4.8	3.3	3.6	11.8
Personal & protective services	2,837	8.9	5.5	3.7	18.1
Sales	2,095	9.0	4.1	1.4	14.5
Plant & machine operatives	2,183	2.9	3.1	1.0	7.0
Other	1,847	3.9	2.3	0.6	6.9
By full-time/part-time work(5,6)					
Full-time	18,124	7.7	5.1	3.6	16.4
Part-time	5,674	10.2	3.2	1.8	15.2
of which:					
students	1,072	26.5	2.4	2.7	31.6
could not find full-time job	558	5.9	3.5	0.9	10.4
did not want full-time job	3,942	6.4	3.3	1.8	11.5
By employment status(5)					
Permanent	22,070	8.1	4.5	3.1	15.7
Temporary	1,576	11.0	6.3	4.1	21.4
of which:					
seasonal/casual work	361	15.2	*	*	19.1
contract for fixed term or task	771	10.9	8.0	5.7	24.6
agency temping	254	7.3	4.0	1.3	12.6
other	189	7.9	10.2	6.5	24.6
By socio-economic group(5)					
Professional	1,449	13.2	6.7	6.0	26.0
Intermediate	7,391	11.0	5.4	4.5	21.0
Skilled (non-manual)	5,779	8.4	4.8	2.3	15.5
Skilled (manual)	4,385	4.6	3.6	2.9	11.1
Partly skilled	3,593	6.2	3.6	1.8	11.6
Unskilled	1,079	3.9	2.3	0.3	6.5
Armed Forces/Other	116	13.3	9.2	7.9	30.4

Source: Labour Force Survey, Spring 2000(7)

(1) Employees are those in employment excluding the self-employed, unpaid family workers and those on government employment and training programmes.
(2) Job-related training includes both on and off-the-job training.
(3) Working age is defined as males aged 16-64 and females aged 16-59.
(4) Expressed as a percentage of the total number of people in each group.
(5) Apart from rounding, figures may not sum to grand totals because of questions in the LFS which were unanswered or did not apply.
(6) The split between employees working full-time and part-time is based on respondents' own assessment.
(7) Users of these data should read the LFS entry in Annex A, as it contains important information about the LFS and the concepts and definitions used.

THIS PAGE HAS BEEN LEFT BLANK

POST COMPULSORY EDUCATION AND TRAINING: JOB-RELATED TRAINING

Participation by employees(1) in job-related training(2) in the last four weeks by region(3) and a range of personal and economic characteristics, 2000

United Kingdom: Employees(1) of working age(4)

Thousands and percentages(5)

			Region(3)				
	United Kingdom	North East	North West	Yorkshire and the Humber	East Midlands	West Midlands	Eastern
All employees	3,833	148	458	329	275	339	355
By gender							
Males	1,872	72	225	149	138	167	180
Females	1,961	76	232	180	138	173	175
By age							
16-19	374	15	57	38	25	33	28
20-24	531	19	59	44	38	48	41
25-29	522	15	61	35	35	43	51
30-39	1,087	47	126	99	81	99	107
40-49	833	37	98	71	59	67	83
50-64	485	15	57	42	37	49	45
By highest qualification held(6)							
Degree or equivalent	997	25	109	75	63	81	92
Higher Education qualification (below degree level)	553	24	65	49	37	49	44
GCE A level or equivalent	951	35	111	78	72	80	88
GCSE grades A* to C or equivalent	878	47	117	84	73	89	88
Other	306	10	35	28	20	22	30
None	126	*	17	13	*	17	11
By occupation							
Managers & administrators	569	22	66	42	38	43	64
Professional	730	21	88	59	49	67	68
Associate professional & technical	604	21	74	49	44	51	58
Clerical & secretarial	547	21	66	50	37	43	48
Craft & related	282	12	38	23	24	31	20
Personal & protective services	514	20	56	45	45	43	47
Sales	304	16	35	30	24	29	22
Plant & machine operatives	153	*	21	17	*	21	16
Other	127	*	13	13	*	12	12
By industry							
Agriculture & fishing	17	*	*	*	*	*	*
Energy & water	52	*	*	*	*	*	*
Manufacturing	509	23	78	54	48	57	47
Construction	158	*	18	14	*	21	13
Distribution, hotels & restaurants	601	24	69	57	51	50	45
Transport & communication	188	*	24	14	*	15	23
Banking, finance & insurance etc	599	11	56	41	36	41	60
Public admin, education & health	1,510	64	183	126	110	133	141
Other services	194	*	20	16	*	18	20
Percentages(5)							
All employees	16.1	15.5	16.8	16.3	15.7	16.0	15.7
By gender							
Males	14.7	14.0	15.3	13.8	14.5	14.4	14.8
Females	17.8	17.3	18.6	19.2	17.0	17.9	16.7
By age							
16-19	26.1	30.7	32.0	31.5	23.9	27.9	20.1
20-24	23.3	20.8	22.8	22.7	25.2	23.7	20.3
25-29	17.3	12.2	17.3	14.5	16.4	16.5	17.6
30-39	16.1	16.6	16.2	17.3	16.6	16.5	17.2
40-49	15.0	16.1	15.1	15.2	14.0	13.5	16.0
50-64	10.2	8.2	11.1	10.0	9.8	11.0	9.1
By highest qualification held							
Degree or equivalent	24.2	22.2	26.2	25.9	23.7	25.1	25.1
Higher Education qualification (below degree level)	23.8	24.5	24.2	24.8	25.0	24.3	22.9
GCE A level or equivalent	16.5	14.7	15.6	15.1	17.3	16.8	16.8
GCSE grades A* to C or equivalent	15.9	19.2	17.3	17.3	17.1	17.5	14.8
Other	9.5	7.2	10.9	9.9	8.2	7.1	9.7
None	4.8	*	5.8	5.6	*	6.0	4.3
By occupation							
Managers & administrators	15.5	18.0	16.2	15.6	15.7	16.1	16.5
Professional	28.5	28.7	31.2	31.6	15.2	30.1	28.3
Associate professional & technical	25.4	24.0	27.8	25.5	27.6	27.8	24.9
Clerical & secretarial	14.3	14.1	14.5	15.5	27.7	12.9	12.7
Craft & related	11.8	11.2	12.8	10.7	13.7	11.5	9.5
Personal & protective services	18.1	17.2	18.0	18.1	11.6	17.4	18.5
Sales	14.5	16.6	14.8	16.6	23.2	15.1	12.3
Plant & machine operatives	7.0	*	8.2	7.5	*	8.2	7.8
Other	6.9	*	6.5	7.8	*	7.4	6.6
By industry							
Agriculture & fishing	8.2	*	*	*	*	*	*
Energy & water	17.7	*	*	*	*	*	*
Manufacturing	11.5	11.2	13.2	12.3	11.3	10.2	11.8
Construction	11.9	*	11.4	12.8	*	17.3	10.2
Distribution, hotels & restaurants	12.8	13.2	12.6	14.0	14.1	12.4	10.5
Transport & communication	11.3	*	12.5	11.4	*	10.8	12.8
Banking, finance & insurance etc	16.8	10.5	16.9	16.7	17.3	16.6	14.8
Public admin, education & health	23.6	23.3	24.9	23.1	25.0	25.3	25.5
Other services	15.9	*	16.7	17.5	*	18.3	15.5

Source: Labour Force Survey, Spring 2000(7)

(1) Employees are those in employment excluding the self-employed, unpaid family workers and those on government employment and training programmes.
(2) Job-related training includes both on and off-the-job training.
(3) Government Office Regions in England and each UK country.
(4) Working age is defined as males aged 16-64 and females aged 16-59.
(5) Expressed as a percentage of the total number of people in each group.
(6) Apart from rounding, figures may not sum to grand totals because of questions in the LFS which were unanswered or did not apply.
(7) Users of these data should read the LFS entry in Annex A, as it contains important information about the LFS and the concepts and definitions used.

3.20 POST COMPULSORY EDUCATION AND TRAINING: JOB-RELATED TRAINING

Participation by employees(1) in job-related training(2) in the last four weeks by region(3) and a range of personal and economic characteristics, 2000

United Kingdom: Employees(1) of working age(4)

Thousands and percentages(5)

	Region(3)						
	London	South East	South West	England	Wales	Scotland	Northern Ireland
All employees	479	551	352	3,287	168	317	60
By gender							
Males	245	252	184	1,612	82	153	25
Females	233	299	169	1,676	86	164	34
By age							
16-19	25	55	37	314	18	37	*
20-24	89	68	42	448	23	49	11
25-29	77	81	49	446	22	45	*
30-39	148	146	86	939	51	80	17
40-49	82	128	93	719	34	70	10
50-64	58	74	45	421	21	37	*
By highest qualification held(6)							
Degree or equivalent	190	146	82	864	44	73	16
Higher Education qualification (below degree level)	53	77	57	456	25	67	*
GCE A level or equivalent	95	135	95	790	41	104	16
GCSE grades A* to C or equivalent	69	128	84	779	42	42	16
Other	55	48	24	272	12	18	*
None	17	10	*	109	*	10	*
By occupation							
Managers & administrators	87	89	49	501	20	43	*
Professional	112	103	68	638	32	54	*
Associate professional & technical	77	90	49	514	26	55	*
Clerical & secretarial	70	83	50	467	22	46	11
Craft & related	15	33	32	229	16	32	*
Personal & protective services	55	81	46	439	24	41	11
Sales	38	44	27	264	11	23	*
Plant & machine operatives	*	12	18	131	*	12	*
Other	15	15	13	107	*	10	*
By industry							
Agriculture & fishing	*	*	*	13	*	*	*
Energy & water	*	*	*	36	*	13	*
Manufacturing	24	54	54	439	27	34	*
Construction	12	18	18	130	*	18	*
Distribution, hotels & restaurants	81	83	59	518	26	49	*
Transport & communication	31	28	12	161	*	18	*
Banking, finance & insurance etc	129	105	51	529	18	46	*
Public admin, education & health	163	230	141	1,291	73	119	26
Other services	38	22	12	163	10	19	*
Percentages(5)							
All employees	16.9	15.9	17.7	16.3	15.9	15.4	10.6
By gender							
Males	16.3	13.5	17.4	14.9	14.5	14.3	8.5
Females	17.6	18.8	18.1	18.0	17.5	16.7	12.9
By age							
16-19	19.7	23.5	27.3	25.9	25.9	28.7	*
20-24	27.9	21.9	23.8	23.5	23.1	24.1	16.0
25-29	19.4	18.3	20.3	17.5	16.5	18.3	*
30-39	16.5	15.5	16.3	16.4	17.4	13.5	10.3
40-49	13.5	16.1	19.7	15.4	13.4	13.8	8.1
50-64	12.0	10.0	10.4	10.3	9.7	9.7	*
By highest qualification held							
Degree or equivalent	24.2	21.5	26.4	24.3	27.5	23.7	17.0
Higher Education qualification (below degree level)	23.1	24.2	27.4	24.5	21.6	22.7	*
GCE A level or equivalent	17.6	16.2	19.8	16.7	17.4	16.1	11.4
GCSE grades A* to C or equivalent	13.8	14.9	16.3	16.2	15.2	12.9	12.5
Other	11.2	11.0	9.0	9.7	8.3	8.8	*
None	6.7	3.5	*	5.1	*	4.0	*
By occupation							
Managers & administrators	15.1	13.5	17.3	15.5	17.1	16.3	*
Professional	28.9	25.0	34.7	29.2	27.4	26.1	*
Associate professional & technical	22.5	24.1	25.6	25.3	25.9	26.6	*
Clerical & secretarial	14.0	15.0	15.9	14.3	14.9	15.4	10.9
Craft & related	9.9	11.7	15.2	11.7	12.7	13.8	*
Personal & protective services	17.0	20.0	18.5	18.7	17.3	15.4	13.4
Sales	16.6	13.8	14.2	14.9	11.7	12.5	*
Plant & machine operatives	*	5.7	9.4	7.2	*	6.4	*
Other	8.8	6.5	8.4	7.0	*	5.0	*
By industry							
Agriculture & fishing	*	*	*	8.2	*	*	*
Energy & water	*	*	*	17.5	*	21.4	*
Manufacturing	9.6	9.9	14.6	11.6	12.3	10.7	*
Construction	10.6	10.8	15.4	12.2	*	12.3	*
Distribution, hotels & restaurants	15.3	11.9	14.1	13.1	13.4	11.8	*
Transport & communication	12.5	10.3	10.4	11.3	*	13.3	*
Banking, finance & insurance etc	17.5	16.5	18.5	16.6	16.6	19.9	*
Public admin, education & health	22.5	25.8	24.7	24.6	21.6	19.9	13.6
Other services	17.6	12.6	14.5	15.9	18.0	16.3	*

Source: Labour Force Survey, Spring 2000(7)

See previous page for footnotes.

POST COMPULSORY EDUCATION AND TRAINING: JOB-RELATED TRAINING

3.21

Length of job-related training(1), 2000

United Kingdom: People of working age(2)

Thousands and percentages(3)

	Total receiving training(5) (thousands)	Length of training(4)							
		Under 1 week	1 week < 1 month	1 month < 6 months	6 months < 1 year	1 year < 2 years	2 years < 3 years	3 years or more	Ongoing or no definite limit
All people	5,196	26.3	3.4	7.0	6.6	8.7	9.3	14.6	17.2
Economic activity									
Employees(6,7)	3,833	33.2	4.2	6.9	5.9	7.1	7.1	9.9	19.4
Self-employed(7,8)	238	34.7	*	9.6	5.4	7.3	5.1	6.5	25.8
ILO unemployed(9)	166	*	*	12.9	11.5	18.0	14.7	16.9	12.1
Economically inactive(10)	841	*	*	4.8	8.6	12.9	17.6	37.9	6.8
All employees	3,833	33.2	4.2	6.9	5.9	7.1	7.1	9.9	19.4
By gender									
Males	1,872	33.8	5.1	6.3	4.3	6.0	6.9	10.9	20.6
Females	1,961	32.7	3.3	7.6	7.5	8.2	7.4	9.0	18.2
By age									
16-19	374	5.0	*	*	6.7	16.7	22.9	21.2	13.9
20-24	531	16.3	3.5	4.8	5.2	7.8	8.6	25.0	19.1
25-29	522	28.0	5.0	7.1	6.3	6.8	6.4	10.5	22.1
30-39	1,087	36.0	4.9	9.3	6.1	6.3	6.1	6.6	19.8
40-49	833	45.1	4.4	7.1	6.3	6.1	4.0	3.6	19.0
50-64	485	52.4	3.5	7.2	4.4	3.0	2.0	2.3	20.7
By highest qualification held(11)									
Degree or equivalent	997	42.6	4.3	5.0	4.3	5.3	5.1	8.0	19.8
Higher Education qualification (below degree level)	553	38.5	3.3	8.2	6.4	5.7	7.3	9.6	17.1
GCE A level or equivalent	951	30.3	4.5	7.0	5.4	6.3	6.6	15.0	18.5
GCSE grades A* to C or equivalent	878	24.8	3.7	8.0	7.8	10.5	10.6	8.8	19.3
Other qualification	306	28.9	6.2	6.2	6.6	9.5	6.3	5.9	22.9
No qualification	126	27.8	*	11.4	*	*	*	*	22.1
By occupation									
Managers & administrators	569	46.1	4.7	6.5	4.0	4.9	5.1	4.4	18.5
Professional	730	44.0	3.0	4.8	4.8	5.5	5.2	8.4	19.2
Associate professional & technical	604	33.5	3.3	7.8	5.7	7.1	7.2	9.7	21.4
Clerical & secretarial	547	30.3	5.3	7.8	7.2	6.8	5.8	9.2	20.7
Craft & related	282	22.2	4.2	6.7	5.7	4.7	9.2	23.2	16.8
Personal & protective services	514	24.2	4.7	7.7	8.5	10.0	8.4	10.9	18.6
Sales	304	21.1	3.2	6.7	5.3	11.7	12.7	14.7	16.0
Plant & machine operatives	153	29.6	7.3	10.0	7.0	*	*	*	25.6
Other occupations	127	18.7	*	8.2	*	12.0	13.6	8.8	18.5
By industry									
Agriculture, forestry & fishing	17	*	*	*	*	*	*	*	*
Energy & water supply	52	47.5	*	*	*	*	*	*	*
Manufacturing	509	30.8	5.5	7.3	6.2	6.7	5.5	12.4	19.6
Construction	158	30.1	*	7.3	*	*	9.4	18.7	13.5
Distribution, hotels & restaurants	601	20.5	2.4	5.8	4.9	11.0	12.6	14.8	19.3
Transport	188	37.7	7.0	6.4	*	5.9	6.4	6.3	17.5
Banking, finance & insurance	599	35.8	5.5	6.7	4.6	3.9	4.6	8.7	22.9
Public administration, education & health	1,510	38.3	3.7	7.6	6.8	7.2	5.8	7.0	19.2
Other services	194	27.1	*	6.0	8.1	8.9	11.7	11.5	17.3
By region(12)									
United Kingdom	3,833	33.2	4.2	6.9	5.9	7.1	7.1	9.9	19.4
North East	148	32.4	*	8.4	7.0	9.9	7.7	6.9	19.6
North West	458	29.8	4.0	6.3	7.4	7.6	9.6	9.5	20.9
Yorkshire and the Humber	329	35.4	3.8	7.5	6.2	6.4	6.7	10.5	19.0
East Midlands	275	31.6	5.2	8.3	6.5	5.9	6.2	9.1	20.1
West Midlands	339	33.0	3.3	5.8	6.6	8.3	8.0	9.9	19.1
Eastern	355	36.8	4.2	5.7	5.0	7.4	7.4	6.7	20.9
London	479	36.1	4.4	5.9	4.7	6.5	5.4	9.5	18.3
South East	551	35.9	5.6	7.0	4.7	6.9	6.6	9.1	17.4
South West	352	33.6	4.2	8.9	6.0	8.8	6.3	9.8	16.0
England	3,287	34.1	4.4	6.9	5.9	7.4	7.1	9.2	18.9
Wales	168	24.5	*	6.6	6.8	6.5	7.6	16.6	22.8
Scotland	317	31.4	*	7.0	5.1	4.7	7.0	13.6	21.6
Northern Ireland	60	19.9	*	*	*	*	*	*	21.8

Source: Labour Force Survey, Spring 2000(13)

(1) Job-related training includes both on and off-the-job training.
(2) Working age is defined as males aged 16-64 and females aged 16-59.
(3) Expressed as a percentage of those in the group who received training in the last four weeks .
(4) The total length of the course was recorded not just the part completed. For people engaged on day or block release, the total length of training is given. For people who dropped out of a course the time spent on the course, not the total length is recorded.
(5) People of working age who received on or off-the-job training in the last four weeks.
(6) Employees are those in employment excluding the self-employed, unpaid family workers and those on government employment and training programmes.
(7) The split into employees and self-employed is based on respondents' own assessment of their employment status.
(8) Self-employed are those in employment excluding employees, unpaid family workers and those on government employment and training programmes.
(9) Unemployed according to the International Labour Office (ILO) definition.
(10) Economically inactive are those who are neither in employment nor ILO unemployed.
(11) Apart from rounding, figures may not sum to grand totals because of questions in the LFS which were unanswered or did not apply.
(12) Government Office Regions in England and each UK country.
(13) Users of these data should read the LFS entry in Annex A, as it contains important information about the LFS and the concepts and definitions used.

POST COMPULSORY EDUCATION AND TRAINING: JOB-RELATED TRAINING
Location of off-the-job training(1), 2000

United Kingdom: People of working age(2)   Thousands and percentages(3)

	Total receiving training(1) (thousands)	Main place of training (percentages)(4)						
		Employer's premises	Another employer's premises	Private training centre	At home(5)	Further Education college or University	Other educational institution	Other
All people	4,037	22.0	4.6	6.2	6.2	40.1	4.0	8.6
Economic activity								
Employees(6,7)	2,729	30.9	5.5	7.4	6.6	30.7	3.2	8.7
Self-employed(7,8)	209	8.1	10.3	11.6	9.4	29.4	6.3	19.3
ILO unemployed(9)	166	*	*	*	7.2	57.1	7.9	9.0
Economically inactive(10)	841	1.2	*	*	4.2	70.4	5.4	4.8
All employees	2,729	30.9	5.5	7.4	6.6	30.7	3.2	8.7
By gender								
Males	1,315	30.1	6.0	8.8	7.7	28.0	2.5	10.0
Females	1,414	31.7	5.1	6.1	5.7	33.2	3.8	7.4
By age								
16-19	281	12.5	*	*	*	64.6	5.6	*
20-24	377	22.7	3.0	5.2	5.1	45.0	*	6.2
25-29	366	30.4	4.7	7.7	9.7	26.6	3.3	9.0
30-39	778	32.8	6.2	7.7	8.7	26.7	2.1	10.2
40-49	600	37.8	7.5	9.5	6.8	20.7	3.7	9.3
50-64	327	40.0	7.3	9.4	4.5	17.6	4.1	12.6
By highest qualification held(4)								
Degree or equivalent	739	33.6	7.7	10.4	7.6	19.4	3.3	11.4
Higher Education qualification (below degree level)	417	33.2	6.5	5.3	8.0	29.7	3.2	9.7
GCE A level or equivalent	683	28.6	4.6	6.5	5.6	37.1	2.4	7.4
GCSE grades A* to C or equivalent	619	28.3	3.4	6.7	5.9	38.0	4.0	6.2
Other qualification	191	31.7	5.6	7.5	6.4	32.8	*	6.5
No qualification	67	33.3	*	*	*	20.7	*	14.3
By occupation								
Managers & administrators	427	33.6	9.0	12.5	6.7	17.8	2.3	12.0
Professional	539	36.0	6.6	8.8	7.2	20.6	3.5	11.4
Associate professional & technical	437	33.6	7.6	7.2	8.7	28.1	*	7.9
Clerical & secretarial	376	32.2	*	7.6	9.2	31.4	4.1	5.7
Craft & related	202	26.2	4.7	5.1	*	42.7	*	7.2
Personal & protective services	358	31.5	4.1	4.5	3.8	38.1	3.2	6.9
Sales	219	16.0	*	*	*	51.3	4.6	6.9
Plant & machine operatives	86	31.1	*	*	*	32.5	*	*
Other occupations	84	12.6	*	*	*	55.4	*	*
By industry(4)								
Agriculture, forestry & fishing	12	*	*	*	*	*	*	*
Energy & water supply	34	34.1	*	*	*	*	*	*
Manufacturing	347	32.3	4.3	7.7	6.5	31.5	*	9.5
Construction	114	19.4	*	9.1	*	45.4	*	*
Distribution, hotels & restaurants	434	17.9	4.3	3.7	5.2	47.5	4.3	6.7
Transport	123	32.8	*	9.6	11.8	22.9	*	8.8
Banking, finance & insurance	430	27.8	7.0	11.6	12.0	20.1	2.8	10.6
Public administration, education & health	1,087	38.8	6.0	6.7	5.2	26.6	3.1	8.8
Other services	143	25.3	*	7.1	*	38.7	*	7.2
By region(11)								
United Kingdom	2,729	30.9	5.5	7.4	6.6	30.7	3.2	8.7
North East	109	33.2	*	9.6	*	34.9	*	*
North West	322	30.8	4.8	5.4	5.2	36.9	3.6	9.1
Yorkshire and the Humber	231	35.7	6.3	5.3	5.7	29.0	*	11.3
East Midlands	184	30.1	7.9	5.4	*	34.0	*	9.6
West Midlands	243	31.5	4.7	7.6	5.5	34.0	*	7.6
Eastern	259	35.7	5.1	8.7	8.5	23.4	*	10.3
London	359	27.2	5.3	12.3	6.0	26.6	4.1	8.4
South East	388	30.9	6.4	8.5	9.2	28.8	2.8	7.8
South West	259	30.6	6.6	6.8	5.8	31.2	4.2	9.6
England	2,354	31.4	5.9	7.9	6.4	30.5	3.3	8.9
Wales	118	33.6	*	*	10.0	34.5	*	*
Scotland	217	29.9	*	5.6	8.7	36.4	*	8.3
Northern Ireland	39	*	*	*	*	*	*	*

Source: Labour Force Survey, Spring 2000(12)

(1) Excludes those receiving on-the-job training only.
(2) Working age is defined as males aged 16-64 and females aged 16-59.
(3) Expressed as a percentage of those in the group who received training in the last four weeks.
(4) Apart from rounding, figures may not sum to grand totals because of questions in the LFS which were unanswered or did not apply.
(5) Includes open university, open tech, correspondence course and college.
(6) Employees are those in employment excluding the self-employed, unpaid family workers and those on government employment and training programmes.
(7) The split into employees and self-employed is based on respondents' own assessment of their employment status.
(8) Self-employed are those in employment excluding employees, unpaid family workers and those on government employment and training programmes.
(9) Unemployed according to the International Labour Office (ILO) definition.
(10) Economically inactive are those who are neither in employment nor ILO unemployed.
(11) Government Office Regions in England and each UK country.
(12) Users of these data should read the LFS entry in Annex A, as it contains important information about the LFS and the concepts and definitions used.

POST COMPULSORY EDUCATION AND TRAINING: JOB-RELATED TRAINING
Hours spent on job-related training(1) in the last week, 2000

United Kingdom: People of working age(2)　　　　　　　　　　　　　　　　Thousands and percentages(3)

	Total receiving training(4) (thousands)	Hours spent on training						Average number of hours per week
		Less than 7.5 hours	7.5 to <15 hours	15 to < 22.5 hours	22.5 to < 30 hours	30 to < 37.5 hours	37.5 hours or more	
All people	2,787	37.0	19.7	13.0	6.1	10.0	13.7	17.4
Economic activity								
Employees(5,6)	1,904	44.5	22.9	12.1	4.2	7.3	8.7	13.8
Self-employed(6,7)	108	61.0	20.0	9.1	*	*	*	9.9
ILO unemployed(8)	111	26.1	13.3	22.6	8.9	15.3	13.7	20.1
Economically inactive(9)	578	12.1	10.6	14.8	12.1	18.5	30.7	29.4
All employees	1,904	44.5	22.9	12.1	4.2	7.3	8.7	13.8
By gender								
Males	908	39.3	24.4	12.5	4.6	8.0	10.8	15.1
Females	997	49.2	21.6	11.6	3.9	6.7	6.8	12.7
By age								
16-19	235	18.1	16.3	15.2	10.0	21.3	18.6	22.9
20-24	313	33.4	20.9	14.6	4.6	11.5	14.6	18.2
25-29	267	43.4	24.4	11.4	4.0	6.3	10.2	14.1
30-39	522	49.4	25.0	12.5	3.1	3.4	6.1	11.7
40-49	370	54.3	24.8	11.0	3.2	3.2	3.5	10.1
50-64	197	63.3	23.1	6.0	*	*	*	8.3
By highest qualification held(10)								
Degree or equivalent	445	51.4	22.8	11.6	2.8	4.3	7.0	12.0
Higher Education qualification (below degree level)	273	44.7	26.5	14.1	3.9	4.9	5.8	12.2
GCE A level or equivalent	494	39.1	24.5	12.6	5.5	8.3	9.6	15.1
GCSE grades A* to C or equivalent	479	40.5	21.6	11.8	5.2	10.9	9.8	15.2
Other qualification	145	49.0	20.5	10.9	2.4	*	10.8	13.7
No qualification	58	58.2	*	*	*	*	*	13.6
By occupation								
Managers & administrators	240	48.7	28.4	11.8	*	*	5.4	11.2
Professional	332	52.8	23.7	10.8	*	3.6	6.2	11.3
Associate professional & technical	303	44.8	24.8	13.6	3.5	6.2	7.0	12.9
Clerical & secretarial	281	53.8	21.5	9.5	3.6	5.9	5.5	11.5
Craft & related	157	31.8	31.2	8.9	*	10.5	13.4	16.3
Personal & protective services	275	39.3	20.3	14.0	6.3	6.7	12.6	16.4
Sales	168	31.8	12.1	18.2	8.6	17.6	11.7	18.8
Plant & machine operatives	78	38.7	26.8	*	*	*	12.7	15.2
Other occupations	69	37.3	*	*	*	18.7	13.9	18.8
By industry(10)								
Agriculture, forestry & fishing	*	*	*	*	*	*	*	12.1
Energy & water supply	23	41.4	*	*	*	*	*	16.9
Manufacturing	261	44.7	25.5	8.9	*	7.5	10.0	13.5
Construction	85	31.4	31.3	*	*	*	13.2	15.9
Distribution, hotels & restaurants	336	32.2	15.9	16.1	7.4	14.8	13.3	18.6
Transport	82	40.0	28.4	*	*	*	*	14.4
Banking, finance & insurance	279	47.1	22.8	14.9	*	5.7	6.4	12.5
Public administration, education & health	728	50.7	24.7	10.6	3.5	3.7	6.3	11.8
Other services	100	46.0	19.1	11.0	*	10.3	*	14.2
By region(11)								
United Kingdom	1,904	44.5	22.9	12.1	4.2	7.3	8.7	13.8
North East	82	43.0	24.6	12.5	*	*	*	13.5
North West	248	44.2	24.1	10.9	4.5	8.3	7.9	13.5
Yorkshire and the Humber	155	45.2	23.1	11.8	*	7.1	7.8	13.1
East Midlands	135	47.0	21.3	12.8	*	7.8	7.2	12.8
West Midlands	183	46.1	23.0	11.9	*	6.9	7.8	13.6
Eastern	165	47.9	21.3	12.5	*	7.1	7.1	13.0
London	221	42.6	22.6	13.6	4.5	7.7	8.5	14.7
South East	260	43.5	23.1	12.0	*	7.3	10.5	14.2
South West	177	43.9	22.7	12.4	6.1	6.2	8.4	13.5
England	1,625	44.7	22.9	12.2	4.4	7.3	8.4	13.6
Wales	85	43.4	24.0	*	*	*	*	14.4
Scotland	160	44.0	23.1	12.2	*	8.1	10.0	14.1
Northern Ireland	35	38.6	*	*	*	*	*	20.7

Source: Labour Force Survey, Spring 2000(12)

(1) Job-related training includes both on and off-the-job training.
(2) Working age is defined as males aged 16-64 and females aged 16-59.
(3) Expressed as a percentage of those in the group who received training in the last week, who specified a valid length of training.
(4) Those who specified a valid length of training.
(5) Employees are those in employment excluding the self-employed, unpaid family workers and those on government employment and training programmes.
(6) The split into employees and self-employed is based on respondents' own assessment of their employment status.
(7) Self-employed are those in employment excluding employees, unpaid family workers and those on government employment and training programmes.
(8) Unemployed according to the International Labour Office (ILO) definition.
(9) Economically inactive are those who are neither in employment nor ILO unemployed.
(10) Apart from rounding, figures may not sum to grand totals because of questions in the LFS which were unanswered or did not apply.
(11) Government Office Regions in England and each UK country.
(12) Users of these data should read the LFS entry in Annex A, as it contains important information about the LFS and the concepts and definitions used.

THIS PAGE HAS BEEN LEFT BLANK

POST COMPULSORY EDUCATION AND TRAINING: JOB-RELATED TRAINING

3.24 Participation by employees(1) in job-related training(2) in the last thirteen weeks by a range of personal and economic characteristics — time series

United Kingdom: Employees(1) of working age(3)   Thousands

	1995(4)			1998(4)			2000		
	All	Males	Females	All	Males	Females	All	Males	Females
All employees(1)	5,559	2,865	2,703	6,454	3,292	3,162	6,972	3,519	3,453
By age									
16-19	288	151	137	438	228	209	491	250	241
20-24	694	348	346	751	384	367	827	429	398
25-29	925	492	433	1,010	538	472	961	501	459
30-39	1,619	861	759	1,899	1,017	881	2,031	1,077	954
40-49	1,382	663	719	1,495	709	786	1,622	749	873
50-64	651	342	309	861	416	445	1,040	512	528
By highest qualification held(5,6)									
Degree or equivalent	1,297	752	545	1,538	841	697	1,808	970	838
Higher Education qualification (below degree level)	900	378	523	1,003	418	585	1,001	404	597
GCE A level or equivalent	1,314	853	461	1,525	961	564	1,672	1,020	652
GCSE grades A* to C or equivalent	1,162	471	691	1,476	541	836	1,550	664	886
Other	595	279	316	626	305	321	638	317	322
None	282	119	164	256	112	145	261	121	140
By industry(5)									
Agriculture, forestry & fishing	30	19	10	33	23	10	39	31	*
Energy & water supply	111	88	23	100	79	21	104	79	26
Manufacturing	839	636	204	971	744	227	940	719	221
Construction	193	164	29	254	220	33	297	256	41
Distribution, hotels & restaurants	784	376	408	966	460	506	1,017	505	512
Transport	313	221	92	336	232	104	398	275	122
Banking, finance & insurance	900	517	383	1,065	591	474	1,112	612	500
Public administration, education & health	2,145	719	1,426	2,436	803	1,634	2,730	884	1,846
Other services	236	111	125	289	137	152	326	152	174
By occupation(5)									
Managers & administrators	978	624	354	1,087	700	387	1,147	734	413
Professional	1,030	544	486	1,104	579	525	1,267	645	622
Associate professional & technical	832	363	469	992	418	574	1,059	426	633
Clerical & secretarial	884	242	642	1,009	269	740	1,030	278	752
Craft & related	387	362	24	468	442	26	503	479	23
Personal & protective services	636	253	383	795	310	486	903	342	560
Sales	366	149	217	461	177	284	492	193	299
Plant & machine operatives	258	221	37	309	265	45	322	272	49
Other	178	92	85	227	132	95	249	147	102
By full-time/part-time work(7)									
Full-time	4,529	2,693	1,836	5,169	3,056	2,113	5,561	3,273	2,289
Part-time	1,030	163	867	1,284	236	1,048	1,409	246	1,163
of which:									
students	247	106	141	355	152	204	405	166	239
could not find full-time job	127	35	91	130	41	89	112	31	81
did not want full-time job	643	19	624	780	39	741	873	44	828
By employment status									
Permanent	5,132	2,670	2,462	5,945	3,074	2,872	6,416	3,281	3,135
Temporary	401	172	230	487	206	281	533	224	309
of which:									
seasonal/casual work	60	26	33	90	37	51	95	41	54
contract for fixed term or task	275	117	157	292	126	167	312	123	189
agency temping	27	11	16	48	19	28	57	26	31
other	40	17	23	58	24	34	70	35	35
By socio-economic group									
Professional	474	359	115	555	408	146	635	450	185
Intermediate	2,434	1,181	1,253	2,706	1,295	1,410	2,899	1,366	1,533
Skilled (non-manual)	1,314	447	867	1,516	493	1,023	1,592	528	1,064
Skilled (manual)	693	533	161	830	654	176	916	713	203
Partly skilled	500	244	256	687	328	360	748	338	410
Unskilled	83	40	43	104	60	44	122	68	54
Armed Forces/Other	50	47	*	55	54	*	58	53	*

Source: Labour Force Survey, Spring 1995, 1998, 2000(8)

(1) Employees are those in employment excluding the self-employed, unpaid family workers and those on government employment and training programmes.
(2) Job-related training includes both on and off-the-job training.
(3) Working age is defined as males aged 16-64 and females aged 16-59.
(4) Figures have been revised as a result of revisions to quarterly LFS data from Autumn 1993 to Autumn 1999 to better reflect population changes over this period.
(5) Apart from rounding, figures may not sum to grand totals because of questions in the LFS which were unanswered or did not apply.
(6) Highest qualifications held figures for 1995 are not directly comparable with later years due to changes in the level of detail collected for qualifications from the 1996 LFS onwards.
(7) The split between employees working full-time and part-time is based on respondents' own assessment.
(8) Users of these data should read the LFS entry in Annex A, as it contains important information about the LFS and the concepts and definitions used.
(9) Expressed as a percentage of the total number of people in each group.

3.24

Participation by employees(1) in job-related training(2) in the last thirteen weeks by a range of personal and economic characteristics – time series

United Kingdom: Employees(1) of working age(3)

Percentages (9)

	1995(4)			1998(4)			2000		
	All	Males	Females	All	Males	Females	All	Males	Females
All employees(1)	25.6	24.9	26.5	28.1	26.8	29.5	29.3	27.6	31.3
By age									
16-19	25.6	27.5	23.8	32.0	33.1	30.9	34.3	34.9	33.8
20-24	28.8	27.8	29.9	33.3	32.1	34.7	36.4	35.1	37.8
25-29	29.7	29.6	29.8	32.1	31.5	32.9	31.9	30.4	33.7
30-39	27.6	27.1	28.2	29.2	28.8	29.8	30.0	29.2	31.0
40-49	26.2	24.9	27.4	28.0	26.3	29.6	29.2	26.6	32.0
50-64	16.8	15.7	18.1	19.6	16.8	23.1	21.8	19.2	25.1
By highest qualification held(6)									
Degree or equivalent	42.6	39.7	47.5	43.4	40.1	48.0	43.9	40.4	48.9
Higher Education qualification (below degree level)	42.7	38.5	46.5	43.7	38.7	48.0	43.1	36.8	48.6
GCE A level or equivalent	25.7	24.2	29.1	28.3	26.1	32.9	29.0	26.4	34.2
GCSE grades A* to C or equivalent	24.8	25.0	24.7	27.1	28.0	26.3	28.0	28.3	27.8
Other	17.9	16.6	19.3	18.8	17.2	20.6	19.9	18.8	21.1
None	8.4	8.1	8.7	9.2	8.8	9.6	10.0	9.8	10.1
By industry									
Agriculture, forestry & fishing	14.0	12.6	17.5	15.9	14.9	18.5	18.6	19.1	*
Energy & water supply	33.8	33.4	35.7	37.3	36.5	40.3	35.6	34.8	38.8
Manufacturing	18.4	19.3	16.2	20.8	21.6	18.6	21.2	21.7	19.7
Construction	19.7	19.5	20.8	21.1	20.8	23.0	22.3	21.9	25.6
Distribution, hotels & restaurants	18.2	19.5	17.2	21.2	21.8	20.7	21.7	23.3	20.4
Transport	22.1	20.4	27.6	22.0	20.5	26.1	24.0	22.6	27.9
Banking, finance & insurance	30.3	34.0	26.4	32.2	34.2	30.1	31.1	32.0	30.2
Public administration, education & health	37.5	39.4	36.7	40.1	42.0	39.2	42.7	44.4	42.0
Other services	20.4	20.9	19.9	24.6	25.3	23.9	26.8	26.1	27.5
By occupation									
Managers & administrators	30.1	28.6	33.2	31.2	29.8	34.1	31.3	29.6	34.7
Professional	46.2	42.8	50.8	46.4	42.0	52.4	49.5	43.7	57.4
Associate professional & technical	41.4	36.7	46.0	44.6	39.1	49.7	44.4	37.9	50.3
Clerical & secretarial	24.6	26.4	24.0	26.6	27.4	26.4	26.9	27.5	26.7
Craft & related	17.2	18.5	8.7	19.8	20.8	10.8	21.0	21.6	12.6
Personal & protective services	25.9	28.9	24.2	29.4	33.4	27.3	31.8	35.2	30.1
Sales	20.2	24.1	18.2	24.1	26.8	22.6	23.5	26.7	21.8
Plant & machine operatives	11.7	12.7	8.2	13.5	14.4	10.0	14.8	15.4	11.8
Other	9.6	10.4	8.9	12.3	13.7	10.8	13.5	14.9	11.8
By full-time/part-time work(5)									
Full-time	27.2	25.0	31.2	29.5	26.8	34.5	30.7	27.7	36.2
Part-time	20.5	23.2	20.0	23.4	26.0	22.9	24.8	25.6	24.7
of which:									
students	33.2	31.6	34.5	36.6	35.3	37.7	37.8	35.4	39.7
could not find full-time job	17.9	16.5	18.6	20.1	18.1	21.2	20.0	15.2	22.7
did not want full-time job	18.4	14.4	18.5	20.6	17.6	20.8	22.1	17.3	22.5
By employment status									
Permanent	25.7	25.1	26.4	28.0	26.8	29.4	29.1	27.5	30.9
Temporary	26.8	24.6	28.8	30.4	28.5	32.0	33.8	30.6	36.7
of which:									
seasonal/casual work	16.9	16.7	16.5	25.5	31.1	25.4	26.2	26.5	26.0
contract for fixed term or task	33.6	30.1	36.8	35.4	32.8	37.6	40.4	34.6	45.4
agency temping	17.1	14.3	19.7	19.1	15.9	22.1	22.3	19.6	25.2
other	24.4	22.1	26.4	34.0	35.2	33.2	37.1	37.5	36.6
By socio-economic group									
Professional	40.7	39.0	46.7	42.1	40.0	49.5	43.8	40.8	53.4
Intermediate	37.0	32.9	41.8	38.4	33.6	44.2	39.2	33.8	45.7
Skilled (non-manual)	24.8	30.6	22.6	27.5	32.7	25.5	27.5	32.2	25.7
Skilled (manual)	16.7	16.1	18.8	19.4	18.9	21.3	20.9	20.2	23.9
Partly skilled	15.6	15.4	15.7	18.8	18.0	19.7	20.8	18.8	22.8
Unskilled	7.6	8.5	7.0	9.7	11.5	8.0	11.3	12.7	9.9
Armed Forces/Other	37.0	36.5	*	50.0	49.8	*	50.5	50.2	*

Source: Labour Force Survey, Spring 1995, 1998, 2000(8)

See previous page for footnotes.

3.25

POST COMPULSORY EDUCATION AND TRAINING: JOB-RELATED TRAINING
Employees(1) of working age(2) in the UK – summary of job-related training(3) received

United Kingdom: Employees(1) of working age(2)   Thousands and percentages

	Total receiving training (thousands)	Number who received training in the last			Never offered training by current employer	Percentage who received training in the last			Never offered training by current employer (percentage)
		13 weeks	4 weeks	1 week		13 weeks	4 weeks	1 week	
All employees(1)	23,802	6,972	3,833	2,114	7,759	29.3	16.1	8.9	32.6
By gender									
Males	12,758	3,519	1,872	1,011	4,036	27.6	14.7	7.9	31.6
Females	11,044	3,453	1,961	1,103	3,383	31.3	17.8	10.0	30.6
By age									
16-19	1,432	491	374	278	400	34.3	26.1	19.4	27.9
20-24	2,275	827	531	366	749	36.4	23.3	16.1	32.9
25-29	3,016	961	522	296	893	31.9	17.3	9.8	29.6
30-39	6,762	2,031	1,087	563	2,081	30.0	16.1	8.3	30.8
40-49	5,546	1,622	833	398	1,779	29.2	15.0	7.2	32.1
50-64	4,772	1,040	485	213	1,855	21.8	10.2	4.5	38.9
By ethnic origin									
White	22,607	6,614	3,620	1,984	7,332	29.3	16.0	8.8	32.4
Non-white	1,193	357	211	130	422	29.9	17.7	10.9	35.4
of which:									
Black	366	122	68	43	101	33.3	18.6	11.7	27.6
Indian, Pakistani & Bangladeshi	537	137	82	49	229	25.5	15.2	9.1	42.6
Other non-white	291	98	61	38	96	33.7	21.1	13.1	33.0
By highest qualification held									
Degree or equivalent	4,116	1,808	997	489	712	43.9	24.2	11.9	17.3
Higher Education qualification (below degree level)	2,325	1,001	553	294	431	43.1	23.8	12.6	18.5
GCE A level or equivalent	5,767	1,672	951	546	1,854	29.0	16.5	9.5	32.1
GCSE grades A* to C or equivalent	5,540	1,550	878	537	1,828	28.0	15.8	9.7	33.0
Other qualification	3,202	638	306	162	1,346	19.9	9.5	5.1	42.0
No qualification	2,611	261	126	73	1,495	10.0	4.8	2.8	57.3
Don't know	241	42	22	14	93	17.4	9.1	5.8	38.6
By occupation(4)									
Managers & administrators	3,664	1,147	569	261	916	31.3	15.5	7.1	25.0
Professional	2,559	1,267	730	364	375	49.5	28.5	14.2	14.7
Associate professional & technical	2,383	1,059	604	326	390	44.4	25.4	13.7	16.4
Clerical & secretarial	3,826	1,030	547	316	1,263	26.9	14.3	8.3	33.0
Craft & related	2,400	503	282	171	1,027	21.0	11.8	7.1	42.8
Personal & protective services	2,837	903	514	312	858	31.8	18.1	11.0	30.2
Sales	2,095	492	304	192	836	23.5	14.5	9.2	39.9
Plant & machine operatives	2,183	322	153	87	1,093	14.8	7.0	4.0	50.1
Other occupations	1,847	249	127	84	998	13.5	6.9	4.5	54.0
By industry(4)									
Agriculture, forestry & fishing	210	39	17	10	110	18.6	8.1	4.8	52.4
Energy & water supply	292	104	52	25	59	35.6	17.7	8.6	20.2
Manufacturing	4,430	940	509	286	1,782	21.2	11.5	6.5	40.2
Construction	1,329	297	158	97	571	22.3	11.9	7.3	43.0
Distribution, hotels & restaurants	4,684	1,017	601	387	1,967	21.7	12.8	8.3	42.0
Transport	1,657	398	188	92	584	24.0	11.3	5.6	35.2
Banking, finance & insurance	3,570	1,112	599	313	1,050	31.1	16.8	8.8	29.4
Public administration, education & health	6,388	2,730	1,510	788	1,169	42.7	23.6	12.3	18.3
Other services	1,218	326	194	113	461	26.8	15.9	9.3	37.8
By region(4,5)									
United Kingdom	23,802	6,972	3,833	2,114	7,759	29.3	16.1	8.9	32.6
North East	958	274	148	87	349	28.6	15.5	9.1	36.4
North West	2,726	826	458	271	863	30.3	16.8	9.9	31.7
Yorkshire and the Humber	2,018	610	329	169	682	30.2	16.3	8.4	33.8
East Midlands	1,758	485	275	149	585	27.6	15.7	8.5	33.3
West Midlands	2,123	605	339	203	772	28.5	16.0	9.6	36.4
Eastern	2,266	662	355	185	744	29.2	15.7	8.2	32.8
London	2,831	869	479	253	844	30.7	16.9	8.9	29.8
South East	3,459	1,039	551	290	1,027	30.0	15.9	8.4	29.7
South West	1,986	616	352	194	617	31.0	17.7	9.8	31.1
England	20,125	5,986	3,287	1,802	6,482	29.7	16.3	9.0	32.2
Wales	1,059	296	168	91	363	28.0	15.9	8.6	34.3
Scotland	2,056	572	317	182	722	27.8	15.4	8.9	35.1
Northern Ireland	562	118	60	39	192	21.0	10.6	6.9	34.2

Source: Labour Force Survey, Spring 2000(6)

(1) Employees are those in employment excluding the self-employed, unpaid family workers and those on government employment and training programmes.
(2) Working age is defined as males aged 16-64 and females aged 16-59.
(3) Job-related training includes both on and off-the-job training.
(4) Apart from rounding, figures may not sum to grand totals because of questions in the LFS which were unanswered or did not apply.
(5) Government Office Regions in England and each UK country.
(6) Users of these data should read the LFS entry in Annex A, as it contains important information about the LFS and the concepts and definitions used.

Chapter 4
Qualifications

CHAPTER 4: QUALIFICATIONS

Key Facts

GCE, GCSE, SCE and GNVQ/GSVQ qualifications

- In 1998/99, 33.7 per cent of young students in schools and FE colleges in the United Kingdom obtained 2 or more passes at GCE A level or equivalent. At GCSE or SCE (Scottish Certificate of Education) (S Grade) level, of pupils in their last year of compulsory schooling:

  - 49.1 per cent gained 5 or more passes at grades A*-C / 1-3

  - 24.8 per cent gained 1-4 passes at grades A*-C / 1-3

  - 20.3 per cent gained no passes at grades A*-C / 1-3 but gained at least one grade D-G

  - 5.9 per cent had no graded results **(Table 4.1)**

- Over 5.4 million entries were made for GCSE/SCE (S grade) examinations by pupils in their last year of compulsory education in schools in Great Britain in 1998/99. 56% of all entries achieved passes at grade A* -C. **(Table 4.2)**

- For pupils aged 16-18, a total of 875,600 entries were made for GCE A level / SCE (H grade) examinations in Great Britain in 1998/99. 60% of all entries achieved grades A- C. **(Table 4.3)**

Subject Choice

- Most frequently studied subjects at GCE A level / SCE (H grade) were English (English 49,600, English Literature 64,900), General Studies (85,200), Mathematics (84,600) and Biological Sciences (60,700). **(Table 4.3)**

- Of the 14,200 Intermediate and Foundation GNVQ entries in England, Wales and Northern Ireland in 1998/99, 74% achieved GNVQ Part One, and 17% achieved a Full GNVQ. Of the 40,700 Advanced GNVQ entries, 22% obtained a Distinction; the proportions of males and females achieving a distinction were 16% and 27% respectively. **(Table 4.4)**

Vocational Awards

- There was an increase of almost 60% in the numbers of NVQs/SVQs awarded between 1994/95 and 1998/99 and awards of GNVQs/GSVQs more than doubled over the same period. **(Table 4.5)**

National Learning Targets for England, 2002

- In Spring 2000 progress towards the targets was:

  - 75% of 11-year-olds reaching the expected standard for their age in literacy

  - 72% of 11-year-olds reaching the standard in numeracy

  - 49% of 16-year-olds gaining at least five good GCSE passes

  - 94% of 16-year-olds gaining at least one exam pass

  - 75% of 19-year-olds with a "level 2" qualification

  - 54% of 21-year-olds with a "level 3" qualification

  - 47% of adults with a "level 3" qualification

  - 27% of adults with a "level 4" qualification **(Table 4.7)**

Higher Education Qualifications

- A total of 446,900 higher education qualifications were awarded in higher education institutions in the United Kingdom in 1998/99. Of these 67,700 were sub-degree qualifications, 263,700 were first degrees, 11,300 were PhD or equivalent and 104,300 were at Masters / other postgraduate level. **(Table 4.8)**

Highest Qualification Held

- Attainment levels vary by Government Office region with London having a higher proportion of better-qualified people (i.e. qualified to NVQ level 4 & 5) than other UK regions in Spring 2000. **(Table 4.9)**

- Attainment levels varied greatly by economic activity with 23% of unemployed people having no qualifications compared to 11% of employees. **(Table 4.9)**

- 91% of employees in professional occupations held two or more A levels or higher level qualification compared with 62% of managers and administrators and only 21% of plant and machine operatives. **(Table 4.9)**

- 42% of the workforce were qualified to NVQ level 3 equivalent and above and 23% of the workforce were qualified to NVQ level 4 equivalent and above, while 16% had no qualification (a decrease of 3 percentage points since 1997). **(Table 4.9)**

People Working Towards a Qualification

- 60% of leavers from Advanced Modern Apprenticeships in England in 1999 gained a full qualification, 12 percentage points higher than the previous 12 months. The proportion of Other Training leavers, who gained a full qualification was 45%, compared to 46% in 1998. **(Table 4.6)**

- 39% of leavers from Work-based Learning for Adults in England in 1999 gained a full qualification compared to 40% in 1998. **(Table 4.6)**

- Around 16% of all people of working age were studying towards a qualification in Spring 2000. Young people aged 16-24 were far more likely to be working towards a qualification than people in any other age group. **(Table 4.10)**

- Members of non-white ethnic groups were far more likely to be studying towards a qualification than people of white ethnic origin; 23.7% compared to 15.3%. **(Table 4.10)**

CHAPTER 4: QUALIFICATIONS – LIST OF TABLES

4.1 QUALIFICATIONS

GCE, GCSE and SCE qualifications obtained by pupils and students at a typical age(1,2), and GCE, GCSE, SCE and GNVQ/GSVQ qualifications obtained by students of all ages — time series

United Kingdom
(i) Students at a typical age
Percentages and thousands

| | Pupils in their last year of compulsory education(1) | | | | | Pupils/students in education(2) | | | |
| | | | | | | % Achieving GCE A Levels and equivalent | | | |
	5 or more grades A*-C (%)(3)	1-4 grades A*-C (%)(3)	Grades D-G(4) only (%)	No graded results (%)	Total (=100%) (thousands)	2 or more passes(5,6)	1 pass(7)	1 or more passes	population aged 17 (thousands)
1995/96(8)									
All	45.2	25.9	21.3	7.5	696.4	29.5	8.0	37.5	648.3
Males	40.4	25.4	25.4	8.7	355.7	26.7	7.3	34.0	333.6
Females	50.2	26.4	17.0	6.3	340.7	32.5	8.8	41.3	314.6
1996/97									
All	46.2	25.5	20.9	7.4	713.3	29.6	7.4	37.0	723.5
Males	41.4	25.3	24.9	8.5	363.5	26.5	6.7	33.2	372.4
Females	51.3	25.7	16.7	6.3	349.7	33.0	8.1	41.1	351.0
1997/98									
All	47.5	25.2(8)	21.1 (8)	6.5	698.4	33.5	6.5	40.1	751.0
Males	42.3	25.4(8)	24.9 (8)	7.5	356.1	29.9	6.0	35.9	384.9
Females	52.8	25.0(8)	17.1 (8)	5.3	342.3	37.4	7.2	44.5	366.1
1998/99									
All	49.1	24.8	20.3	5.9	703.6	33.7	6.7	40.3	744.2
Males	43.8	25.2	24.1	6.9	359.6	30.1	6.1	36.2	381.4
Females	54.6	24.3	16.3	4.8	344.0	37.4	7.3	44.7	362.8

United Kingdom
(ii) Students of any age achieving
Thousands

| | GCSE and SCE S Grade | | | | GCE A Level and SCE Higher Grade | | |
	5 or more grades A*-C(3,9)	1-4 grades A*-C(3,9)	Grades D-G(4,10) only	No graded results	2 or more passes(5,6)	1 pass(7)	Total 1 or more passes
1995/96(11)							
All	331.4	371.7	236.5	51.3	204.5	78.2	282.6
Males	151.3	175.3	130.9	25.4	95.2	33.8	129.0
Females	180.1	196.4	105.6	25.9	109.3	44.3	153.6
1996/97(11)							
All	333.3	358.7	240.5	52.5	219.3	76.6	295.9
Males	152.3	169.6	133.5	26.1	101.2	33.2	134.3
Females	181.0	189.1	107.0	26.5	118.1	43.4	161.6
1997/98(11)							
All	335.3	336.4	233.9	47.4	260.4	70.3	330.6
Males	152.8	162.3	129.5	23.3	119.2	30.5	149.7
Females	182.5	174.1	104.5	24.1	141.2	39.8	181.0
1998/99							
All	341.0	323.7	229.8	40.8	257.9	69.9	327.8
Males	162.3	150.6	128.1	20.5	118.4	30.6	149.0
Females	178.7	173.2	101.7	20.3	139.5	39.3	178.8

Source: Department for Education and Employment; National Assembly for Wales; Scottish Executive; Northern Ireland Department of Education

(1) Pupils aged 15 at the start of the academic year, pupils in Year S4 in Scotland.

(2) Pupils in schools and students in further education institutions aged 16-18 at the start of the academic year in England, Wales and Northern Ireland as a percentage of the 17 year old population. Pupils in Scotland generally sit Highers one year earlier and the figures tend to relate to the results of pupils in Year S5/S6 as a percentage of the 16 year old population.

(3) Standard Grades 1-3 in Scotland.

(4) Grades D-G at GCSE and Scottish Standard Grades 4-7.

(5) 3 or more SCE Higher Grades in Scotland.

(6) Includes Advanced level GNVQ/GSVQ which is equivalent to 2 GCE A levels or AS equivalents/3 SCE Higher grades.

(7) 2 AS levels count as 1 A level pass.

(8) Great Britain only.

(9) Includes GNVQ/GSVQ Intermediate Part 1, Full and Language unit which are equivalent to 2, 4 and 0.5 GCSE grades A*-C/SCE Standard grades 1-3 respectively. Figures include those with 4.5 GCSEs.

(10) Includes GNVQ/GSVQ Foundation Part 1, Full and Language unit which are equivalent to 2, 4 and 0.5 GCSE grades D-G/SCE Standard grades 4-7 respectively.

(11) Figures for Scotland have been revised to include students in Year S7, which were not included in the 1999 Volume.

QUALIFICATIONS

4.2 GCSE/SCE (S grade) entries and achievements(1) by pupils in their last year of compulsory education(2), in all schools by subject and gender by the end of 1998/99

Great Britain

Thousands and percentages

Subject group	Number of entries (000s)			Percentage achieving grade A*-C			Percentage achieving grade D-G		
	All	Males	Females	All	Males	Females	All	Males	Females
Biological Science	64.7	31.2	33.4	85	86	84	15	14	16
Chemistry	63.8	35.6	28.2	87	87	88	12	13	11
Physics	59.8	38.0	21.9	87	87	88	12	12	11
Science Single Award(3)	69.8	36.1	33.8	20	18	22	72	74	71
Science Double Award(4)	465.4	231.6	233.9	50	48	51	48	50	47
Other Science(4)	4.2	3.1	1.1	46	47	43	49	48	53
Mathematics(5)	639.6	323.8	315.8	49	49	50	47	47	47
Computer Studies(6)	103.6	62.7	40.9	57	54	61	40	42	36
Design and Technology(7)	438.6	236.6	202.0	51	44	59	46	52	39
Business Studies	113.7	55.8	57.9	55	51	58	41	44	38
Home Economics	52.7	5.1	47.6	46	31	48	48	59	47
Art and Design	215.5	101.2	114.3	66	55	75	32	42	23
Geography	267.5	151.4	116.1	57	55	61	40	43	36
History	221.8	108.1	113.6	61	57	64	37	40	34
Economics	6.4	4.5	2.0	64	65	63	33	32	34
Humanities(4)	20.7	9.9	10.8	42	36	48	53	58	49
Religious Studies	103.1	41.4	61.7	57	47	64	39	47	33
Social Studies	16.6	4.9	11.7	51	41	55	43	52	40
English	620.5	310.8	309.8	59	52	67	40	47	32
Welsh(8)	4.0	1.8	2.1	67	58	75	33	42	25
English Literature(4)	489.0	235.3	253.7	63	55	69	36	43	30
Drama	88.2	33.9	54.3	68	58	75	30	40	24
Communication Studies(4)	33.5	14.8	18.7	55	46	62	42	50	36
Modern Languages									
French	377.5	179.2	198.3	52	44	60	45	53	38
German	157.8	75.3	82.5	56	49	63	41	48	35
Spanish	44.0	18.5	25.5	55	46	61	43	50	37
Other languages(9)	28.1	12.2	15.9	70	64	75	27	32	23
Classical Studies	15.6	8.1	7.5	87	86	89	11	12	9
Physical Education	117.6	76.2	41.5	54	53	56	44	45	42
Vocational Studies	18.7	7.7	11.0	50	43	55	44	50	40
Modern Studies(10)	13.5	5.8	7.7	65	59	69	35	41	31
Music	52.5	21.7	30.8	71	65	75	26	31	23
Other subjects	6.8	3.4	3.3	55	47	63	43	50	35
All entries(11)	**5,460.4**	**2,717.1**	**2,743.3**	**56**	**51**	**61**	**42**	**46**	**37**
English and Mathematics(12,13)	611.5	306.3	305.2	45	42	48	52	55	49
English, Maths and a Science(12,13)	601.7	301.3	300.4	41	39	44	56	58	53
English, Maths, Science and Modern Languages(14)	497.0	240.0	256.9	39	34	43	58	62	54
Mathematics and Science(14)	582.2	293.9	288.3	44	43	45	53	54	52
Any Subject	644.6	326.4	318.2	77	73	82	22	25	18

Source: Department for Education and Employment; National Assembly for Wales; Scottish Executive

(1) Where a candidate attempted an examination in the same subject more than once, only the highest value pass has been counted. However, some double counting may occur if a student enters for more than one subject within a subject category.
(2) Those in all schools who were 15 at the start of the academic year, i.e. 31 August 1998. Pupils in Year S4 in Scotland.
(3) Standard Grade in General Science in Scotland.
(4) England and Wales only.
(5) Includes related subjects such as Statistics.
(6) Includes Information Systems in England and Wales.
(7) Craft and Design, Graphic Communications and Technological Studies in Scotland.
(8) Welsh as a first language.
(9) Includes Welsh as a second language.
(10) Scotland only.
(11) Science Double Award are counted twice in this row.
(12) English or Welsh as a first language in Wales.
(13) Only includes successful entries (grade A* to G) in Wales so the number of entries is an underestimate.
(14) England and Scotland only.

QUALIFICATIONS

4.3 GCE A level(1)/SCE H grade entries and achievements by pupils aged 16-18(2) in all Schools and Further Education Sector Colleges by subject and gender, 1998/99

Great Britain

Thousands and percentages

Subject group	Number of entries(000s)			Percentage achieved grades A-C			Percentage achieved grades D-E			Percentage with no graded results		
	All	Males	Females	All	Males	Females	All	Males	Females	All	Males	Females
Biological Sciences	60.7	23.1	37.6	58	55	60	30	32	29	12	13	11
Chemistry	48.5	25.3	23.2	67	65	68	24	25	24	9	10	8
Physics	41.8	31.6	10.2	65	63	70	24	25	21	11	12	9
Other Science	10.6	4.5	6.1	54	51	56	33	34	31	14	14	13
Mathematics	84.6	52.0	32.7	65	64	68	23	24	22	11	12	10
Computer Studies(3)	20.9	16.4	4.5	48	48	50	35	35	35	17	17	15
Design and Technology(4)	19.0	14.4	4.6	58	56	64	31	32	29	11	12	7
Business Studies(5)	42.7	20.3	22.4	59	56	61	29	31	27	12	12	12
Home Economics	2.5	0.2	2.4	50	38	51	34	38	34	16	24	16
Art and Design	41.3	15.1	26.2	70	64	74	24	28	22	6	8	4
Geography	47.2	25.6	21.6	64	61	68	28	31	26	7	8	6
History	42.8	18.9	23.9	62	62	62	27	27	27	11	11	11
Economics	20.6	13.1	7.5	59	59	58	30	29	30	12	11	12
Religious Studies	6.9	1.7	5.2	61	59	61	27	26	28	12	15	11
Social Studies(6)	62.8	18.9	43.8	54	50	55	31	32	31	15	18	14
English	49.6	19.0	30.7	62	61	62	27	27	28	11	13	10
Welsh(7,8)	0.5	0.1	0.4	66	61	67	28	32	27	6	8	6
Gaelic	0.2	-	0.1	92	91	92	5	4	5	3	4	3
English Literature(6)	64.9	19.1	45.8	61	62	61	33	32	34	6	7	5
Welsh Literature(7)	0.3	0.1	0.3	61	66	60	30	22	32	9	12	8
Drama	3.6	1.0	2.6	77	72	78	20	24	19	3	3	3
Communication studies(6)	28.1	9.7	18.4	55	49	58	35	39	34	10	13	8
Modern Languages	43.5	12.8	30.7	69	71	68	24	22	25	7	7	7
of which												
French	23.2	6.5	16.7	67	68	67	25	24	26	7	7	7
German	10.9	3.1	7.7	68	72	67	25	22	26	7	6	7
Spanish	5.6	1.5	4.1	70	72	69	23	21	24	7	6	8
Other Languages	3.8	1.6	2.2	77	74	80	16	18	14	7	9	5
Classical Studies(9)	6.0	2.4	3.6	73	70	76	20	23	18	7	8	6
Creative Arts(10)	9.8	4.0	5.8	74	72	76	21	23	20	5	6	4
Physical Education	19.5	12.2	7.3	49	44	57	39	43	34	12	13	10
Vocational Studies(6)	3.4	1.7	1.7	43	40	45	31	29	32	27	30	23
General Studies(6)	85.2	40.7	44.5	49	51	46	35	34	37	16	15	17
Modern Studies(11)	7.9	2.9	4.9	75	72	77	16	17	15	9	10	8
All entries	**875.6**	**406.8**	**468.8**	**60**	**59**	**62**	**29**	**29**	**28**	**11**	**12**	**10**

Sources: Department for Education and Employment; National Assembly for Wales; Scottish Executive

(1) Includes AS equivalent for Wales.
(2) Pupils in schools and students in further education institutions aged 16-18 at the start of the academic year in England, Wales and Northern Ireland. Pupils in Scotland generally sit Highers one year earlier and the figures tend to relate to the result of pupils in Year S5/S6.
(3) Includes Information Systems.
(4) Craft and Design, Graphic Communication and Technological Studies in Scotland.
(5) Includes Accounting, Management and Information Studies and Secretarial Studies in Scotland.
(6) England and Wales only.
(7) Wales only.
(8) Welsh as a second language.
(9) Includes Classical Greek and Latin.
(10) Includes music.
(11) Scotland only.

QUALIFICATIONS
Intermediate, Foundation and Advanced GNVQ entries and results, by subject and gender, 1998/99(1)

England, Wales and Northern Ireland   Numbers

	Intermediate and Foundation GNVQ Pupils aged 15 in all schools(2,3)								Advanced GNVQ Students aged 16 -18 years old in schools and colleges(4)			
			Qualifications obtained									
	Total Entries		GNVQ Part One		Full GNVQ(3)		GNVQ Language Unit(5)		Total Entries	Grade obtained		
	Interm-ediate	Found-ation	Interm-ediate	Found-ation	Interm-ediate	Found-ation	Interm-ediate	Found-ation	Advanced	Distin-ction	Merit	Pass
All												
Art & Design	749	95	596	51	92	44	-	-	4,203	969	1,622	874
Business	3,284	896	2,527	722	553	173	-	-	14,736	3,638	5,633	2,506
Health & Social Care	1,903	827	1,493	652	265	162	-	-	5,751	1,401	2,336	940
Leisure and Tourism	1,102	555	724	345	217	175	-	-	7,131	1,377	2,813	1,735
Manufacturing	834	537	751	441	51	91	-	-	99	31	22	28
Construction	35	68	-	-	11	67	-	-	606	112	193	116
Hospitality and Catering	12	45	-	-	12	45	-	-	826	117	252	240
Science	65	-	-	-	39	-	-	-	1,292	211	403	261
Engineering	502	146	415	110	71	36	-	-	1,119	154	384	300
Information Technology	1,689	346	1,352	293	253	36	-	-	3,415	585	1,245	895
Media: Communication and Production	25	-	-	-	15	-	-	-	1,180	303	449	171
Retail and Distribution	-	-	-	-	-	-	-	-	102	21	39	20
Performing Arts	-	-	-	-	-	-	-	-	198	66	73	19
Total(6)	**10,299**	**3,893**	**7,903**	**2,615**	**1,580**	**843**	**53**	**363**	**40,702**	**8,993**	**15,482**	**8,119**
Males												
Art & Design	374	62	298	37	37	25	-	-	2,032	356	745	530
Business	1,630	508	1,267	403	264	105	-	-	7,513	1,388	2,943	1,677
Health & Social Care	80	103	64	90	8	13	-	-	250	42	94	50
Leisure and Tourism	506	289	344	192	86	90	-	-	2,833	307	1,095	952
Manufacturing	565	430	490	347	45	78	-	-	86	26	20	26
Construction	35	65	-	-	11	64	-	-	576	102	187	112
Hospitality and Catering	7	16	-	-	7	16	-	-	324	35	92	115
Science	45	-	-	-	27	-	-	-	772	92	226	204
Engineering	449	132	367	100	68	32	-	-	1,081	149	369	293
Information Technology	1,013	253	831	204	124	33	-	-	2,957	480	1,088	821
Media: Communication and Production	10	-	-	-	8	-	-	-	612	131	233	126
Retail and Distribution	-	-	-	-	-	-	-	-	53	8	21	13
Performing Arts	-	-	-	-	-	-	-	-	62	13	24	12
Total(6)	**4,749**	**2,058**	**3,677**	**1,373**	**685**	**457**	**19**	**199**	**19,172**	**3,132**	**7,145**	**4,939**
Females												
Art & Design	375	33	298	14	55	19	-	-	2,171	613	877	344
Business	1,654	388	1,260	319	289	68	-	-	7,223	2,250	2,690	829
Health & Social Care	1,823	724	1,429	562	257	149	-	-	5,501	1,359	2,242	890
Leisure and Tourism	596	266	380	153	131	85	-	-	4,298	1,070	1,718	783
Manufacturing	269	107	261	94	6	13	-	-	13	5	2	2
Construction	-	3	-	-	-	3	-	-	30	10	6	4
Hospitality and Catering	5	29	-	-	5	29	-	-	502	82	160	125
Science	20	-	-	-	12	-	-	-	520	119	177	57
Engineering	53	14	48	10	3	4	-	-	38	5	15	7
Information Technology	676	93	521	89	129	3	-	-	458	105	157	74
Media: Communication and Production	15	-	-	-	7	-	-	-	568	172	216	45
Retail and Distribution	-	-	-	-	-	-	-	-	49	13	18	7
Performing Arts	-	-	-	-	-	-	-	-	136	53	49	7
Total(6)	**5,550**	**1,835**	**4,226**	**1,242**	**895**	**386**	**34**	**164**	**21,530**	**5,861**	**8,337**	**3,180**

Source: Department for Education and Employment; National Assembly for Wales; Northern Ireland Department of Education

(1) Including attempts and achievements by these students in previous years.
(2) Those in all schools who were 15 at the start of the academic year, i.e. 31 August 1998.
(3) In Northern Ireland, Full Intermediate and Foundation GNVQ figures relate to pupils aged 16 and 17 in schools and FE colleges at the start of the academic year.
(4) Pupils in schools and students in further education institutions aged 16-18 at the start of the academic year i.e. 31 August 1998.
(5) England only. GNVQ Language Units include French, German and Spanish.
(6) Includes subjects in England which are not specified in the table.

QUALIFICATIONS
4.5 Full vocational awards by gender(1,2), type of qualification and equivalent level – time series

United Kingdom

Thousands and percentages

	Year(3)				
	1994/95	1995/96	1996/97	1997/98(4)	1998/99
All (thousands)(5)					
Full vocational awards:					
By qualification & level					
NVQs/SVQs					
Level 1	55	62	79	72	62
Level 2	165	218	277	271	261
Level 3	49	65	93	102	104
Level 4 and 5	8	9	10	12	15
Total	**278**	**354**	**459**	**458**	**442**
GNVQs/GSVQs					
Level 1	3	6	9	9	12
Level 2	32	44	48	49	54
Level 3	12	34	36	44	47
Total	**47**	**84**	**93**	**103**	**113**
Other Vocational Qualifications(6)					
Level 1	173	188	235	252	279
Level 2	126	89	75	82	96
Level 3	115	94	75	66	74
Level 4 and 5	47	53	54	48	52
Total	**460**	**423**	**439**	**449**	**501**
Males *(percentages)(1,5)*					
Full vocational awards:					
By qualification					
NVQs/SVQs(7)	*41*	*41*	*43*	*47*	*47*
GNVQs/GSVQs	*43*	*47*	*48*	*49*	*50*
Other vocational qualifications(8,9)	*59*	*57*	*49*	*47*	*47*
Females *(percentages)(1,5)*					
Full vocational awards:					
By qualification					
NVQs/SVQs(7)	*59*	*59*	*57*	*53*	*53*
GNVQs/GSVQs	*57*	*53*	*52*	*51*	*50*
Other vocational qualifications(8,9)	*41*	*43*	*51*	*53*	*53*

Source: National Information System for Vocational Qualifications/Qualifications & Curriculum Authority (QCA)

(1) Due to change in methodology these figures are not directly comparable to those in previous volumes.
(2) Based on all awards where the gender of the candidate is identified.
(3) Academic years from October to September.
(4) Includes revised figures for Other Vocational Qualifications.
(5) Awards are excluded if the centre or qualification was not identified.
(6) Numbers may not add to column totals due to rounding.
(7) Prior to 1997/98 data available on gender for NVQs/SVQs was limited therefore this table may not be representative of the gender split for all NVQs/SVQs awarded nationally for these years.
(8) Other Vocational Qualifications made by City & Guilds, RSA, Edexcel and Scottish Qualifications Agency (SQA) only, not UK estimates. For other vocational qualifications, notional NVQ levels are allocated by QCA for analytical purposes as part of the NISVQ project.
(9) Due to limited data available, awards for other non regulated vocational qualifications in this table may not be representative of the gender split for all other vocational qualifications awarded nationally.

QUALIFICATIONS
Work-Based Training for Young People (1,2) and Work-Based Learning for Adults(3): qualifications of leavers – time series

England   Percentages

| Month of survey(5) | Month of leaving | Work-Based Training for Young People | | | | | | | WBLA |
| | | Advanced Modern Apprenticeships(1) survey respondents who: | | Other Training(1,2) survey respondents who: | | Total survey respondents who: | | | survey respondents who: |
		Gained any full qualification	Gained any full qualification at Level 3 or above(4)	Gained any full qualification	Gained any full qualification at Level 2 or above(4)	Gained any full qualification	Gained any full qualification at Level 2 or above(4)	Gained any full qualification at Level 3 or above(4)	Gained any full qualification (4)
July 1990 to September 1991	(1990-91)	..	..	39	..	39	..	..	28
October 1991 to September 1992	(1991-92)	..	..	34	23	34	15	7	29
October 1992 to September 1993	(1992-93)	..	..	35	27	35	18	8	34
October 1993 to September 1994	(1993-94)	..	..	38	31	38	20	10	36
October 1994 to September 1995	(1994-95)	..	..	40	34	40	22	12	39
October 1995 to September 1996	(1995-96)	28	9	43	38	43	25	13	42
October 1996 to September 1997	(1996-97)	43	22	44	40	44	26	14	38
October 1997 to September 1998	(1997-98)	47	27	45	40	45	27	14	37
October 1998 to September 1999	(1998-99)	57	36	46	41	49	27	17	40
1999 Jan to March	(July to Sept 1998)	59	39	49	44	52	29	19	41
April to June	(Oct to Dec1998)	54	34	41	36	46	25	16	38
July to Sept	(Jan to March 1999)	60	40	44	39	50	26	20	40
Oct to Dec	(April to June1999)	63	41	48	41	53	27	20	40
2000 Jan to March	(July to Sept 1999)	71	52	46	40	56	23	28	40
April to June	(Oct to Dec1999)	66	47	40	34	52	21	26	38
Current and previous years data									
July 1998 to June 1999	**(January to December 1998)**	54	33	46	40	48	28	16	40
July 1999 to June 2000	**(January to December 1999)**	66	46	45	39	53	25	24	39

Sources: WBTYP and WBLA trainee databases

(1) Other Training (shown as Youth Training (YT) in the 1997 Volume and which includes Youth Credits) forms part of Work-Based Training for Young People (WBTYP) along with Modern Apprenticeships (MA).

(2) From April 1995 the definition of Other Training leavers changed, no longer counting those making planned transfers from one training provider to another as leavers. Many of these transferring trainees will not have gained a job or qualification or completed their training. Therefore the change in definition will increase slightly the proportions with jobs and qualifications and those completing their training. The way that data on qualifications gained are collected was changed from August 1991 on. The effect appears to have been to decrease the proportion recorded as gaining full qualifications, but to increase by a similar amount the proportion gaining part qualifications. Data for 1990-91 are therefore not strictly comparable with those for later years.

(3) Work-Based Learning for Adults (WBLA) superseded Work-Based Training for Adults (WBTA) in April 1999. Figures for 1990-91 are for Employment Training.

(4) Information on levels of qualifications is not available for 1990-91 leavers and is not published for WBLA leavers.

(5) Leavers to September 1990 surveyed three months after leaving. Leavers in October and November 1990 surveyed in June 1991. Leavers from December 1990 surveyed six months after leaving.

QUALIFICATIONS
National Learning Targets(1) for England, 2002 – time series

4.7

England
Percentages

	1991(2)			1998			1999			2000		
	All	Males	Females	All	Males	Females	All	Males	Females	All	Males	Females
Targets for 11-year-olds												
By 2002												
80% of 11-year olds reaching the expected standard(3) for their age in literacy	..	..	..	65	57	73	71	65	76	75	70	79
75% of 11-year olds reaching the expected standard(3) for their age in numeracy	..	..	..	59	59	58	69	69	69	72	72	71
Targets for 16-year-olds												
By 2002												
50% of 16-year olds should gain at least five good GCSE passes(4)	..	..	..	46	41	52	48	43	53	49	44	54
95% of 16-year olds should gain at least one exam pass(5)	..	..	..	93	92	·95	94	93	95	94	93	95
Targets for Young people												
By 2002												
85% of 19-year-olds with a level 2 qualification(6)	54	54	53	72	70	74	75	74	75	75	72	77
60% of 21-year-olds with a level 3 qualification(7)	30	31	28	50	51	49	54	55	52	54	56	52
Targets for Adults(1,8)												
By 2002												
28% of adults with a level 4 qualification(9)	..	..	..	25	25	25	26	26	26	27	27	27
50% of adults with a level 3 qualification(7)	..	..	..	44	48	38	45	49	40	47	51	41

Source: Department for Education and Employment; Labour Force Survey, Spring Quarter of each year(10)

(1) There is a further 'learning participation' target for adults, and targets for organisations which are not included in this table. These targets are
  - a 7% reduction in non-learners - the learning participation target
  - 45% of medium sized or large organisations recognised as Investors in People
  - 10,000 small organisations recognised as Investors in People
(2) Due to changes in the coverage of the Labour Force Survey, 1991 figures are not directly comparable to later years.
(3) The expected standard = level 4 or above in the national tests set for 11-year-olds in English and mathematics.
(4) 5 higher grade GCSEs = GCSEs at grades A*-C, or the equivalent of.
(5) 1 GCSE = any GCSE grade A*-G, or the equivalent of.
(6) "level 2" = 5 GCSEs at grades A*-C, an NVQ level 2, an Intermediate GNVQ or the equivalent of.
(7) "level 3" = 2 A levels, an NVQ level 3, an Advanced GNVQ or the equivalent of.
(8) Adults consist of males aged 18-64 and females aged 18-59, who are in employment or actively seeking employment.
(9) "level 4" = NVQ level 4, i.e. having a degree or higher level vocational qualification.
(10) More up-to-date information may be available through the DfEE Statistics Website 'www.dfee.gov.uk/statistics'.

4.8 QUALIFICATIONS

Students(1) obtaining higher education qualifications(2,3) by type of course, gender and subject group, 1998/99

United Kingdom

Thousands

	Sub-degree(4)	First Degree	Postgraduate PHD's & equivalent	Postgraduate Masters and Others	Postgraduate Total	Total Higher Education
All						
Medicine & Dentistry	-	5.8	0.9	1.9	2.8	8.7
Subjects Allied to Medicine	19.3	17.6	0.5	4.5	5.1	41.9
Biological Sciences	1.3	17.4	1.7	2.5	4.2	22.8
Vet. Science, Agriculture & related	1.3	2.9	0.3	0.8	1.1	5.3
Physical Sciences	1.0	13.1	1.9	2.4	4.3	18.4
Mathematical and Computer Sciences	4.9	14.6	0.7	4.5	5.2	24.7
Engineering & Technology	4.2	22.0	1.8	6.7	8.5	34.7
Architecture, Building & Planning	1.6	7.2	0.1	3.4	3.5	12.4
Social Sciences	6.0	31.6	1.0	15.3	16.4	54.0
Business & Financial Studies	11.1	30.9	0.4	20.0	20.4	62.4
Librarianship & Info Science	0.3	3.8	-	2.1	2.1	6.2
Languages	1.1	16.0	0.6	2.6	3.2	20.3
Humanities	0.8	10.4	0.6	2.5	3.1	14.3
Creative Arts & Design	2.9	20.3	0.1	3.3	3.4	26.6
Education(5)	3.9	13.5	0.4	26.3	26.7	44.1
Combined, general	8.0	36.6	0.2	5.3	5.5	50.1
All subjects	**67.7**	**263.7**	**11.3**	**104.3**	**115.6**	**446.9**
Males						
Medicine & Dentistry	-	2.8	0.4	1.0	1.4	4.2
Subjects Allied to Medicine	2.0	3.7	0.3	1.1	1.4	7.0
Biological Sciences	0.6	6.5	0.8	0.9	1.8	8.9
Vet. Science, Agriculture & related	0.7	1.3	0.2	0.4	0.6	2.6
Physical Sciences	0.7	7.9	1.3	1.4	2.8	11.4
Mathematical and Computer Sciences	3.5	10.8	0.5	3.2	3.8	18.0
Engineering & Technology	3.8	18.8	1.5	5.5	7.0	29.5
Architecture, Building & Planning	1.2	5.5	0.1	2.2	2.3	9.1
Social Sciences	1.9	12.9	0.6	6.8	7.5	22.2
Business & Financial Studies	4.7	14.5	0.3	11.4	11.7	30.9
Librarianship & Info Science	0.1	1.4	-	0.7	0.8	2.3
Languages	0.4	4.4	0.3	0.9	1.2	5.9
Humanities	0.3	4.6	0.4	1.2	1.6	6.5
Creative Arts & Design	1.4	8.2	0.1	1.4	1.5	11.1
Education(5)	1.2	3.1	0.2	7.9	8.1	12.3
Combined, general	3.2	15.3	0.1	3.3	3.4	21.9
All subjects	**25.6**	**121.7**	**7.2**	**49.4**	**56.6**	**203.9**
Females						
Medicine & Dentistry	-	3.0	0.5	1.0	1.4	4.4
Subjects Allied to Medicine	17.3	13.9	0.3	3.4	3.7	34.9
Biological Sciences	0.6	10.8	0.9	1.6	2.4	13.9
Vet. Science, Agriculture & related	0.6	1.6	0.1	0.4	0.5	2.6
Physical Sciences	0.4	5.1	0.6	1.0	1.6	7.0
Mathematical and Computer Sciences	1.4	3.9	0.1	1.3	1.4	6.7
Engineering & Technology	0.4	3.3	0.3	1.2	1.5	5.2
Architecture, Building & Planning	0.4	1.7	-	1.2	1.2	3.3
Social Sciences	4.2	18.6	0.4	8.5	8.9	31.7
Business & Financial Studies	6.4	16.4	0.1	8.6	8.7	31.5
Librarianship & Info Science	0.2	2.4	-	1.3	1.4	3.9
Languages	0.8	11.6	0.3	1.7	2.0	14.3
Humanities	0.5	5.8	0.2	1.3	1.5	7.8
Creative Arts & Design	1.5	12.1	-	1.9	1.9	15.5
Education(5)	2.7	10.5	0.2	18.4	18.6	31.8
Combined, general	4.8	21.4	-	2.1	2.1	28.3
All subjects	**42.0**	**142.0**	**4.2**	**54.8**	**59.0**	**243.0**

Sources: Department for Education and Employment; Higher Education Statistics Agency (HESA)

(1) Includes students on Open University courses.
(2) Excludes qualifications from the private sector.
(3) Includes higher education in higher education ostitutions in the United Kingdom only. Higher education qualifications in further education institutions (approximately 6% of the total number of students) are excluded.
(4) Excludes students who successfully completed courses for which formal qualifications are not awarded.
(5) Including ITT and INSET.

QUALIFICATIONS

Highest qualification held by people of working age(1), by gender, age, ethnicity, region and economic activity and, for employees of working age(1), by occupation, 2000

United Kingdom

Thousands & percentages

	All people of working age (1) (000s)	Percentage of people of working age					
		NVQ level 5(2)	NVQ level 4(3)	NVQ level 3(4)	NVQ level 2(5)	Below NVQ level 2(6)	No qualifications
Personal and economic characteristics							
By gender							
Males	19,020	5	20	23	22	17	14
Females	17,292	3	19	14	22	23	19
By age							
16-19	2,903	*	1	16	41	22	21
20-24	3,473	1	19	33	22	17	7
25-29	4,066	5	26	18	21	21	9
30-39	9,425	5	22	17	21	25	11
40-49	7,842	5	22	17	20	19	17
50-64	8,604	4	17	17	19	16	27
By ethnic origin							
White	33,872	4	19	19	22	20	16
Non-white	2,430	5	18	16	20	22	20
of which:							
Black	651	4	20	16	21	23	16
Indian, Pakistani & Bangladeshi	1,181	4	16	15	19	21	25
Other non-white	598	7	20	17	21	22	12
By Government Office region(7)							
United Kingdom	36,312	4	19	19	22	20	16
North East	1,573	2	15	19	24	20	20
North West	4,180	3	18	19	23	19	17
Yorkshire & the Humber	3,078	3	17	19	22	21	17
East Midlands	2,569	3	17	19	22	22	18
West Midlands	3,239	3	17	17	21	21	20
Eastern	3,301	4	18	18	22	22	15
London	4,619	6	23	16	20	20	15
South East	4,907	5	22	20	22	20	11
South West	2,921	4	20	19	23	22	13
England	30,386	4	19	18	22	21	16
Wales	1,750	4	18	17	23	20	20
Scotland	3,160	4	21	21	20	16	18
Northern Ireland	1,017	3	16	18	23	14	26
By economic activity							
Employees(8)	23,802	5	22	19	23	20	11
of which:							
Managers & administrators	3,664	7	34	21	20	14	4
Professional	2,559	27	57	7	5	3	1
Associate professional & technical	2,383	6	54	16	14	8	2
Clerical & secretarial	3,826	1	14	19	30	29	7
Craft & related	2,400	*	7	37	27	17	12
Personal & protective services	2,837	1	11	20	29	25	14
Sales	2,095	1	10	19	31	24	16
Plant & machine operatives	2,183	*	3	18	24	33	22
Other	1,847	*	3	12	21	30	33
Self-employed(8)	2,930	4	23	24	21	15	12
ILO unemployed(9)	1,602	2	9	16	23	27	23
Inactive(10)	7,744	2	10	16	20	20	33
Time series							
1997(11)	35,844	3	17	17	22	22	19
1998(11)	36,026	3	18	18	22	21	18
1999(11)	36,177	4	19	18	22	20	17
2000	36,312	4	19	19	22	20	16

Labour Force Survey, Spring Quarters(12,13)

(1) Working age is defined as males aged 16 - 64 and females aged 16 - 59.
(2) Includes Higher degrees and other qualifications at Level 5.
(3) Includes First degree, Other degree and sub-degree higher education qualifications such as teaching and nursing certificates, HNC/HNDs, other HE diplomas and other qualifications at Level 4.
(4) Vocational qualifications include those with RSA Advanced Diploma, BTEC Nationals, ONC/ONDs, City and Guilds Advanced Craft or trade apprenticeships and other professional or vocational qualifications at Level 3. Academic qualifications include those with Advanced GNVQs, more than one GCE A level or SCE Highers/Scottish Certificates of Sixth Year Studies (CSYS) at Level 3.
(5) Vocational qualifications include those with RSA Diplomas, City and Guilds Craft, BTEC Firsts or trade apprenticeships and other professional or vocational qualifications at Level 2. Academic qualifications include those with one GCE A level, five or more GCSE grades A*-C or equivalent or AS examinations/SCE Highers/CSYS at Level 2.
(6) Vocational qualifications include those with BTEC general certificates, YT certificates, other RSA qualifications, other City and Guilds or other professional or vocational qualifications at Level 1. Academic qualifications include those with one or more GCSE grade G or equivalent (but less than five at grades A*-C) or AS examinations at Level 1.
(7) Usual region of residence - Government Office Regions in England and each UK country.
(8) The split into employees and self employed is based on respondents own assessment of their employment status.
(9) Unemployed according to the International Labour Office (ILO) definition.
(10) People who are neither in employment nor ILO unemployed.
(11) Figures have been revised as a result of revisions to quarterly LFS data from Autumn 1993 to Autumn 1999 to better reflect population changes over this period.
(12) Users of these data should read the LFS entry Annex A, as it contains important information about the LFS and the concepts and definitions used.
(13) More up-to-date information may be available through the DfEE Statistics Website 'www.dfee.gov.uk/statistics'.

4.10 QUALIFICATIONS
People(1) currently working towards a qualification(2), 2000

United Kingdom

Thousands & percentages

	Total working towards a qualification		Of which, percentage working towards(3)					
	Number (thousands)	Percentage (%)(4)	Degree or equivalent	Higher Education qualification (below degree level)	GCE A level or equivalent	GCSE grades A* to C or equivalent	Other qualification	Don't know/ no answer
All people(1)	5,776	15.9	25.8	9.3	22.0	13.3	27.4	2.1
Economic activity								
Employees(5,6)	3,497	14.7	21.2	11.2	22.8	9.4	33.5	1.9
Self-employed(6,7)	167	5.7	25.9	8.9	8.5	7.2	48.2	1.4
ILO unemployed(8)	256	16.0	16.3	7.8	20.8	22.9	27.9	4.3
Economically inactive(9)	1,739	22.5	37.7	6.2	21.2	20.1	12.8	2.0
All aged								
All	5,776	15.9	25.8	9.3	22.0	13.3	27.4	2.1
16-19	1,921	66.2	11.8	4.1	47.5	26.6	8.2	1.8
20-24	1,070	30.8	57.1	10.0	9.9	4.2	17.1	1.7
25-29	622	15.3	30.4	11.7	8.5	7.0	39.3	3.0
30-39	1,117	11.8	23.4	13.6	9.2	7.4	44.0	2.3
40-49	711	9.1	21.0	13.8	10.1	8.5	44.7	1.9
50-64	336	3.9	16.0	9.0	7.9	8.3	55.9	2.9
Males aged								
All	2,727	14.3	27.1	8.1	23.1	12.8	26.8	2.2
16-19	951	64.0	10.9	3.4	49.8	25.8	8.0	2.0
20-24	541	30.6	56.6	9.6	11.7	3.8	16.7	1.6
25-29	299	14.4	33.5	11.9	6.2	5.7	40.6	2.1
30-39	524	10.9	26.1	11.4	8.1	5.8	45.7	3.0
40-49	276	7.0	24.0	11.2	7.8	9.5	45.6	1.9
50-64	136	2.7	18.7	7.5	7.3	7.5	56.4	2.7
Females aged								
All	3,049	17.6	24.7	10.4	21.1	13.8	27.9	2.0
16-19	970	68.4	12.6	4.8	45.3	27.3	8.5	1.5
20-24	529	31.0	57.5	10.4	8.1	4.7	17.5	1.9
25-29	323	16.2	27.6	11.5	10.7	8.2	38.0	3.9
30-39	593	12.8	21.1	15.6	10.2	8.9	42.5	1.7
40-49	435	11.1	19.1	15.5	11.5	7.9	44.2	1.9
50-59	200	5.5	14.2	10.1	8.3	8.8	55.6	3.1
By highest qualification held								
Degree or equivalent	847	15.9	46.1	11.4	3.3	2.7	35.2	1.4
Higher Education qualification (below degree level)	537	17.8	32.7	20.5	6.5	3.3	35.1	1.8
GCE A level or equivalent	1,608	18.7	47.7	11.4	12.3	3.9	23.1	1.5
GCSE grades A* to C or equivalent	1,724	21.5	3.8	6.4	53.2	10.9	23.9	1.7
Other qualification	493	9.8	15.7	5.8	12.8	17.8	43.9	4.1
No qualification	527	8.9	0.9	1.5	5.5	73.6	16.1	2.5
By ethnic origin								
White	5,198	15.3	25.0	9.3	22.3	13.5	28.0	1.9
Non-white	576	23.7	33.1	9.6	19.5	12.0	22.1	3.8
of which:								
Black	169	26.0	26.2	13.7	17.0	10.4	26.5	6.3
Indian, Pakistani & Bangladeshi	226	19.1	29.8	8.1	23.3	13.8	21.9	3.0
Other non-white	180	30.1	43.8	7.5	17.0	11.2	18.1	2.3
Employees								
Full-time & part-time								
All	3,497	14.7	21.2	11.2	22.8	9.4	33.5	1.9
Males	1,648	12.9	22.3	9.9	23.6	8.5	33.8	1.9
Females	1,849	16.7	20.3	12.4	22.0	10.2	33.1	2.0
Full-time								
All	2,135	11.8	20.9	12.5	15.1	6.5	42.7	2.3
Males	1,194	10.1	21.4	10.6	16.3	6.0	43.5	2.3
Females	941	14.9	20.3	14.8	13.7	7.2	41.8	2.2
Part-time								
All	1,362	24.0	21.8	9.3	34.8	13.8	19.0	1.4
Males	453	47.1	24.8	7.9	43.1	14.7	8.5	*
Females	909	19.3	20.3	10.0	30.6	13.3	24.2	1.7

Source: Labour Force Survey, Spring 2000(10)

(1) Only those of working age; males aged 16-64 and females aged 16-59.
(2) For those who are working towards more than one qualification the highest is recorded.
(3) Expressed as a percentage of those in the group working towards a qualification.
(4) Expressed as a percentage of the total number of people in the group.
(5) Employees are those in employment excluding the self-employed, unpaid family workers and those on government employment and training programmes.
(6) The split into employee and self-employed is based on respondents' own assessment of their employment status
(7) Self-employed are those in employment excluding employees, unpaid family workers and those on government employment and training programmes.
(8) Unemployment according to the International Labour Office (ILO) definition.
(9) People who are neither in employment nor ILO unemployed.
(10) Users of these data should read the LFS entry in Annex A, as it contains important information about the LFS and the concepts and definitions used..

Chapter 5
Destinations

CHAPTER 5: DESTINATIONS

Key Facts

- The number of school leavers in England increased by 10,200 between 1998 and 1999, with the proportion of school leavers continuing their education increasing from 68% to 71% – some 10 percentage points higher than in 1991 (61%). In Scotland the proportion remained at 49%, while in Northern Ireland the proportion increased to 68%. Data for Wales are no longer collected. **(Table 5.1)**

- 70% of leavers from *Work-Based Training for Young People* in 1999 were in a job 6 months after leaving the programme, compared to 68% in 1998. The proportion who were unemployed 6 months after leaving, remained at 12%. **(Table 5.2)**

- 40% of leavers from *Work-Based Learning for Adults* in 1999 were in a job 6 months after leaving the programme, one percentage point less than a year earlier. The proportion in a positive outcome showed a similar trend, with the proportion who were unemployed increasing by one percentage point. **(Table 5.2)**

- 123,100 first-degree graduates from the academic year 1998/99 were known to go into employment, 10,300 graduates were believed to be unemployed and 39,500 graduates continued their education/training. **(Table 5.3)**

- Of those with a known destination, 64.6% were in employment, 20.7% continued their education/training and 5.4 % were believed unemployed. **(Table 5.3)**

CHAPTER 5: DESTINATIONS – LIST OF TABLES

DESTINATIONS

5.1

Destinations of school leavers by country – time series

United Kingdom   Thousands and percentages(1)

	1991	1997(2)	1998(2)	1999(2)
United Kingdom				
Number of school leavers	638.3	647.9 (2)	638.7 (2)	647.4 (2)
England				
Number of school leavers	522.8	561.2	553.7	563.9
of which(%):				
Education	61	68	68	71
Government supported training(3)	15	10	9	8
Employment	10	8	9	9
Unemployed or not available for work	9	7	7	5
Unknown or left area(4)	6	7	6	5
Wales				
Number of school leavers	34.9	..	..	..
of which(%):				
Education	62	..	..	..
Government supported training(3)	16	..	..	..
Employment	8	..	..	..
Unemployed or not available for work	8	..	..	..
Unknown or left area(4)	6	..	..	..
Scotland(5)				
Number of school leavers	55.2	60.4	59.3	57.2
of which(%):				
Education	32	47	49	49
Training	25	11	10	8
Employment	24	25	26	26
Unemployed	9	..	..	..
Miscellaneous/other known destinations	11	13	13	14
Destinations not known(4)	..	3	3	3
Northern Ireland				
Number of school leavers	25.4	26.3	25.7	26.3
of which(%):				
Education	58	66	67	68
Training	27	22	21	20
Employment	5	6	6	6
Unemployed or not available for work	4	4	3	3
Unknown or left area(4)	6	2	3	3

Sources: School Leavers Destinations Surveys; Careers Service Activity Survey

(1) Figures may not sum to 100% due to rounding.

(2) Data for Wales are no longer collected and are therefore excluded from the UK aggregate.

(3) Including those who have employed status under Work-based training for young people schemes.

(4) Those who failed to let the Careers Service or school know what they were doing, and who failed to respond to at least two attempts at follow-up by the Careers Office.

(5) These figures cannot be directly compared with those for England and Wales as they cover the destinations of pupils from classes S4, S5 and S6 who left school during or at the end of the years academic session. England and Wales figures relate to destinations of year 11 pupils leaving secondary school.

5.2 DESTINATIONS

Work-Based Training for Young People (1,2) and Work-Based Learning for Adults(3): destinations of leavers — time series

England   Percentages

		Advanced Modern Apprenticeships(1) survey respondents who were:			Other Training(1,2) survey respondents who were:		
		In a job	In a positive outcome(4)	Unemployed	In a job	In a positive outcome(4)	Unemployed
Month of survey(5)	**Month of leaving**						
July 1990 to September 1991	(1990-91)	..	..	..	58	74	20
October 1991 to September 1992	(1991-92)	..	..	..	51	67	25
October 1992 to September 1993	(1992-93)	..	..	..	50	67	28
October 1993 to September 1994	(1993-94)	..	..	..	54	70	25
October 1994 to September 1995	(1994-95)	..	..	..	58	72	22
October 1995 to September 1996	(1995-96)	67	84	12	63	76	18
October 1996 to September 1997	(1996-97)	75	85	9	66	79	15
October 1997 to September 1998	(1997-98)	80	88	7	65	79	14
October 1998 to September 1999	(1998-99)	82	89	6	64	77	15
1999 Jan to March	(July to Sept 1998)	80	89	6	62	79	13
April to June	(Oct to Dec 1998)	84	89	6	62	74	17
July to Sept	(Jan to March 1999)	84	89	6	66	78	15
Oct to Dec	(April to June 1999)	83	89	6	66	77	15
2000 Jan to March	(July to Sept 1999)	82	91	5	60	77	15
April to June	(Oct to Dec 1999)	86	91	5	60	73	18
Current and previous years data							
July 1998 to June 1999	**(January to December 1998)**	82	89	6	64	77	15
July 1999 to June 2000	**(January to December 1999)**	83	90	5	63	76	16

		Work-Based Training for Young People(1) survey respondents who were:			Work-Based Learning for Adults(3) survey respondents who were:		
		In a job	In a positive outcome(4)	Unemployed	In a job	In a positive outcome(4)	Unemployed
Month of survey(5)	**Month of leaving**						
July 1990 to September 1991	(1990-91)	58	74	20	33	36	53
October 1991 to September 1992	(1991-92)	51	67	25	31	36	55
October 1992 to September 1993	(1992-93)	50	67	28	34	40	52
October 1993 to September 1994	(1993-94)	54	70	25	36	43	48
October 1994 to September 1995	(1994-95)	58	72	22	38	42	48
October 1995 to September 1996	(1995-96)	63	76	18	39	44	47
October 1996 to September 1997	(1996-97)	67	80	15	44	49	42
October 1997 to September 1998	(1997-98)	68	81	13	44	48	45
October 1998 to September 1999	(1998-99)	69	81	12	40	45	47
1999 Jan to March	(July to Sept 1998)	65	81	11	40	45	47
April to June	(Oct to Dec 1998)	69	79	14	40	44	48
July to Sept	(Jan to March 1999)	72	81	12	39	43	49
Oct to Dec	(April to June 1999)	71	81	12	41	46	47
2000 Jan to March	(July to Sept 1999)	68	82	11	40	46	48
April to June	(Oct to Dec 1999)	71	80	13	40	45	49
Current and previous years data							
July 1998 to June 1999	**(January to December 1998)**	68	80	12	41	46	47
July 1999 to June 2000	**(January to December 1999)**	70	81	12	40	45	48

Sources: WBTYP and WBLA trainee databases

(1) Other Training (shown as Youth Training (YT) in the 1997 Volume and which includes Youth Credits) forms part of Work-Based Training for Young People (WBTYP) along with Modern Apprenticeships (MA).

(2) From April 1995 the definition of Other Training leavers changed, no longer counting those making planned transfers from one training provider to another as leavers. Many of these transferring trainees will not have gained a job or qualification or completed their training. Therefore the change in definition will increase slightly the proportions with jobs and qualifications and those completing their training. The way that data on qualifications gained are collected was changed from August 1991 on. The effect appears to have been to decrease the proportion recorded as gaining full qualifications, but to increase by a similar amount the proportion gaining part qualifications. Data for 1990-91 are therefore not strictly comparable with those for later years.

(3) Work-Based Learning for Adults (WBLA) superseded Work-Based Training for Adults (WBTA) in April 1999. Figures for 1990-91 are for Employment Training.

(4) In a positive outcome = in a job, full-time education or other TEC-Delivered Government Supported Training.

(5) Leavers to September 1990 surveyed three months after leaving. Leavers in October and November 1990 surveyed in June 1991. Leavers from December 1990 surveyed sixth months after leaving.

THIS PAGE HAS BEEN LEFT BLANK

United Kingdom   (i) Numbers of first degree graduates — by destination   Thousands

	UK Employment		Overseas employment (5)	Total Employment (6)	Continuing education/ training (7)	Believed unemployed	Other known destinations (8)	Unknown destinations (9)	All First Degree Graduates (10)
	Permanent (4)	Temporary							
All									
Medicine & Dentistry	1.3	3.2	.	**4.6**	0.3	.	.	0.4	**5.4**
Subjects Allied to Medicine	6.6	1.7	0.2	**9.4**	1.2	0.3	0.4	1.8	**13.2**
Biological Sciences	5.1	1.6	0.4	**7.6**	4.3	0.8	1.1	2.7	**16.5**
Vet. Science, Agriculture & related	1.3	0.2	0.1	**1.7**	0.3	0.1	0.2	0.4	**2.8**
Physical Sciences	3.9	1.1	0.3	**5.7**	3.6	0.6	0.8	1.7	**12.4**
Mathematical and Computer Sciences	6.2	0.7	0.4	**7.9**	1.7	0.7	0.5	3.0	**13.8**
Engineering & Technology	7.1	0.7	0.9	**9.5**	2.8	0.9	0.8	6.1	**20.1**
Architecture, Building & Planning	2.2	0.6	0.3	**3.4**	0.7	0.2	0.2	1.4	**5.9**
Social Sciences	8.8	2.2	0.7	**12.9**	7.7	1.2	1.6	6.0	**29.5**
Business & Financial Studies	11.6	1.7	1.1	**15.9**	2.3	1.3	1.5	7.2	**28.1**
Librarianship & Info Science	1.5	0.3	0.1	**2.1**	0.3	0.2	0.2	0.8	**3.7**
Languages	4.4	1.4	1.1	**7.5**	3.6	0.6	1.0	2.7	**15.5**
Humanities	2.7	1.1	0.3	**4.5**	2.6	0.5	0.7	1.7	**10.0**
Creative Arts & Design	6.8	1.5	0.4	**10.0**	2.6	1.2	1.3	4.9	**19.9**
Education	6.0	2.7	0.3	**10.2**	0.4	0.4	0.4	1.6	**12.9**
Combined, general	8.8	2.1	0.8	**12.9**	5.1	1.3	1.7	5.2	**26.2**
All subjects	**84.3**	**22.7**	**7.3**	**126.0**	**39.5**	**10.3**	**12.4**	**47.6**	**235.8**
Males									
Medicine & Dentistry	0.6	1.5	.	**2.2**	0.2	.	.	0.2	**2.6**
Subjects Allied to Medicine	1.2	0.5	.	**1.9**	0.4	0.1	0.1	0.5	**3.0**
Biological Sciences	1.8	0.5	0.1	**2.7**	1.6	0.4	0.4	1.1	**6.2**
Vet. Science, Agriculture & related	0.6	0.1	0.1	**0.8**	0.1	.	0.1	0.2	**1.2**
Physical Sciences	2.3	0.6	0.2	**3.4**	2.1	0.5	0.5	1.1	**7.5**
Mathematical and Computer Sciences	4.6	0.5	0.3	**5.9**	1.1	0.6	0.3	2.2	**10.1**
Engineering & Technology	5.9	0.6	0.8	**8.0**	2.3	0.8	0.7	5.3	**17.0**
Architecture, Building & Planning	1.7	0.4	0.2	**2.6**	0.5	0.1	0.2	1.1	**4.4**
Social Sciences	3.5	0.8	0.3	**5.0**	3.1	0.5	0.6	2.7	**12.0**
Business & Financial Studies	5.3	0.7	0.5	**7.3**	1.1	0.7	0.7	3.6	**13.3**
Librarianship & Info Science	0.5	0.1	.	**0.8**	0.1	0.1	0.1	0.3	**1.3**
Languages	1.2	0.3	0.3	**2.0**	0.9	0.2	0.2	0.9	**4.3**
Humanities	1.2	0.4	0.1	**1.9**	1.1	0.3	0.3	0.9	**4.5**
Creative Arts & Design	2.8	0.5	0.1	**3.9**	0.9	0.6	0.5	2.2	**8.1**
Education	1.4	0.4	0.1	**2.1**	0.1	0.1	0.1	0.5	**2.9**
Combined, general	3.7	0.8	0.3	**5.2**	1.9	0.6	0.7	2.4	**10.7**
All subjects	**38.4**	**8.9**	**3.5**	**55.7**	**17.4**	**5.5**	**5.4**	**25.1**	**109.2**
Females									
Medicine & Dentistry	0.7	1.7	.	**2.4**	0.2	.	.	0.2	**2.8**
Subjects Allied to Medicine	5.4	1.2	0.2	**7.5**	0.8	0.2	0.3	1.3	**10.2**
Biological Sciences	3.3	1.1	0.2	**5.0**	2.7	0.4	0.7	1.6	**10.3**
Vet. Science, Agriculture & related	0.7	0.2	.	**1.0**	0.2	0.1	0.1	0.2	**1.6**
Physical Sciences	1.5	0.5	0.1	**2.3**	1.4	0.2	0.3	0.6	**4.9**
Mathematical and Computer Sciences	1.5	0.2	0.1	**2.0**	0.6	0.2	0.2	0.7	**3.7**
Engineering & Technology	1.2	0.1	0.2	**1.6**	0.5	0.1	0.1	0.8	**3.1**
Architecture, Building & Planning	0.4	0.2	0.1	**0.8**	0.2	.	0.1	0.4	**1.5**
Social Sciences	5.4	1.4	0.4	**7.9**	4.6	0.6	1.0	3.3	**17.5**
Business & Financial Studies	6.3	1.0	0.6	**8.7**	1.2	0.6	0.8	3.5	**14.8**
Librarianship & Info Science	1.0	0.2	.	**1.4**	0.2	0.1	0.2	0.5	**2.3**
Languages	3.3	1.0	0.8	**5.5**	2.7	0.4	0.7	1.8	**11.2**
Humanities	1.5	0.6	0.1	**2.5**	1.6	0.2	0.4	0.8	**5.5**
Creative Arts & Design	4.1	0.9	0.3	**6.0**	1.7	0.6	0.8	2.7	**11.8**
Education	4.6	2.3	0.2	**8.0**	0.3	0.3	0.3	1.1	**10.0**
Combined, general	5.1	1.4	0.5	**7.7**	3.2	0.6	1.0	2.9	**15.5**
All subjects	**45.8**	**13.9**	**3.9**	**70.3**	**22.1**	**4.7**	**7.0**	**22.5**	**126.6**

Source: Department for Education and Employment; Higher Education Statistics Agency (HESA)

(1) The categorisation of destination of graduates reflects that collected since 1994/95 by HESA. Consequently direct comparisons with earlier years cannot be made.
(2) Higher education institutions only.
(3) Destinations from the academic year 1998/99.
(4) Includes the self-employed.
(5) Home and overseas students.
(6) Includes those employed in the UK with unknown employment termination date. These figures are not included in the preceding 'employment' columns.
(7) Continuing education/training in the United Kingdom or overseas.
(8) Including students not available for employment.
(9) Includes those Overseas graduates reported as returning overseas (no other information available).
(10) Includes known and unknown destinations.
(11) As a percentage of known destinations.

DESTINATIONS

Destinations(1) of full-time first degree graduates(2) by gender and subject group, 1998/99(3)

United Kingdom　　　　　　　　(ii) Percentage of known destinations　　　　Percentages(11) and Thousands

	UK Employment		Overseas employment (5)	Total Employment (6)	Continuing education/ training (7)	Believed unemployed	Other known destinations (8)	Total of known destinations (000s) (=100%)	All First Degree Graduates (000s)(10)
	Permanent (4)	Temporary							
All									
Medicine & Dentistry	27.0	64.5	0.5	**92.8**	6.7	0.2	0.3	5.0	5.4
Subjects Allied to Medicine	58.0	14.8	2.0	**82.3**	10.9	3.1	3.7	11.4	13.2
Biological Sciences	36.8	11.2	2.7	**55.4**	31.0	5.8	7.8	13.8	16.5
Vet. Science, Agriculture & related	52.7	10.4	4.2	**72.6**	14.0	5.0	8.4	2.4	2.8
Physical Sciences	36.0	10.6	2.5	**53.6**	33.1	6.0	7.2	10.7	12.4
Mathematical and Computer Sciences	57.0	6.2	3.6	**73.3**	15.2	6.9	4.6	10.8	13.8
Engineering & Technology	50.4	5.0	6.7	**67.8**	20.1	6.4	5.6	14.0	20.1
Architecture, Building & Planning	48.8	12.5	7.3	**75.3**	15.9	3.6	5.2	4.5	5.9
Social Sciences	37.7	9.5	2.9	**55.1**	33.0	4.9	6.9	23.4	29.5
Business & Financial Studies	55.3	8.1	5.0	**75.9**	10.9	6.0	7.2	21.0	28.1
Librarianship & Info Science	51.1	11.4	2.8	**74.4**	10.9	6.6	8.0	2.9	3.7
Languages	34.6	10.6	8.7	**58.9**	28.5	4.8	7.8	12.8	15.5
Humanities	32.6	12.7	3.2	**53.9**	31.8	5.8	8.5	8.3	10.0
Creative Arts & Design	45.6	9.8	2.9	**66.5**	17.2	8.0	8.4	15.0	19.9
Education	53.4	24.1	2.5	**90.2**	3.4	3.1	3.3	11.3	12.9
Combined, general	41.8	10.2	3.7	**61.8**	24.1	6.1	8.0	21.0	26.2
All subjects	**44.8**	**12.1**	**3.9**	**67.0**	**21.0**	**5.5**	**6.6**	**188.2**	**235.8**
Males									
Medicine & Dentistry	26.5	64.3	0.5	**92.2**	7.3	0.2	0.2	2.4	2.6
Subjects Allied to Medicine	49.7	18.8	1.5	**76.3**	16.1	4.0	3.6	2.5	3.0
Biological Sciences	36.0	9.9	2.6	**53.2**	31.3	7.4	8.1	5.0	6.2
Vet. Science, Agriculture & related	55.8	9.2	5.2	**74.2**	12.3	4.8	8.6	1.0	1.2
Physical Sciences	36.3	10.0	2.4	**53.0**	32.8	7.2	7.0	6.5	7.5
Mathematical and Computer Sciences	59.0	5.8	3.6	**75.1**	13.7	7.0	4.3	7.9	10.1
Engineering & Technology	50.4	4.7	6.7	**67.7**	19.8	6.9	5.6	11.7	17.0
Architecture, Building & Planning	51.8	12.0	6.4	**76.8**	14.3	3.5	5.4	3.4	4.4
Social Sciences	37.5	8.8	3.3	**54.3**	33.3	5.8	6.6	9.2	12.0
Business & Financial Studies	54.8	7.5	5.1	**74.8**	11.1	6.7	7.5	9.7	13.3
Librarianship & Info Science	49.5	10.2	3.2	**72.0**	10.7	9.8	7.6	1.0	1.3
Languages	34.8	9.8	9.1	**59.3**	26.7	6.7	7.3	3.4	4.3
Humanities	32.4	12.5	3.5	**53.7**	30.1	7.4	8.8	3.6	4.5
Creative Arts & Design	46.7	9.1	2.3	**66.6**	15.0	10.0	8.4	5.9	8.1
Education	58.4	18.3	3.4	**88.6**	5.2	3.0	3.1	2.4	2.9
Combined, general	43.8	9.3	3.7	**62.4**	22.1	7.6	7.9	8.4	10.7
All subjects	**45.7**	**10.5**	**4.1**	**66.3**	**20.7**	**6.6**	**6.5**	**84.1**	**109.2**
Females									
Medicine & Dentistry	27.4	64.7	0.4	**93.3**	6.2	0.1	0.4	2.6	2.8
Subjects Allied to Medicine	60.4	13.7	2.1	**84.1**	9.4	2.8	3.8	8.9	10.2
Biological Sciences	37.3	12.0	2.7	**56.7**	30.8	4.9	7.6	8.8	10.3
Vet. Science, Agriculture & related	50.3	11.2	3.4	**71.3**	15.3	5.2	8.2	1.3	1.6
Physical Sciences	35.5	11.6	2.6	**54.5**	33.7	4.2	7.5	4.3	4.9
Mathematical and Computer Sciences	51.9	7.0	3.5	**68.4**	19.4	6.5	5.6	3.0	3.7
Engineering & Technology	50.4	6.1	6.6	**68.3**	21.9	4.1	5.7	2.3	3.1
Architecture, Building & Planning	39.5	13.7	10.1	**70.6**	20.8	4.0	4.7	1.1	1.5
Social Sciences	37.8	9.9	2.6	**55.7**	32.7	4.4	7.2	14.2	17.5
Business & Financial Studies	55.6	8.7	5.0	**76.9**	10.7	5.5	7.0	11.3	14.8
Librarianship & Info Science	52.1	12.1	2.6	**75.8**	11.1	4.9	8.3	1.8	2.3
Languages	34.6	10.8	8.6	**58.7**	29.1	4.2	7.9	9.4	11.2
Humanities	32.7	12.9	3.0	**54.0**	33.0	4.6	8.4	4.7	5.5
Creative Arts & Design	44.8	10.3	3.2	**66.4**	18.6	6.7	8.4	9.1	11.8
Education	52.0	25.6	2.3	**90.6**	2.9	3.1	3.4	8.9	10.0
Combined, general	40.6	10.8	3.8	**61.4**	25.5	5.0	8.1	12.6	15.5
All subjects	**44.0**	**13.3**	**3.7**	**67.5**	**21.3**	**4.5**	**6.7**	**104.1**	**126.6**

Source: Department for Education and Employment; Higher Education Statistics Agency (HESA)

See previous page for footnotes

Chapter 6
Population

CHAPTER 6: POPULATION

Key Facts

- UK population aged 2 and over at January 2000 was 58.2 million (28.6 million males and 29.5 million females). **(Table 6.1)**

- UK working age population at Spring 2000 was 36.3 million, of which 23.8 million were Employees, 2.9 million were Self employed, 1.6 million were ILO unemployed and 7.7 million were Economically inactive. **(Table 6.1)**

- UK population aged 2 and over increased by 4.6 per cent between 1991 (55.6 million) and 2000 (58.2 million). Over the same period the working age population increased by 3.4 per cent, from 35.1 million to 36.3 million. **(Table 6.2)**

- Of people of working age, between 1991 and 2000, Employees increased by 9 per cent (21.9 million to 23.8 million), Self employed decreased by 10 per cent (2.9 million from 3.3 million), Economically inactive increased by 11 per cent (7.0 million to 7.7 million), while ILO unemployed decreased by 36 per cent from 2.5 million to 1.6 million. **(Table 6.2)**

CHAPTER 6: POPULATION - LIST OF TABLES

POPULATION

6.1

Population(1) at 1 January by age(2) and gender at the beginning of the academic year(2), 2000

United Kingdom

Thousands

	2000(2)														
	All(3)					Males					Females				
	UK	England	Wales	Scotland	NI	UK	England	Wales	Scotland	NI	UK	England	Wales	Scotland	NI
Ages															
Under 5	2,196	1,839	105	179	73	1,126	943	54	92	37	1,070	896	51	87	36
5-10	4,677	3,904	229	388	156	2,397	2,001	117	198	80	2,280	1,903	112	189	76
11-15	3,816	3,160	197	324	135	1,958	1,622	101	166	69	1,858	1,538	96	158	66
16-19	2,976	2,460	153	262	101	1,526	1,263	78	133	52	1,450	1,197	75	129	49
20-24	3,545	2,951	163	317	114	1,818	1,511	86	162	59	1,727	1,440	77	155	55
25-29	4,246	3,574	189	357	127	2,182	1,837	98	181	65	2,065	1,737	91	176	61
30-39	9,519	8,015	426	820	258	4,854	4,101	216	409	127	4,665	3,914	210	410	131
40-49	7,850	6,560	383	697	209	3,936	3,296	191	345	104	3,914	3,264	192	352	106
50-59	7,180	6,015	371	613	181	3,568	2,996	184	300	89	3,612	3,020	187	313	92
60-64	2,864	2,381	151	259	73	1,402	1,170	74	123	35	1,462	1,211	77	136	38
65+	9,296	7,783	508	785	220	3,850	3,235	211	316	89	5,446	4,548	297	469	132
Total aged 2 +	**58,164**	**48,643**	**2,874**	**5,002**	**1,646**	**28,617**	**23,976**	**1,410**	**2,426**	**806**	**29,547**	**24,667**	**1,464**	**2,576**	**840**
of which working age(4)	36,312	30,386	1,750	3,160	1,017	19,020	15,940	921	1,635	524	17,292	14,446	829	1,524	493
of which															
Employees(5,6)	23,802	20,125	1,059	2,056	562	12,758	10,826	564	1,071	297	11,044	9,298	495	985	265
Self employed(6,7)	2,930	2,511	142	194	83	2,174	1,849	106	148	70	756	661	36	45	12
ILO unemployed(8)	1,602	1,282	80	190	51	984	775	51	124	34	618	507	29	66	17
Economically inactive(9)	7,744	6,285	455	698	306	2,987	2,400	191	280	116	4,758	3,885	264	419	190

Sources: Department for Education and Employment; Labour Force Survey(10); Office for National Statistics; Government Actuary's Department

(1) Estimated and projected numbers based on demographic data provided by the Office for National Statistics and Surveys and the Government Actuary's Department.

(2) Age at 31 August 1999. For the Labour Force Survey economic data only, age is based on the age of respondents at the time of the survey.

(3) Males and Females may not sum to All totals due to rounding.

(4) Working age is defined as males aged 16-64 and females 16-59.

(5) Employees are those in employment excluding the self-employed, unpaid family workers and those on government employment and training programmes.

(6) The split into employees and self-employed is based on respondents' own assessment of their employment status.

(7) Self-employed are those in employment excluding employees, unpaid family workers and those on government employment and training programmes.

(8) Unemployed according to the International Labour Office (ILO) definition.

(9) Economically inactive are those who are neither in employment nor ILO unemployed.

(10) Users of these data should read the LFS entry in Annex A, as it contains important information about the LFS and the concepts and definitions used.

6.2

POPULATION

Population(1) at 1 January by age(2) at the beginning of the academic year — time series

United Kingdom   Thousands

	1991	1996	1998	1999(3)	2000
Ages					
Under 5	2,300	2,337	2,248	2,226	2,196
5-10	4,399	4,625	4,705	4,696	4,677
11-15	3,407	3,665	3,697	3,743	3,816
16-19	3,204	2,730	2,895	2,967	2,976
20-24	4,569	3,968	3,610	3,509	3,545
25-29	4,759	4,624	4,477	4,345	4,246
30-39	8,251	8,971	9,311	9,405	9,519
40-49	6,823	7,896	7,800	7,781	7,850
50-59	6,070	6,358	6,802	7,011	7,180
60-64	3,040	2,782	2,789	2,825	2,864
65+	8,774	9,229	9,269	9,268	9,296
Total aged 2 +	**55,596**	**57,185**	**57,605**	**57,775**	**58,164**
of which working age(4)	35,103	35,663	36,026	36,177	36,312
of which					
Employees(5,6)	21,920	22,092	23,006	23,392	23,802
Self employed(6,7)	3,250	3,109	3,080	2,999	2,930
ILO unemployed(8)	2,501	2,321	1,757	1,732	1,602
Economically inactive(9)	6,980	7,790	7,929	7,818	7,744

Source: Department for Education and Employment; Labour Force Survey(10); Office for National Statistics; Government Actuary's Department

(1) Estimated and projected numbers based on demographic data provided by the Office for National Statistics and Surveys and the Government Actuary's Department.

(2) Age at 31 August of the previous year. For the Labour Force Survey economic data only, age is based on the age of respondents at the time of the survey.

(3) Population figures have been revised to include more recent estimates and projections than those shown in the 1999 volume.

(4) Working age is defined as males aged 16-64 and females 16-59.

(5) Employees are those in employment excluding the self-employed, unpaid family workers and those on government employment and training programmes.

(6) The split into employees and self-employed is based on respondents' own assessment of their employment status.

(7) Self-employed are those in employment excluding employees, unpaid family workers and those on government employment and training programmes.

(8) Unemployed according to the International Labour Office (ILO) definition.

(9) Economically inactive are those who are neither in employment nor ILO unemployed.

(10) Users of these data should read the LFS entry in Annex A, as it contains important information about the LFS and the concepts and definitions used.

Chapter 7
International Comparisons

CHAPTER 7: INTERNATIONAL COMPARISONS

Introduction

International comparisons of the functioning of education and training systems can help countries to identify their strengths and weaknesses and evaluate their performance against their main competitors. Governments are increasingly looking towards these comparisons as they develop and monitor education and training policies.

The United Kingdom participates in the continuing development of international comparisons of education and training. With help from the National Assembly for Wales, Scottish Executive, Northern Ireland Department of Education and the Northern Ireland Department of Higher and Further Education, Training and Employment, DfEE supply detailed statistics on education and training in the UK, drawn from this volume and other sources, to the Organisation for Economic Co-operation and Development (OECD), the Statistical Office of the European Union (EUROSTAT) and the United Nations Educational, Scientific and Cultural Organisation (UNESCO).

Based on information supplied by various countries to the international bodies, and the results of international studies, a range of 'indicators' is now available, seeking to compare different aspects of countries' education and training systems and their respective performance.

The comparative tables shown here draw from OECD's "Education at a Glance" (2000 Edition), which includes *trends* in international comparisons.

It is important to note however that international comparisons of education and training are very difficult and should therefore be treated with caution. In addition, some knowledge of the underlying systems in different countries is extremely useful in interpreting the data.

To ensure comparability, most educational activity in different countries has been assigned to 6 internationally-agreed "ISCED" (International Standard Classification of Education) levels of education. The best comparisons are based on such internationally agreed definitions and procedures, backed up by controls to ensure that each country meets these. Despite these efforts, there may still be comparability problems that persist - some of the more important ones are noted below:

Notes:

Classifying education

- Coverage of what is considered to be "education" may vary, especially at the pre-compulsory and post-compulsory level e.g. early childhood provision, apprenticeships, adult learning etc. The UK are participating in a revision of ISCED, attempting to address any inconsistencies between countries.

Expenditure on education

- Where institutions cover more than one of the education levels (e.g. "lower" (age 11-13) and "upper" (age 14+) secondary school education in the UK), estimates are often required to assign expenditure figures between levels.

- The range of public and private provision varies considerably between countries. In Japan and the United States, private expenditure on educational institutions is almost one-third of that from public sources.

- Public expenditure on education, as a percentage of GDP, is influenced by a number of factors. An obvious one is the proportion of the population of school age, which can vary widely between different countries.

- Expenditure coverage, especially at the HE level, differs according to the extent to which countries include elements such as student support and research and development.

Participation in education

- Many of the measures shown are on the basis of headcounts, no distinction being possible between full-time and part-time study. Some countries do not even recognise the concept of part-time study, although many of their students would be classified as "part-time" in the UK.

- When comparing expected years of schooling in different countries, the length of the school year and the quality of education offered is not necessarily the same.

- The reasons why adults in some countries are so much less likely than others to participate in university-level education are varied. One important factor may be the extensive provision of vocational education and apprenticeships in continental Europe, likely to have reduced the perceived need to enrol in formal university-level studies as preparation for work.

Teachers
- A clear definition of a "teacher", especially in higher education, has not been well established in international data collections. Some countries include professional staff such as guidance counsellors and school psychologists in their "teacher" counts.

CHAPTER 7: INTERNATIONAL COMPARISONS

Key Facts
- Public expenditure on all levels of education in the UK was 5.1% of Gross Domestic Product in 1997, slightly below the OECD average. This was higher than in Germany (4.8 %), and Japan (3.6%), but lower than France (6.0 %), the US (5.2%) and all the Scandinavian countries. **(Table 7.1)**

- The UK provided average public subsidies of US$2,505 per higher education student in 1997, higher than the OECD mean (US$1,856), but lower than all the Scandinavian countries. However, Norway and Sweden paid most of their student support in the form of loans, whereas only around a quarter of the student support provided in the UK at that time was in the form of loans. **(Table 7.1)**

- Expenditure per pupil in early childhood education was well above the OECD average in the UK in 1997, although expenditure per primary and secondary school pupil, and higher education student were all slightly below the OECD average. Expenditure at all these levels was higher than the UK in Germany, Japan and the US - the US spent over twice the amount per higher education student as the UK. **(Table 7.2)**

- Between 1990 and 1996, expenditure per primary and secondary school pupil increased in real terms in the UK, however, along with the Netherlands and Canada, expenditure per higher education student fell, due to a sharp increase in higher education enrolments. **(Table 7.2)**

- Over 90% of the population are enrolled in education in the UK, each year between the ages of 4 to 15. In some other countries, compulsory education does not start until later, but continues to age 18. **(Table 7.3)**

- In 1998, given current conditions, a UK 5 year old could expect to enrol in 17.1 years of full-time and part-time education. Expected years in education in the UK increased by 1.7 years between 1990 and 1998. They were highest in Australia, increasing from 16.4 years in 1990 to 20.0 years in 1998. **(Table 7.3)**

- The ratio of students to teaching staff in the UK was above the OECD average in 1998, at all levels of education. **(Table 7.4)**

- At age 16, 81% of the UK population were enrolled, full- or part-time, in educational institutions in 1998. Participation was near-universal in France (95%), Germany (96%), Japan (96%) and Australia (97%). At age 18, UK participation rates were 49%, compared with participation rates of over 80% in Germany, France and Sweden. **(Table 7.5)**

- In 1998, the entry rate to university-level (first and higher degree) higher education was 48% in the UK, above the OECD average. However UK higher education courses are on average shorter than those in other countries, so that "expected years" of higher education in the UK were around average for OECD countries. **(Table 7.6)**

- 10.8% of all higher education students in the UK in 1998 were overseas-domiciled, over double the OECD average, and lower than only Australia, Austria, Switzerland and Luxembourg. **(Table 7.6)**

- UK dropout rates from higher education (19%) are the second lowest in the OECD, behind Japan (11%). In 1998, the United Kingdom had the highest graduation rate from first degrees in the European Union (35%, compared with 16% in Germany and 24% in France). **(Table 7.7)**

- 56% of all employed adults aged 25-64 in the UK participated in job-related education in 1994/95 - the highest for countries participating in the International Adult Literacy Survey. However, the average duration of training per participant was relatively low. **(Table 7.8)**

CHAPTER 7: INTERNATIONAL COMPARISONS - LIST OF TABLES

7.1 Expenditure on education, as a percentage of GDP and public subsidies per higher education student 1997

7.2 Expenditure on education, per student per year 1997, and index of change between 1990 and 1996

7.3 Participation in compulsory education 1990 and 1998

7.4 Ratio of students to teaching staff by level of education (based on full-time equivalents) 1998

7.5 Participation in education of 16 to 18 year olds 1998

7.6 Higher education: Entry, participation and overseas students 1998

7.7 Higher education: Drop-out and graduation rates 1998

7.8 Rates of participation in job-related education and training by age 1994/95

INTERNATIONAL COMPARISONS
Expenditure on Education, as a percentage of GDP and public subsidies per higher education student 1997

| | Public expenditure on education(1) as a percentage of GDP | | | Public Subsidies per higher education student(2) | | | |
| | | | | (US$ converted using purchasing power parities) | | | |
	Primary and Secondary Education	Higher Education	All levels(3)	Attributable for educational institutions (tuition)	Attributable for student living costs and educational expenditure outside educational institutions	Total	of which loans
Australia	3.6	1.3	5.0	675	803	1,478	672
Austria	4.2	1.5	6.2	x	x	1,526	-
Belgium (Flemish)	3.4	1.1	5.1	..	..	..	..
Canada	4.0	1.8	6.0	570	773	1,345	201
Czech Republic	3.4	0.8	4.8	-	419	419	.
Denmark	4.9	1.8	7.9	-	4,629	4,629	736
Finland	4.0	2.1	6.9	-	1,464	1,464	-
France	4.2	1.1	6.0	165	388	553	.
Germany	3.0	1.1	4.8	-	1,090	1,090	239
Greece	2.5	1.0	3.5	..	..	..	..
Hungary	3.0	0.9	4.7	140	304	444	.
Iceland	4.0	0.9	5.4	x	x	2,057	2,057
Ireland	3.6	1.4	5.0	515	1,564	2,080	-
Italy	3.4	0.7	4.7	..	..	..	..
Japan	2.8	0.5	3.6	..	..	..	..
Korea	3.4	0.5	4.4	-	-	-	-
Luxembourg	4.2	0.2	4.4	.	.	6,809	.
Mexico	3.3	0.9	4.6	x	x	276	90
Netherlands	3.1	1.4	5.0	862	1,877	2,739	899
New Zealand	5.1	1.8	7.3	x	x	2,109	2,086
Norway	4.4	2.0	6.6	x	x	4,737	3,132
Poland	3.9	1.3	6.2	.	130	130	.
Portugal	4.5	1.1	5.9	.	187	187	.
Spain	3.5	1.0	4.8	108	234	341	-
Sweden	5.5	2.2	6.8 (4)	-	5,535	5,535	3,564
Switzerland	4.1	1.2	5.6	x	x	500	24
Turkey	..	0.8	..	..	..	..	..
United Kingdom	**3.5**	**1.2**	**5.1**	992	1,514	2,505	633
United States	3.5	1.4	5.2	x	x	1,599	x
Country Mean	**3.8**	**1.3**	**5.5**	**237**	**1,230**	**1,856**	**651**

Source: OECD, Education at a Glance, 2000

(1) Direct expenditure for institutions and public subsidies to students e.g. for tuition fees and living costs. For some countries, expenditure on public subsidies to students is missing and so excluded from the total.
(2) Average public subsidy to ALL HE students i.e. including students not eligible for support.
(3) Includes expenditure for early childhood education and other miscellaneous expenditure.
(4) Expenditure on public subsidies to students at all levels is missing and excluded from the total. However, expenditure data are available and included at the primary and secondary, and HE levels.
x - included in another column of the table

Expenditure on Education, per student per year 1997, and index of change between 1990 and 1996

| | Expenditure per full-time equivalent student per year: 1997(1) | | | | Index of change in spending per student between 1990 and 1996 | |
| | (USS converted using purchasing power parities) | | | | | |
	Early childhood education	Primary education	Secondary education	Higher Education	Primary and Secondary education	Higher education
Australia	..	3,633	5,570	11,240	114	114
Austria(2)	4,867	6,258	8,213	9,993	120	109
Belgium (Flemish)(3)	2,768	3,813	6,938	7,834	..	..
Canada	3,942	..	..	14,809	104	93
Czech Republic	2,526	1,954	3,641	5,351	..	..
Denmark	5,487	6,596	7,198	7,294	..	..
Finland	6,340	4,639	5,065	7,145	86	98
France	3,462	3,621	6,564	7,177	113	100
Germany	4,288	3,490	6,149	9,466	..	..
Greece(3)	x	2,351	2,581	3,990	..	..
Hungary(2)	2,106	2,035	2,093	5,430	..	..
Iceland(2)	3,591	..	..	..	..	..
Ireland	2,559	2,574	3,864	7,998	136	107
Italy	4,462	5,073	6,284	5,972	95	70
Japan	3,096	5,202	5,917	10,157	..	..
Korea	1,676	3,308	3,518	6,844	..	..
Mexico	979	935	1,726	4,519	166	101
Netherlands	3,310	3,335	4,992	9,989	110	89
Norway(2)	..	6,315	6,973	10,108	114	94
Poland	..	1,435	..	4,395	..	..
Portugal(2)	2,044	3,248	4,264	..	153	56
Spain	2,520	3,180	4,274	5,166	125	127
Sweden	2,943	5,491	5,437	12,981	..	..
Switzerland(2)	2,451	6,237	9,045	16,376	101	86
Turkey(2)	..	..	..	2,397	..	..
United Kingdom(3)	**5,312**	**3,206**	**4,609**	**8,169**	**101**	**84**
United States	6,158	5,718	7,230	17,466	..	..
Country Mean	**3,463**	**3,851**	**5,273**	**8,612**	**117**	**95**

Source: OECD, Education at a Glance, 2000

(1) Calendar year 1997. Where the financial year and / or school year does not match the calendar year, corresponding weightings are made.
(2) Public institutions only.
(3) Public and Government-dependent private institutions only.

x - included in another column of the table

INTERNATIONAL COMPARISONS
Participation in compulsory education 1990 and 1998

	Context			Expected years of full-time and part-time education (all levels) from age 5(1)	
	Compulsory school starting age	Ending age of compulsory schooling	Age range at which over 90% of the population are enrolled	1990	1998
Australia	6	15	6 - 16	16.4	20.0
Austria	6	15	5 - 15	14.3	16.0
Belgium (Flemish)	6	18	3 - 17	..	17.3
Canada	6	16	6 - 17	16.5	16.7
Czech Republic	6	15	5 - 16	13.9	15.1
Denmark	7	16	5 - 16	16.1	17.5
Finland	7	16	7 - 17	15.5	17.9
France	6	16	3 - 17	..	16.6
Germany	6	18	6 - 17	..	16.8
Greece	6	14.5	6 - 15	..	15.5
Hungary	6	16	5 - 16	13.8	15.6
Iceland	6	16	6 - 15	16.0	17.7
Ireland	6	15	5 - 16	14.5	15.9
Italy	6	14	3 - 14	..	15.7
Japan	6	15	4 - 17	..	..
Korea	6	14	6 - 17	..	15.5
Luxembourg	6	15	..	..	..
Mexico	6	15	6 -11	11.8	12.2
Netherlands	5	18	4 - 17	16.7	17.2
New Zealand	6	16	4 - 15	14.8	17.1
Norway	7	16	6 - 17	16.0	17.7
Poland	7	15	6 - 16	..	15.6
Portugal	6	14	6 - 15	13.7	16.9
Spain	6	16	4 - 15	15.4	17.3
Sweden	7	16	6 - 18	..	19.4
Switzerland	6	15	6 - 16	15.3	16.2
Turkey	6	14	7 - 10	..	9.7
United Kingdom	**5**	**16**	**4 - 15**	**15.4**	**17.1**
United States	6	17	6 - 15	16.3	16.8
Country Mean				**15.1**	**16.4**

Sources: OECD, Education at a Glance, 2000; UNESCO Statistical Yearbook, 1999

(1) Calculated as the sum of the net enrolment rates in education for each single year of age from age 5 onwards, divided by 100.

INTERNATIONAL COMPARISONS
Ratio of students to teaching staff(1) by level of education (based on full-time equivalents) 1998

	Early childhood education	Primary education	Secondary education	Higher education
Australia	..	17.9	15.5	..
Austria	18.6	12.7	9.5	..
Belgium (Flemish)	18.0	14.0	..	..
Canada	16.2	21.0	22.1	..
Czech Republic	15.9	19.2	15.4	13.5
Finland	11.9	17.7	..	..
Germany	23.2	21.6	15.5	12.4
Greece	15.9	13.6	11.5	26.3
Hungary	12.1	11.0	10.8	11.8
Iceland	5.6	14.1	..	9.3
Ireland	14.7	22.6	16.3	16.6
Japan	19.3	21.4	15.7	11.8
Korea	23.6	31.0	22.8	..
Netherlands	x	17.8	18.5	18.7
New Zealand	5.6	24.7	21.0	15.5
Norway	..	12.6	..	13.0
Spain	18.3	16.0	12.1	17.2
Sweden	..	13.4	15.3	9.0
Switzerland(2)	18.7	16.3	14.0	..
United Kingdom	**21.5**	**22.0**	**16.7**	**17.7**
United States	18.0	16.5	15.9	14.6
Country Mean	**15.5**	**17.1**	**15.2**	**14.6**

Source: OECD, Education at a Glance, 2000

(1) Includes headteachers and administrative personnel involved in teaching, pro-rata.
(2) Public institutions only.
x - included in another column of the table

INTERNATIONAL COMPARISONS
Participation in education(1) of 16 to 18 year olds(2) 1998

	Age at end of compulsory education	Age 16	Age 17	Age 18
OECD countries				
Australia	15	97	87	66
Austria	15	89	86	68
Belgium	18	94	93	80
Canada	16	99	92	51
Czech Republic	15	96	88	64
Denmark	16	93	82	75
Finland	16	89	93	85
France	16	95	90	82
Germany	18	96	92	86
Greece	14.5	90	67	71
Hungary	16	98	87	62
Iceland	16	89	77	67
Ireland	15	91	82	71
Italy	14	78	73	68
Japan	15	96	94	..
Korea	14	96	91	54
Mexico	15	42	35	25
Netherlands(3)	18	96	90	78
New Zealand	16	89	73	55
Norway	16	94	93	88
Poland	15	90	88	72
Portugal	14	84	84	66
Spain	16	88	79	66
Sweden	16	98	97	96
Switzerland	15	90	86	80
Turkey	14	43	26	18
United Kingdom	**16**	**81**	**68**	**49**
United States	17	84	77	63
Country Mean		**88**	**80**	**68**

Source: OECD, Education at a Glance, 2000

(1) Includes all education taking place in educational institutions, so includes apprenticeships in countries which operate a dual system e.g. Austria, Germany. Age participation rates are based on a full-time and part-time headcount.
(2) Age at start of academic year.
(3) Only educational programmes lasting more than 12 months are included.

	Entry	Participation	Overseas students
	Net entry rate(1) to university-level higher education(2)	Expected years of higher education for all 17 year olds(3)	Foreign students as a percentage of all students
OECD countries			
Australia	53	3.1	12.6
Austria	28	2.2	11.5
Belgium (Flemish)	28	2.4	4.0
Canada	..	2.7	3.8 (4)
Czech Republic	22	1.3	1.9
Denmark	30	2.4	6.0
Finland	58	3.8	1.7
France	..	2.6	7.3
Germany	28	2.0	8.2
Greece	..	2.4	..
Hungary	45	1.6	2.6
Iceland	38	2.0	2.4
Ireland	28	2.3	4.8
Italy	42	2.3	1.2
Japan	36 (5)	..	0.9
Korea	43 (5)	3.3	0.1
Luxembourg	..	..	30.5
Mexico	21	0.9	..
Netherlands	52	2.2	..
New Zealand	68	2.9	3.7
Norway	56	3.0	3.2
Poland	..	2.0	0.5
Portugal	..	2.2	..
Spain	41	2.7	1.7
Sweden	59	2.4	4.5
Switzerland	..	1.6	15.9
Turkey	20	1.2	1.3
United Kingdom	**48**	**2.5**	**10.8**
United States	44	3.5	3.2
Country Mean	**40**	**2.3**	**4.8**

Source: OECD, Education at a Glance, 2000

(1) Calculated as the sum over all age groups of new university-level entrants within an age group divided by the total population for that age group.

(2) "University-level" higher education refers to "largely theoretically based" courses with a minimum of 3 years full-time-equivalent duration. In the UK, this comprises first and higher degrees. "Non university-level higher education" courses are "more practically-oriented and occupationally specific". In the UK, this level comprises "sub-degree" higher education courses, such as HNCs, HNDs, Dip HEs.

(3) Calculated as the sum of the net enrolment rates (full-time and part-time) in higher education for each single year of age from age 17 onwards, divided by 100.

(4) University-level higher education students only.

(5) "Gross" entry rate.

| | Drop-out and survival rates(1) | | Non-university level higher education(3) | Graduation Rates(2) — University level higher education(3) | | | |
| | | | | First Degree | | Higher Degree | |
	Survival	Drop-Out		Short(4)	Long(5)	Masters or equivalent	PhD or equivalent
OECD countries							
Australia	65	35	..	25.8	.	7.5	1.1
Austria(6)	53	47	10.5	0.5	13.2	-	1.6
Belgium (Flemish)	63	37	25.8	10.8	6.5	4.9	0.7
Canada	..	..	5.5	27.0	2.4	4.5	0.8
Czech Republic(6)	79	21	4.5	2.9	8.3	1.7	0.5
Denmark	67	33	..	..	..	..	..
Finland	75	25	28.4	15.7	14.6	..	2.3
France(6)	55	45	17.5	18.0	6.0	6.3	1.2
Germany	72	28	12.5 (6)	4.8	11.2	.	1.8
Hungary	77	23	..	24.7	x	3.3	0.9
Iceland	..	..	9.8	22.3	2.5	1.1	-
Ireland(6)	77	23	17.7	23.8	1.4	11.9	0.8
Italy	35	65	0.3	0.9	13.6	3.1	0.4
Japan(6)	90	11	29.9	27.7	x	2.5	0.5
Korea(6)	..	..	29.8	25.1	0.4	2.5	0.6
Luxembourg(6)	..	..	7.4	.	.	.	.
Mexico	68	32	..	10.1	..	..	x
Netherlands	70	30	0.8	33.3	1.3	2.2	x
New Zealand	76	24	12.7	26.1	7.3	14.1	0.7
Norway	..	..	6.3	33.3	5.1	5.2	1.1
Poland(6)	..	..	0.8	12.0	13.0	5.3	..
Portugal(6)	49	51	6.5	7.4	10.1	..	1.4
Spain	..	..	4.1	12.5	15.4	..	0.9
Sweden	..	..	1.5	23.0	2.1	0.4	2.2
Switzerland(6)	74	30	..	7.8	12.3	1.2	2.5
Turkey	55	45	6.4	9.6	.	1.0	0.2
United Kingdom	**81**	**19**	**11.1**	**33.2**	**2.0**	**12.3**	**1.2**
United States(6)	63	37	9.2	32.9	.	14.6	1.3
Country Mean	**67**	**33**	**11.2**	**17.5**	**5.7**	**4.4**	**1.0**

Source: OECD, Education at a Glance, 2000

(1) From university-level higher education. Calculated using a variety of methods agreed between member states and validated by OECD. Reference dates vary

(2) Calculated as the sum over all age groups of graduates within an age group divided by the total population for that age group.

(3) "University-level" higher education refers to "largely theoretically based" courses with a minimum of 3 years full-time-equivalent duration. In the UK, this comprises first and higher degrees. ""Non university-level higher education" courses are "more practically-oriented and occupationally specific". In the UK, this level comprises "sub-degree" higher education courses, such as HNCs, HNDs, Dip HEs.

(4) 3 to less than 5 years duration.

(5) 5 years or longer duration.

(6) "Gross" graduation rates.

x - included in another column of the table

7.8

Rates of participation in job related education and training by age 1994/95

	Percentage of employed adults(1) participating in job-related education and training in the previous year				Mean number of hours per trainee (all ages)	Mean number of hours per employee (all ages)(2)
	25-34	35-44	45-64	All		
Australia	45	44	35	41	110	45
Belgium (Flemish)	24	19	24	22	123	27
Canada	40	42	31	38	104	39
Ireland	27	25	20	24	196	47
Netherlands	39	39	28	35	161	57
New Zealand	54	53	47	51	130	66
Poland	18	18	14	17	116	20
Switzerland (French)	32	29	20	26	117	31
Switzerland (German)	40	33	31	35	106	37
United Kingdom	**63**	**59**	**47**	**56**	**95**	**53**
United States	48	49	46	47	80	38
Country Mean	**39**	**37**	**31**	**36**	**122**	**42**

Source: OECD and Statistics Canada / International Adult Literacy Survey

(1) Employed adults include 25 to 64 year olds employed mostly full-time (more than 30 hours per week) for at least 42 weeks in the past 12 months whose primary work situation is not student.

(2) Mean number of hours per trainee multiplied by participation rate, divided by100.

SOURCES OF EDUCATION AND TRAINING STATISTICS

This section gives details of the current major sources of education and training statistics used in this publication. Previous editions of "Education Statistics for the United Kingdom" and "Training Statistics" give earlier sources used.

List of Sources

1   Education Expenditure

2   Further Education Statistics

3   Higher Education Statistics Agency (HESA)

4   Labour Force Survey (LFS)

5   Public Examinations: GCSE/GNVQ, GCE and Scottish Certificate of Education (SCE)

6   School Leavers Destinations

7   Schools Statistics

8   TEC/CCTE-Delivered Government Supported Training:

  –   TEC Management Information

  –   Work-based Training for Young People: trainee database

  –   Work-based Learning for Adults: trainee database

9   Vocational Qualifications

1 EDUCATION EXPENDITURE

HM Treasury provided education expenditure figures in Tables 1.1 and 1.2 from their Public Expenditure Statistical Analysis (PESA). The tables show Total Managed Expenditure (TME) on services, which is a definition of aggregate public spending on services based on the national accounts aggregate TME. It is the consolidated sum of current and capital expenditure, but excludes public sector debt interest, net public service pensions and other accounting adjustments. Gross Domestic Product (GDP) figures and deflators are based on the September 2000 National Accounts first release.

2 FURTHER EDUCATION STATISTICS

Statistical information on further education students in England, Scotland and Wales are produced by the respective Further Education Funding Councils. Institutes of further education provide data for Northern Ireland to the Department of Higher and Further Education, Training and Employment (DHFETE). The Higher Education Statistics Agency (HESA) provides data on FE students in higher education institutions in the UK.

3 HIGHER EDUCATION STATISTICS AGENCY (HESA)

From the academic year 1994/95 onwards, the Higher Education Statistics Agency (HESA) has collected analogous information for HE students within UK HE institutions. The data collected includes enrolment numbers, qualifiers and first destinations of qualifiers.

4 LABOUR FORCE SURVEY (LFS)

Please note that in the LFS tables some separate analyses will not sum to base figures shown because of unpaid family workers, those on government-supported training and employment programmes, or those who did not answer, who are excluded from the separate analyses (see below for details).

The Labour Force Survey (LFS) was first carried out in the United Kingdom in 1973, as part of the UK's obligations as members of the European Economic Community, and was repeated every two years until 1983. Between 1984 and 1991, the survey was carried out annually, with results published relating to the March to May quarter.

From spring (March to May) 1992 the survey was carried out in Great Britain on a quarterly basis. In Northern Ireland the LFS was conducted in spring 1992 and spring 1993, and was then carried out quarterly from winter (December to February) 1994-95. So for about

the last five years, there has been a quarterly survey covering the whole of the UK. The International Labour Organisation (ILO) – an agency of the United Nations – agrees the concepts and definitions used in the LFS.

The survey is based on a random sample throughout the whole of the United Kingdom. Every three months almost 65 thousand households are contacted and information is collected about the personal circumstances and work of everyone living in these households. As well as these private households, the survey covers two groups of people living in a type of accommodation called *communal establishments*. These two groups are students in halls of residence (whose parents usually answer the survey questions on the students' behalf) and people living in NHS accommodation (which used to be called nurses' homes). The survey does not sample people living in other forms of accommodation – for example, army camps, local authority homes, or hospitals.

The results of each survey are processed, 'grossed', to provide estimates that cover the whole population. This allows us to say that there are about 27 million people in employment, even though the sample itself has only identified about 70 thousand employed people.

Users of the LFS data contained in this volume should be aware that in April 2000 ONS released revised (reweighted or 'regrossed') LFS estimates for the period between September-November 1993 to September-November 1999 inclusive, which are now based on more up-to-date population totals. This has meant that time-series data that fall between these periods needed updating to reflect the new population estimates. All LFS time series data used in this volume have been updated to reflect the new population totals.

Concepts and Definitions

All People
This group includes everyone of working age (Males aged 16-64 and Females aged 16-59) and comprises; employees, the self-employed, those on government supported programmes, unpaid family workers, the ILO unemployed and the economically inactive.

Economically active – people aged 16 and over who are either in employment (did some paid work in the reference week) or ILO unemployed.

Employees / Self-employed – the division between employees and self-employed is based on survey respondents' own assessment of their employment status.

Full-time / part-time – the classification of employees, self-employed, those on government work-related training programmes and unpaid family workers in their main job and as full-time or part-time is on the basis of self-assessment. People on Government-supported training and employment programmes who are at college in the survey reference week are classified, by convention, as part-time.

Temporary employees – in the LFS these are defined as those employees who say that their main job is non-permanent in one of the following ways: fixed period contract; agency temping; casual work; seasonal work; other temporary work.

Government-supported training and employment programmes – This group comprises all people aged 16 and over participating in one of the Government's employment and training programmes administered by Training and Enterprise Councils in England and Wales, local enterprise companies in Scotland, or the Training and Employment Agency in Northern Ireland. This group of people has been excluded from the separate economic analyses in the tables as the LFS generally undercounts the numbers involved. Administrative sources provide much more reliable information about this group (see separate source number 8).

Unpaid Family Workers – This group comprises persons doing unpaid work for a business they own or for a business that a relative owns. This group of people has been excluded from the separate economic analyses as it is relatively small (around 100,000) and when disaggregated many of the estimates fall below the publication threshold of 10,000.

ILO unemployment – the International Labour Office (ILO) measure of unemployment refers to people without a job who were available to start work in the two weeks following their LFS interview and who had either looked for work in the four weeks prior to interview or were waiting to start a job they had already obtained.

Economically inactive – people who are neither in employment nor unemployed on the ILO measure. This group includes, for example, all those who were looking after a home or retired (as well as those aged under 16).

Industry – the classification of respondents' industry of employment is based on the Standard Industrial Classification 1992: SIC (92).

Occupation – the classification of respondents' occupations are based on the Standard Occupational Classification (SOC), introduced in 1991.

5 PUBLIC EXAMINATIONS: GCSE/GNVQ, GCE A LEVEL AND SCOTTISH CERTIFICATE OF EDUCATION (SCE)

Data for England and Wales are produced from data provided by the GCSE and GCE examining boards and groups. GCSE and GCE data for Northern Ireland are derived from the School Performance Survey and Further Education examination results. In Scotland pupils study for the SCE Standard grade (a two-year

course leading to examinations at the end of the fourth year of secondary schooling) and Higher grade, which requires at least a further year of secondary schooling. The data source is the Scottish Qualifications Authority (formerly Scottish Examination Board).

6 SCHOOL LEAVERS DESTINATIONS

From 1996, information on the early destinations of year 11 pupils in England has been collected via the Careers Service Activity Survey. This replaced the former School Leavers Destination Survey, which collected information on the destinations of year 11 pupils in England and Wales. It provides data about the choices of around half a million young people finishing compulsory education each year. Similar information is available for Scotland and Northern Ireland but data for Wales are no longer collected.

7 SCHOOLS STATISTICS

The Department for Education and Employment carries out an annual Census of schools in England on the third Thursday in January. Data are collected on the number of schools by type; number of pupils by age and sex; number of admissions; pupils' school meal arrangements; number of teaching and non-teaching staff; course of study followed by pupils aged 16 and over; number of classes as taught and number of pupils with statements of special educational needs. Data collected each January becomes available towards the end of the same calendar year.

Corresponding annual schools census counts are also carried out in January for pupils in Wales, September for pupils in Scotland and October for pupils in Northern Ireland.

8 TEC-DELIVERED GOVERNMENT SUPPORTED TRAINING

The main TEC/CCTE-delivered Government Supported Training programmes are Advanced Modern Apprenticeships (formerly Modern Apprenticeships), Foundation Modern Apprenticeships (formerly National Traineeships), Other Training for Young People and Work-based Learning for Adults. All of these programmes are funded in England by the Department for Education and Employment, and delivered through the network of Training and Enterprise Councils (TECs) and CCTEs (Chambers of Commerce Training and Enterprise). The TECs and CCTEs themselves work with local and national training providers and employers. Because the programmes delivered in Wales are virtually identical, the information collected is also consistent with that for England.

The statistics come from three sources. Numbers joining and participating in the programmes come from aggregate management information returns, which are provided by TECs and CCTEs as part of their contract with the DfEE, (National Assembly in Wales). Information on characteristics of trainees (age, sex, ethnic origin etc.) comes from starts certificates, which TECs and CCTEs are required to complete for each individual joining a programme. Six months[1] after leaving the programme each trainee[2] is sent a postal questionnaire asking for information on whether they completed their training, usefulness of the training, their current activity and what qualifications they gained. While the questionnaires have changed several times since their introduction, the core questions have remained consistent.

Further details of the programmes and data sources can be obtained from the Statistical First Releases (SFRs) shown in section 3(iii) of Annex B.

9 VOCATIONAL QUALIFICATIONS

Information on awards of National Vocational Qualifications (NVQs)/Scottish Vocational Qualifications (SVQs), General National Vocational Qualifications (GNVQs)/General Scottish Vocational Qualifications (GSVQs), and Other Vocational Qualifications made by UK awarding bodies has been taken from the National Information System for Vocational Qualifications (NISVQ) held by DfEE. As part of the NISVQ project the Qualifications and Curriculum Authority (QCA) provides annual totals (October-September) of NVQ awards by framework area and level, which are used for grossing up the more detailed NVQ award information, collected from the awarding bodies who participate in NISVQ, in order to produce UK NVQ estimates. QCA's totals are based on quarterly returns sent to QCA by all NVQ awarding bodies. UK NVQ/SVQ estimates are based on grossed-up numbers of NVQs plus all SVQs.

NISVQ receives detailed information on awards of NVQs/SVQs, GNVQs/GSVQs and Other VQs (made by four of the largest awarding bodies: City and Guilds, Edexcel, OCR and SQA). Information on GNVQs/GSVQs is complete, because all the relevant awarding bodies are included. SQA also provides complete information on SVQs.

More detailed statistical information on the awards of Vocational Qualifications is presented in the DfEE Statistical Bulletin: Vocational Qualifications in the UK 1998/99, which can be found on the DfEE Statistical Website. (www.dfee.gov.uk/statistics).

---

1   In the past, follow-up surveys have been carried out 3 months after leaving up to December 1990 leavers for Employment Training and up to September 1990 leavers for Youth Training.

2   Apart from those known to have ceased training as a result of serious injury, serious illness or death.

UNITED KINGDOM EDUCATION AND TRAINING STATISTICS: OTHER REFERENCE MATERIAL

1 GENERAL

1.1 Various summaries of education and training statistics for all four parts of the United Kingdom are contained in the *Annual Abstract of Statistics*, *Regional Trends* and *Social Trends* publications prepared by the Office for National Statistics. Some education statistics also appear in the *Digest of Welsh Statistics*, the *Scottish Abstract of Statistics* and the *Annual Abstract of Statistics, Northern Ireland*.

1.2 Each of the home education departments also publish statistics in a variety of press notices, bulletins and statistical volumes. Details of those published by or in conjunction with the Department for Education and Employment are given in Section 3. The relevent websites are as follows:

England: http://www.dfee.gov.uk/statistics
Wales: http://www.wales.gov.uk/index_e.hmtl
Scotland: http://www.scotland.gov.uk
N. Ireland: http://www.deni.gov.uk
            http://www.dhfete.gov.uk

2 OFFICE FOR NATIONAL STATISTICS (ONS) PUBLICATIONS

The Office for National Statistics publishes a quarterly journal entitled Statistical News (price £59.00 pa, or £16 per issue) which contains short articles and notes on the latest developments in all fields of government statistics, including education and training.

Social Trends is produced annually, No 30 2000 (£39.50. ISBN 0 11 621242 X) being the current edition. This publication brings together some of the more significant statistical series relating to social polices and conditions and presents a series of articles, followed by tables and charts. One chapter concentrates on education and training.

Regional Trends is also published annually, No 35 2000 (£39.50. ISBN 0 11 621271 3) being the current edition. This publication brings together detailed information highlighting regional variations in the United Kingdom and covering a wide range of social, demographic and economic topics. One chapter concentrates on education and training.

Guide to Official Statistics 2000 Edition (£32.00. ISBN 0 11 621 161 X) is a comprehensive guide to UK statistics, listing all the statistical censuses, surveys, administrative systems, press releases, publications, databases, CD-ROMs, and other services, by industry sector. The information is also available on StatBase at http://www.statistics.gov.uk .

Labour Market Trends (incorporating the Employment Gazette) is a monthly publication with 70-plus pages of labour market statistical tables. It also contains regular analytical articles using Labour Force Survey data and every month includes an LFS Help Line feature which presents information frequently requested by users of the LFS. The price per issue is £9.50 or £95.00 for annual subscription (UK). Available from The Stationery Office Bookshops.

Social Focus on Young People 2000 (£30.00. ISBN 0 11 621366 3) draws together statistics and research from a wide range of sources to paint a broad picture of the lives of young people in the United Kingdom today and changes over the years.

The Office for National statistics on behalf of The Government Statistical Service (GSS) has created StatBase® as an on-line access system for deposited official data. The data comes from a variety of individual sources throughout GSS. This can be accessed via the ONS website – the home page can be found at, http://www.ons.gov.uk .

3 DEPARTMENT FOR EDUCATION AND EMPLOYMENT (DFEE) RELATED PUBLICATIONS (copies of statistical publications and related information can be downloaded from http://www.dfee.gov.uk/statistics)

(i) Education and Training reports
A number of important education and training reports of recent years contain statistical tables and results of special surveys and are set out below. Previous editions of this publication include a list of pre-2000 reports:

Learning and Training at Work 1999. IFF Research Ltd for DfEE, 2000.

School and College Performance Tables 2000:16-18 Age Group. DfEE, 2000.

Secondary School Performance Tables 2000. DfEE, 2000.

Autumn package of Pupil Performance Information; contains Key Stage results, GCSE/ GNVQs. DfEE 2000. Also on DfEE website http://www.dfee.gov.uk/

(ii) Annual Volumes
The Department publishes education Statistics for England, or England and Wales for Education and Employment as follows in various annual volumes of tabulations:

Schools in England 2000
Gives information on numbers of schools by type and size, numbers of pupils by age and type of school;

pupil:teacher ratios; class sizes; courses of study and school meals. Many of the tables provide information by Government Office Region (£24.95. ISBN 0 11 271095 6)

Children's Day Care Facilities in England 2000

Gives information covering various types of day care facilities for children aged under 8 -day nurseries, playgroups, childminders, out of school clubs, holiday schemes and family centres. Figures are collected on the number of providers of day care facilities, places provided and children receiving local authority provision. Where collected, provision for children under five is separately identified (£14.95. ISBN 0 11 271097 2).

National Curriculum Assessments of 7, 11 and 14 Year Olds by Local Education Authority, 1999

This Statistical Volume is an update based on final data of the provisional figures in Statistical First Release SFR29/1999 published on 6 October 1999. This Volume provides the results of further analyses carried out on the attainments of pupils in England under the National Curriculum.

Public Examinations, GCSE/GNVQ and GCE/AGNVQ in England 1999

Gives information on candidates for the GCSE/GNVQ and GCE/AGNVQ examinations and the results attained in individual subjects for school pupils and further education students (£15.95. ISBN 0 11 271089 1).

Further Education statistics

From 1994/95 statistical information on further education students has been collected and published by the Further Education Funding Council for England (FEFC), Cheylesmore House, Quinton Road, Coventry CV1 2WT.

The FEFC also produces three Press Notices annually on FE students; in April, July and December.

Teachers, England and Wales 1999

The 'Teachers, England and Wales' volume is split into distinct sections, each relating to an aspect of the professional career of teachers. The sections are: initial teacher training, new entrants, teacher flows, teachers in service, teacher's pay, promotions, vacancies, retirements, out of service teachers, further education and higher education (£14.95. ISBN 0 11 271 079 4).

Student Support, England and Wales 1997/98

This volume provides information on awards by Local Education Authorities to students domiciled in England and Wales for the academic year 1997/98.

Information is provided for both mandatory and discretionary awards to students in higher and further education; on the award of educational maintenance allowances; and on awards for postgraduate students. Details are also given on loans made to students in the United Kingdom administered by the Student Loans Company; on access funds administered by education institutions and on career development loans in Great Britain administered by banking institutions. Also included are some time series tables (£14.95. ISBN 0 11 271081 6).

Higher Education Statistics for the UK 1998/99 [published by the Higher Education Statistics Agency (HESA)]

The purpose of the volume is to present an overview of all aspects of higher education in the UK. It is unique in drawing together the basic figures not only on student enrolments in higher education institutions (HEIs) but also on qualifications obtained, staff, finance, applicants, and student support. In addition, the volume now contains summary statistics on higher education study in further education colleges. A further feature of the volume is the inclusion of separate data for England, Scotland, Wales and Northern Ireland some of which has not been published previously (£32.00. ISBN 1 84177013 2).

(iii) Statistical Bulletins and Statistical First Releases

A number of Statistical Bulletins and Statistical First Releases (SFRs) are also released throughout the year. Those issued between October 1999 and September 2000 cover the following topics:

Statistical Bulletins

October-99

| No 11/99 | Education and Labour Market Status of Young People in England Aged16-18: 1992-1998 |
| No 12/99 | Special Educational Needs in England: January 1999 |

November-99

| No 13/99 | Survey of Information and Communications Technology in Schools |

December-99

| No 14/99 | Participation in Education and Training by Young People aged 16 and 17 in each Local Area and Region, England, 1993/94 to 1997/98 |
| No 15/99 | Pupil Absence and Truancy from Schools in England 1998/99 |

March-00

| No 1/00 | GCSE/GNVQ and GCE A/AS Level Performance of Candidates attempting two or More GCE A Levels or AS Equivalents: 1998/99 |

May-00

No 02/00	Youth Cohort Study: Education, Training and Employment of 16-18 Year olds in England and the Factors Associated with Non-Participation
No 03/00	National Curriculum Assessments of 7, 11 and 14 Year Olds in England – 1999
No 04/00	GCSE/GNVQ and GCE A/AS level & Advanced GNVQ Examination Results 1998/99 – England

June-00

No 05/00	Vocational Qualifications in the UK: 1998/99

September-00

No 06/00	Education and Training Expenditure since 1990-91

Statistical First Releases

October-99

SFR 28/1999	Children's Day Care Facilities at 31 March 1999 England (Provisional)
SFR 29/1999	National Curriculum Assessments of 7, 11 and 14 Year Olds by Local Education Authority: 1999
SFR 30/1999	New Deal for Lone Parents: statistics (Latest monthly statistics)
SFR 31/1999	GCSE/GNVQ and GCE A/AS and Advanced GNVQ Results for Young People in England, 1998/99 (Early Statistics)
SFR 32/1999	Infant Class Sizes in England: September 1999
SFR 33/1999	New Deal for Young People and Long-Term Unemployed People aged 25+: statistics (Latest monthly statistics)

November-99

SFR 34/1999	New Deal for Lone Parents: statistics (Latest monthly statistics)
SFR 35/1999	GCSE/GNVQ and GCE A/AS and Advanced GNVQ Results for Young People in England, 1998/99 (Provisional)
SFR 36/1999	New Deal for Young People and Long-Term Unemployed People aged 25+: statistics (Latest monthly statistics)
SFR 37/1999	Student Support: Student Loans in the United Kingdom: Financial Year 1998-99 and Academic Year 1998/99

December-99

SFR 38/1999	New Deal for Lone Parents: statistics (Latest monthly statistics)
SFR 39/1999	TEC Delivered Government-Supported Training: work based training for young people and work-based learning for adults - England & Wales
SFR 40/1999	New Deal for Young People and Long-Term Unemployed People aged 25+: statistics (Latest monthly statistics)

January-00

SFR 1/2000	New Deal for Lone Parents: statistics (Latest monthly statistics)
SFR 2/2000	Infant Class Sizes in England: September 1999 (Revised figures)
SFR 3/2000	New Deal for Young People and Long-Term Unemployed People aged 25+: statistics (Latest monthly statistics)

February-00

SFR 4/2000	New Deal for Lone Parents: statistics (Latest monthly statistics)
SFR 5/2000	New Deal for Young People and Long-Term Unemployed People aged 25+: statistics (Latest monthly statistics)

March-00

SFR 6/2000	New Deal for Lone Parents: statistics (Latest monthly statistics)
SFR 7/2000	Learning and Training for Work: 1999, England
SFR 8/2000	TEC/CCTE Delivered Government - Supported Training: work based training for young people and work-based learning for adults - England & Wales
SFR 9/2000	The Level of Highest Qualification Held by Young People and Adults: England 1999
SFR 10/2000	New Deal for Young Unemployed People and Long Term Unemployed People Aged 25+: statistics (Latest monthly statistics)

April-00

SFR 12/2000	New Deal for Lone Parents: statistics to January 2000

SFR 13/2000	Teachers in Service and Teacher Vacancies: January 2000 (Provisional)
SFR 14/2000	Pupil: Teacher Ratios in Maintained Schools in England: January 2000 (Provisional)
SFR 15/2000	Class Sizes in Maintained Schools in England: January 2000 (Provisional)
SFR 16/2000	Statistics of Student Support: Awards in England and Wales, Academic Year 1998/99
SFR 17/2000	New Deal for Young People and Long-Term Unemployed People aged 25+: statistics to February 2000

May-00

SFR 18/2000	Special Educational Needs in England: January 2000 (Provisional)
SFR 19/2000	New Deal for Lone Parents: statistics to February 2000
SFR 20/2000	Permanent Exclusions from Schools and Exclusion Appeals, England 1998/99 (Provisional)
SFR 21/2000	Teacher Sickness Absence in 1999 (Provisional)
SFR 22/2000	Adult Education Enrolments in England - November 1999
SFR 23/2000	Provision for Children Under Five Years of Age in the Private, Voluntary, Independent and Maintained Sectors England: January 2000 (Provisional)
SFR 24/2000	New Deal for Young People and Long-Term Unemployed People aged 25+: statistics to March 2000

June-00

SFR 25/2000	New Deal for Lone Parents: statistics to March 2000
SFR 26/2000	TEC/CCTE Delivered Government-Supported Training: work-based training for young people and work-based learning for adults - England & Wales
SFR 27/2000	New Deal for Young People and Long-Term Unemployed People aged 25+: statistics to April 2000
SFR 28/2000	Participation in Education, Training and Employment by 16 to 18 year olds, 1998 to 1999

July-00

SFR 29/2000	New Deal for Lone Parents: statistics to April 2000
SFR 30/2000	Admission Appeals for Maintained Primary and Secondary Schools in England 1998/99
SFR 31/2000	New Deal for Young People and Long-Term Unemployed People aged 25+: statistics to May 2000
SFR 32/2000	Children's Day Care Facilities at 31 March 2000 (Provisional)

August-00

SFR 33/2000	New Deal for Lone Parents: statistics to May 2000
SFR 34/2000	New Deal for Young People and Long-Term Unemployed People aged 25+: statistics to June 2000

September-00

SFR 35/2000	Information and Communications Technology in Schools England: 2000
SFR 36/2000	New Deal for Lone Parents: statistics to June 2000
SFR 37/2000	TEC/CCTE Delivered Government - Supported Training: work - based learning for adults - England and Wales: (latest quarterly statistics)
SFR 38/2000	New Deal for Young Unemployed People and Long-term Unemployed People aged 25: statistics to July 2000

The Higher Education Agency (HESA) and Further Education Funding Council also produce Statistical First Releases and Press Notices in conjunction or collaboration with DfEE as follows:

ISR/SFR14 (FEFC)	Student Numbers at Colleges in the Further Education Sector and External Institutions in England in 1998/99 (published December 1999)
ISR/SFR15 (FEFC)	Student Numbers at Colleges in the Further Education Sector and External Institutions in England on 1 November 1999 (published April 2000)
ISR/SFR16 (FEFC)	Student Numbers, In-year Retention, Achievements and Destinations at Colleges in the Further Education Sector, External Institutions and Further Education Student Numbers in Higher Educational Institutions in England in 1998/99 (published July 2000)
SFR37 (HESA)	Qualifications Obtained by and Examinations Results of Higher Education Students at Higher Education Institutions in the United Kingdom for the Academic Year 1998/99 (published February 2000)
SFR38 (HESA)	Student Enrolments on Higher Education Courses at Publicly Funded Higher Education Institution in the United Kingdom for the Academic Year 1999/00 (published April 2000)
SFR41 (HESA)	First Destinations of Higher Education Students in the United Kingdom for the Academic Year 1998/99 (published June 2000)

4 INTERNATIONAL STATISTICS

A number of publications providing comparative statistics and indicators on education and training in different countries are now available - some of the most important are listed below.

Education at a Glance: OECD Indicators 2000. Organisation for Economic Co-operation and Development. Stationery Office, 2000. @ £30.00. ISBN 92 64 17199 1.

Key Data on Vocational Training in the European Union. European Commission, Eurostat, CEDEFOP. Stationery Office, 1999. ISBN 92 828 6215 1.

Key Data on Education in the European Union. Eurydice, Eurostat. Stationery Office, 1999. @ £20.00. ISBN 92 828 8537 2.

Education across the European Union: Statistics and Indicators 1999. European Commission, Eurostat. Stationery Office, 1999. @ £30.00. ISBN 92 827 9797 X.

UNESCO Statistical Yearbook 1999. United Nations Educational, Scientific and Cultural Organisation. UNESCO Publishing and Bernan Press. @ £65.00 + VAT. ISBN 92 3 003635 8.

INDEX (BY TABLE NUMBER)

DEPARTMENT FOR EDUCATION AND EMPLOYMENT
NATIONAL ASSEMBLY FOR WALES
SCOTTISH EXECUTIVE
NORTHERN IRELAND DEPARTMENT OF EDUCATION
HIGHER EDUCATION STATISTICS AGENCY
NORTHERN IRELAND DEPARTMENT OF HIGHER AND FURTHER EDUCATION,
TRAINING AND EMPLOYMENT

EDUCATION AND TRAINING STATISTICS FOR THE UNITED KINGDOM

2000 EDITION

London: The Stationery Office